niverse for the
tor O'Meira and
rimstone Carriage
£ 10.000
Debts paid
£600
Per Annum
&c &c
This will d
Newcastle Pottery
of Silver acts 19d & 19

BY ROYAL APPOINTMENT

Of all the famous mistresses, from Nell Gwynne and Emma Hamilton to Madame de Pompadour and Lily Langtry, Mary Ann Clarke was the most spectacular and the most outrageous. Her career was a rags-to-riches story of a girl from the teeming back streets of Georgian London who rose with premeditated guile to a life of pretentious affluence as the mistress of "The Brave Old Duke of York".

Slight and short, with fair complexion and blue eyes, Mrs. Clarke was as shrewdly intelligent as she was attractive, and as the mistress of the Duke of York, Commander-in-Chief of the Army, it was a short and lucrative step to trafficking in commissions.

A stream of military men fawned upon her to use her influence with the Duke, flattering her vanity and providing the money to finance her reckless extravangance. All was grist to her duplicity, from two Colonels seeking an exchange to an ambitious Colonel aspiring to the rank of Brigadier-General, and a Colonel and a Captain wanting a profitable recruiting levy. For a thousand pounds she placed a devoted admirer in the commissariat; to her footboy she presented a commission; and, with amused condescension, she aided and abetted a preposterous Irish cleric in search of preferment.

When discarded by the Duke in 1806, Mrs. Clarke's fortunes were at a perilously low ebb, but two-and-a-half years later she extended her nefarious practices with spellbinding panache by appearing in the House of Commons to support Colonel Wardle's charge of the misconduct of the Duke of York as Commander-in-Chief.

For several weeks she was a national sensation. People cheered her in the streets. Her wit and effrontery provided the satirists with illimitable scope, and "Mrs. Clarke", wrote one contemporary, "ushers in the first mouthful at meals and waits upon the last".

The aftermath of the inquiry was equally dramatic. A timorous government paid £10,000 for the suppression of her memoirs, and two successful law suits followed in less than six months. At last, in 1814, her luck ran out, and she was sentenced to nine months' imprisonment for libel.

The following year Mrs. Clarke retired to France, where she died, like Emma Hamilton, in obscurity and comparative poverty, but the achievements of her descendants – George du Maurier, the illustrator and author; Sir Gerald du Maurier, the Edwardian actor; and her great-great-granddaughter, Daphne du Maurier – must surely owe much to the intelligence and vitality inherited from the indomitable girl from Bowl and Pin Alley.

By the same Author:—
DAUGHTERS OF CAIN

The sculpture which Mrs. Clarke commissioned in 1811, with her head and shoulders rising from within the petals of a sunflower, symbolizing the woman discarded by her lover.

BY ROYAL APPOINTMENT

A biography of Mary Ann Clarke
Mistress of the Duke of York

PAUL BERRY

A Femina Book

First published 1970 by Femina Books
Second impression 1970
1a Montagu Mews North, London W.1.
SBN: 850 43011 9

Distributed by British Printing Corporation Ltd.,
St. Giles House, Poland Street, London W.1.
Printed by W. & G. Baird Ltd., Belfast.

ACKNOWLEDGEMENTS

I owe special thanks to the Librarian of the House of Commons and his staff, who have given me such valuable help, and to Boris Mollo, Keeper of Books and Archives. The National Army Museum, for his courteous co-operation, and for giving me very useful information regarding the military career of George Clarke.

I acknowledge also with gratitude and appreciation the help and information received from: The Secretary and staff of The National Registrar of Archives (Scotland); The Archivist, Greater London Council; The County Archivist, Royal County of Berkshire; The Archivist, City of Westminster Public Libraries, Buckingham Palace Road; The Archives Department, City of Westminster Public Library, Marylebone Road; The County Archivist, Kent County Council; The County Archivist, East Sussex Record Office; The Superintendent and staff of the British Museum Reading Room; the staff of the Public Record Office; The Department of British and Medieval Antiquities of The British Museum; The Director and staff of Brighton Art Gallery and Museums; The Borough of Camden Librarian; The Area Librarian, Kent County Library, Tonbridge; The Librarian, Devon County Library, Exmouth; The Librarian of The Institute of Criminology, University of Cambridge; The Librarian and staff, Midhurst Public Library; The staff of the Clerk of the Council, Walton and Weybridge Urban District Council; The Clerk and Solicitor, Exmouth Urban District Council; The Law Society; and I am grateful to The National Advertising Benevolent Society for permitting me to see their office, which was once Mrs. Clarke's drawing-room.

From France, M. P. Bangard, Le Directeur des Services d'Archives du Pas-de-Calais, kindly supplied me with valuable information; Le Sénateur-Maire de Boulogne very courteously provided a photostat copy of the death certificate relating to Mrs. Clarke; and to La Bibliothèque Nationale, Paris, I am indebted for the extracts quoted from "The Boulogne Gazette" and "The French Times".

My grateful thanks are due also for permission to quote from the following copyright material: to Cecil Woodham-Smith and Constable & Co. for an extract from "The Reason Why"; and to John Murray (Publishers) Ltd. for allowing me to include passages from "The Correspondence of Charlotte Grenville, Lady Williams Wynn, and her three sons", edited by Rachel Leighton; "The Private Correspondence of Lord Granville Leveson-Gower 1781-1821", edited by Countess Granville; and "A Selection from the Correspondence and Diaries of the late Thomas Creevey, M.P.", edited by Sir Herbert Maxwell. I am particularly grateful to Major J. C. Blackett Ord, the present owner of the Creevey Papers, for the time and trouble taken in providing me with an unpublished sentence from Creevey's Diary, and for allowing me to include it in the present biography. For permission to quote from the letters written to Lord Folkestone by Mrs. Clarke and Colonel Wardle, which are now in the Berkshire Record Office, Reading, I am much obliged to Miss K. Pleydell-Bouverie and The National Trust.

I am indebted also to Sotheby & Co. for permitting me to reproduce their catalogue description of the autograph manuscript of Mrs. Clarke's memoirs included in their sale held on July 2nd, 1930.

A special word of gratitude is due to my friends for their interest and help, and for bearing patiently with me during the three years that I have spent writing this biography. To Mrs. Hilda Cannings I express my appreciation for the thoroughness with which she typed the MS.

Stedham, Sussex.
August, 1969.

ILLUSTRATIONS

Between pp. 176 and 177

No. 9. A broadside by Gillray grimly predicting "Blood an' Thunder when Whore and Rogue are rent asunder".

By courtesy of the National Army Museum

No. 10. In an acrimonious exchange in the House of Commons, Mrs. Clarke accused John Wilson Croker of spying upon her visitors from his garret window, which inspired a bawdy skit by Rowlandson on the activities at her fashionable Chelsea residence.

By courtesy of the Trustees of The British Museum

No. 11. Mrs. Clarke was supplanted in the Duke's affections by the actress Mrs. Carey, which provided Williams with material for an amusing caricature on the amorous escapades of the Duke of York.

By courtesy of the Trustees of The British Museum

No. 12. Cruikshank's satire on the re-instatement of the Duke of York as Commander-in-Chief. The Duke is mounted on the shoulders of the decrepit General Dundas, and the Prince Regent ushers him back into office with a pleased smile. Spencer Perceval, the Prime Minister, clears the way with a broom, pushing aside Wardle, who lies on his back whilst a perky little dog, with the head of Mrs Clarke superimposed, stands over him urinating.

By courtesy of the Trustees of The British Museum

For
my Mother
who asked me to write her a book,
with love and appreciation

Prologue

IN 1772 an art collector returning to England from Naples brought with him a white marble bust. It was believed to be of Clytie, deserted by her lover Helias, who was changed into a flower, but it has since been identified as a portrait of Antonia, the daughter of Mark Antony.

To Mary Ann Clarke, the cast-off mistress of the Duke of York, the idea of having a similar head and shoulders made of herself, appealed to her caustic sense of humour. Not only would it be a memorable record of her as a remarkable personality, but also an inspired gibe at the dubious fame of His Royal Highness, the Commander-in-Chief of the British Army.

In 1811, she therefore commissioned Lawrence Gahagan to execute the twenty-five inch bust on a base of grey marble, which is now in the National Portrait Gallery, with paintings of the Duke and Colonel Wardle (the man instrumental in his disgrace and downfall) grouped appropriately around it. Mrs. Clarke's head and shoulders rise from within the petals of a sunflower, and her head is turned slightly to the left and tilted upwards in a striking pose of quizzical intelligence. Her hair, cut short at the back, is swept up and elaborately curled on the crown and sides of her head, while the vestiges of drapery over her shoulders leave the left breast exposed.

The attendant at the National Portrait Gallery who showed the author the bust of Mrs. Clarke knew about her chaotic life of sex and intrigue.

"You'd go barmy if you didn't take an interest in the people around you. I'm very attached to her," he confided, nodding at the Gahagan head with the slightly-parted lips and elusive smile. "She could be a girl of today – and you can't say that about many of them. When she was in a special display a couple of years ago, some hooligan touched up her breast with lipstick." – a spontaneous tribute to her charms that Mrs. Clarke would have thoroughly appreciated!

Chapter One

AT THE beginning of the nineteenth century the House of Commons was the best club in the world – for men only.

One or two women, the fiery Lady Holland or the indefatigable letter-writing Lady Bessborough, might attempt to exert political influence from the seclusion of their drawing-room or study, but within the precincts of St. Stephen's women were neither to be seen nor heard.

On January 27th, 1809, the House received the first unpalatable intimation that, temporarily at any rate, they might have to screw up their courage to meet a feminine intrusion of the most ribald kind.

That day, Colonel Gwyllym Lloyd Wardle, a forty-six-year-old Welshman and member for Okehampton in Devon, rose to urge the appointment of a Committee to investigate the conduct of the Duke of York as Commander-in-Chief of the Army, "with regard to Promotions, Exchanges and Appointments to Commissions, and in raising Levies for the Army".

He spoke about the point and purpose of the half-pay fund, which provided a reduced rate of pay for officers who had temporarily resigned from service with a regiment, or from the staff, but who would be available for service at a future date. The fund was financed from the sale of commissions vacant through death, by promotion of officers not allowed to sell, or by dismissals from the service, and was, Wardle reminded the House, "an establishment under the direction of the Commander-in-Chief".

He went on to suggest that the Duke of York had off-duty pursuits of a more exhilarating kind. It was absolutely necessary for his purpose, he said, "to call the attention of the House to another establishment of the Commander-in-Chief, which is of a quite different complexion. This establishment, which consisted of a splendid house in Gloucester Place, a variety of carriages and a long retinue of servants, commenced in the year 1803, and at the head of it was placed a lady of the name of Clarke."

The scandal that had been circulating so freely in London was at last confirmed, and who knew what royal linen the Duke's mistress would dredge up for public inspection?

"Here the reader is able to see the puss half out of the bag," wrote Mrs. Clarke some months later on a very different topic, but it is a comment far more appropriate to her own spectacular début.

Colonel Wardle's motion was quickly seconded by the radical Member for Westminster, Sir Francis Burdett who, a year later, was to spend nearly three months in the Tower for a vitriolic denunciation of the House for its use of privilege.

Colonel Wardle asked for a Select Committee to synthesize the evidence in private with the minimum of publicity, and a public debate when its work was done. Many Members heaved a sigh of relief, hoping that the unsavoury allegations could be disposed of without bruiting the sordid details of the Duke's affaire from every house-top and tap-room.

With more valour than discretion, some Members were not to be baulked so easily. William Adam, the Duke's legal adviser and confidant for twenty years, whose private skirmishing with Mrs. Clarke had ended in stalemate, felt capable in public (with other Government supporters at his side) of routing this shameless woman once and for all.

With unctuous concern but little acumen he called for "a public investigation before the world at the bar of the House."

"The authority of the House, when examining witnesses at the bar," he hinted slyly, "would ensure their punishment in case of prevarication.'

The brunt of the responsibility for defending the Duke was to fall on the shoulders of the Chancellor of the Exchequer, "the sepulchral Spencer Perceval*" as Sidney Smith dubbed him in his 'Peter Plymley' letters. Eighteen months earlier, Perceval had discovered the Duke to be £20,000 in debt; an amount which doubled during the next year. To a man less swayed by sentiments of monarchical omnipotence and royal prerogative, such financial instability might have been a warning of other human foibles, but Perceval was in complete agreement with William Adam.

"From the nature of the facts which had been already stated, he would stake his reputation upon it," he declared, "that it was

* Prime Minister 1809–1812, later shot and killed by a madman.

impossible that after the result of the inquiry, any suspicion could even attach to His Royal Highness."

Others believed the charges should be committed to a specially delegated parliamentary commission, among them the perspicacious William Wilberforce. "It would afford the best species of communication" he said, "namely, publicity at the end, but not in the progress of the investigation."

A certain John Ward maliciously questioned the purity of Wilberforce's motives. "He is afraid," he gibed in private, "at the thought of this Babylonish person being brought into his holy presence."

Rumours of Lord Folkestone's relations with Mrs. Clarke being of a highly compromising nature, he, too, plumped for a Select Committee sifting the evidence behind closed doors.

Six months later George Canning and Lord Castlereagh were to find themselves facing each other at dawn on Putney Heath with loaded pistols, but for the moment they also were united in their demand for a public inquiry.

"I am not for leaving it to any Select Committee, nor even to the twelve judges", Lord Castlereagh announced as the House listened attentively, "nor to anything short of that full and open examination which might be had at the bar of the House."

Canning declared emotionally that "to direct unfounded attacks against those in high authority was nearly similar to an attack on an undefended woman", and the House agreed that on the following Wednesday it should resolve itself into a Committee to investigate the charges on the conduct of the Duke of York as Commander-in-Chief of the Army.

For Colonel Wardle the prospect was bewitching. The most that he had hoped for was the appointment of a Select Committee, but instead there was to be a public inquiry and a blaze of publicity, and he saw himself in the leading role of virtuous patriot exposing corruption and abuse. The die was cast. The dirty linen was to be brought out and washed in public, and the public was avid to hear what Mrs. Clarke would have to say about it all as she disseminated the dark secrets of high life in Gloucester Place.

It is always intriguing to see the type of woman a man will choose for an extra-marital romp, and there is added piquancy when that man is George III's second son, the Commander-in-Chief of the Army, and third in succession to the throne.

On Tuesday, January 31st, Mrs. Mary Ann Clarke, of 2 Westbourne Place, Sloane Square, received a summons to attend a Committee of the whole House of Commons on the following day, and her appearance was the moment for which everyone was waiting.

She made clear from the beginning the commotion that she intended to create. "When summoned to the bar," wrote one eyewitness, "she trips with light and airy steps and smirking countenance, as if she was going into a ballroom."

She arrived accompanied by a friend and curtseyed to the House with easy theatrical grace. Mr. Wharton, the Chairman, was momentarily confused by the appearance of two women when only Mrs. Clarke had been called, and her companion, Miss Clifford, was told to withdraw.

Mrs. Clarke was dressed for the occasion with skilful elegance in a long, powder-blue silk pelisse of classical simplicity, with high waist, and décolleté neck-line edged with lace. On her arm she carried a white swan's-down muff. She wore a contrasting lilac-coloured velvet hat with a veil, "which at no time is let down over her face to hide it", one journalist commented caustically.

She was thirty-three, still youthful looking and attractive, and was certainly not the woman to conceal her charms by a conventional show of modesty that she did not feel.

The House gave every Member the right to question the witnesses. Facing more than six hundred men, closely scrutinized by every eye, it was a moment to break the nerve of the strongest woman, destroy even the most self-confident, and to elicit merely the briefest replies.

"Did you reside in Gloucester Place, in a house of the Duke of York's, in July, 1805?" asked Colonel Wardle.

"Yes, I did."

"Did you live under his protection?"

"Yes, I did."

Sir Vicary Gibbs, the Attorney-General, wanted to know a little more about Mrs. Clarke's antecedents. "Are you a married woman or not?"

"You have no reason to doubt it."

The Chairman intervened, telling her to give a direct answer to the question.

"I am a married woman," Mrs. Clarke informed Sir Vicary. Turning to the Chairman she seized the initiative. "There is no question I will not answer, though it may be unpleasant."

"How long have you been married?" Sir Vicary asked.

"I refer you to Mr. Adam," blithely replied Mrs. Clarke, ignoring the instruction she had just received. "He has my certificate."

The Attorney-General repeated the question.

"I believe fourteen or fifteen years."

"Is your husband living?"

"I don't know."

"Have you not sworn yourself to be a widow?"

"No, I did not swear it. I will explain that," she said, launching unchecked into a long explanation. "His Royal Highness, a very short time since, when I sent to ask him to send me a few hundred pounds, sent me word that if I dared speak against him, or write against him, he would put me into the pillory or into the Bastille. He fancies that I swore myself to be a widow woman when I was examined at a Court-Martial. But the Deputy Judge Advocate had more feeling than the gentleman who has examined me now. He told me I might say anything out of court which it might be unpleasant to me to swear to. I told him it would be very improper for me to say that I was a married women, when I had been known to be living with the Duke of York. I did not swear that I was a widow. I said it out of court, and it was put into the Court-Martial minutes as if I had sworn to it, but it was not so. The Judge Advocate, to whom I said it, is at the door, and I think he had better be called in. I know now what he came for."

"Who brought this message from the Duke to you?"

To Mrs. Clarke, Sir Vicary Gibbs was another hard-faced henchman of the Duke of York's, who had treated her abominably; she saw her chance and light-heartedly proceeded to catch him in her web.

"A very particular friend of the Duke of York's."

"Who is he?"

"One Taylor, a shoemaker in Bond Street; very well known to Mr. Adam."

"How did you send the request to the Duke for these few hundred pounds to which the Duke sent this answer by Taylor?"

"By my pen," Mrs. Clarke announced airily. The House laughed at her impudence.

Sir Vicary Gibbs blundered on. "How did you send the letter?"

"By this Ambassador of Morocco," replied Mrs. Clarke smoothly, and the House once more dissolved into laughter.

"What do you mean by this Ambassador of Morocco?"

"The ladies' shoemaker."

This was levity on the grand scale, and Mrs. Clarke had had a good run for her money. The Chairman again intervened, rebuking her for the indiscreet and indecent way she was giving her evidence which was, he said, totally inconsistent with the dignity of the House. He warned her to be more courteous, and added that if she persevered in this attitude it would call for a very heavy censure.

"What is your husband's name?" Sir Vicary continued.

"Clarke."

"What is his Christian name?"

"Joseph, I believe."

"Where were you married to him?"

"At Pancras. Mr. Adam can tell you."

"Have you ever said that you were married at Berkhampstead?"

"I did when I was laughing at Mr. Adam."

"Was it true or not that you were married at Berkhampstead?"

"I tell you, I told him laughing, and I told the Duke I was making a fool of him when I said that, for which His Royal Highness said he was very sorry, for he was entirely in Mr. Adam's clutches."

Mrs. Clarke was making it tantalisingly clear that she had plenty more to say about Mr. Adam.

"Did you not represent your husband as a nephew of Mr. Alderman Clarke?"

"He told me he was." No one could contradict that.

"Did you ever see Mr. Alderman Clarke?"

"I never saw any of Mr. Clarke's relations but two of his brothers and his sister. I have seen the Alderman sometimes about – as anybody else might have seen him."

"Do you now believe that your husband is the nephew of Alderman Clarke?"

Mrs. Clarke was becoming tetchy with all these absurd questions about a husband she would prefer to forget. Perhaps the probing into her past brought back ugly memories of recriminations and unedifying brawls, of cruel words and violence when her husband returned home the worse for drink from the taverns of Hoxton. Was this a public enquiry into her private life, or an investigation into the conduct of the Commander-in-Chief?

The Attorney-General persisted, and Mrs. Clarke decided to dispose of the offensive topic once and for all.

"I have never taken any pains to ask anything concerning him, as I have quitted him. He is nothing to me, nor I to him, nor have I seen him nearly these three years, nor heard of him since he brought an action against the Duke – or threatened. I saw him about a month before that."

"What is your husband?"

"He is nothing . . ." One can almost see the contemptuous curl of the lip, the disdainful glance over the faces of the men filling St. Stephen's hall to capacity. "He is nothing but a man."

"Did you ever live in Tavistock Place?"

"Yes, I did."

"When did you live there?"

"I do not recollect. I lived there with my mother."

"Where did you live when first you knew the Duke?"

Mrs. Clarke was determined that even if he was the Attorney-General, neither Sir Vicary Gibbs nor anyone else should know how, when or where she met the Duke.

"You will excuse me if I do not mention it," she replied, all sweetness and light. The Chairman interjected, telling her to answer, but she had devised an infallible method for circumventing such disagreeable questions.

"I do not recollect," she said.

It is conceivable that one could forget the unimportant particulars of some prosaic event, or chance, inconsequential meeting with a stranger, but is it possible to forget first meeting a new lover when that lover is the Duke of York, the King's favourite son? Sir Vicary Gibbs did not think so.

"If you do not recollect, why did you desire to be excused from answering the question?"

"Because I did not recollect."

"Was that your only reason for desiring to be excused answering the question?" Mrs. Clarke must have felt that she was nearly off the hook, and adopted a more conciliatory approach.

"Yes, because it would be seeming as if I could not answer many of the questions you put to me. I wish to be very fair and honest."

"Recollect yourself, and say positively whether you did not live in Tavistock Place before you knew the Duke?"

"I knew the Duke many years before that. I do not think it is a fair question at all to put to me. You hear that I am a married woman, and I have a family of children, and I have a daughter grown up."

"Do you mean to say that you never lived in Tavistock Place till you were under the protection of the Duke?"

Mrs. Clarke meant to say nothing of the sort. "No, I say I was there with my mother and children. I knew His Royal Highness previous to that but did not live with him."

This was the limit to which Mrs. Clarke was prepared to go about the beginning of her association with the Duke. She had lived previously with William Ogilvie, an army agent whose career ended ignominiously in bankruptcy, and it was generally assumed that it was through his connivance that she first met the Duke of York. She had no intention, however, of permitting her life of protection and promiscuity to become a topic for public discussion, and it is scarcely surprising to find William Wilberforce writing in his diary that night, "Mrs. Clarke elegantly dressed, consummately impudent, and very clever. After two hours of cross-examination in the Old Bailey way she had clearly got the better of the struggle."

Sir Vicary Gibbs next turned the spotlight on some of Mrs. Clarke's more discreditable activities. "Have you not threatened the Duke that if he would not come to the terms you proposed and pay you what you required of him, you would put the letters into the hands of persons who would pay you?"

"Would pay me what?"

"What you required the Duke to pay you."

"What is that? Will you be so good as to state what I wanted him to do."

"Have you not stated that you had put upon paper, or would put upon paper, the transactions for the last fourteen or fifteen years, and that if he did not comply with your demand, that you would put the memoir into the hands of persons who would publish it?"

"No, I have not." A ready denial sprang to Mrs. Clarke's lips, when too late she recalled a certain peremptory letter she had written to Mr. Adam. Hastily she endeavoured to retrieve the situation. "I cannot recollect what I said, but I must beg for the letter and that will convince at once."

Other witnesses were also examined, and at last, at two in the morning, the House adjourned, left with a profusion of unanswered questions.

Who was Mrs. Clarke's husband? How had she cuckolded the Duke of York? When did their intimacy begin – and end? What were the transactions extending over fourteen or fifteen years that she proposed to publish?

A whole host of witnesses were waiting to be heard, not only those at a public inquiry into the conduct of the Duke of York, but the men and women who would piece together the story of Mrs. Clarke's chaotic, kaleidoscopic life: Captain Huxley Sandon serving with the Royal Waggon Train*; Elizabeth Taylor, who ran a boarding school in Chelsea; William Dowler, in charge of the Accounts Department of the Commissariat in Lisbon; John Few, who took her to court for the payment of a Grecian lamp for her back room; Mrs. Favery, her housekeeper and confederate; Dr. Andrew Thynne, her reluctant physician; Dominigo Corri, an improbable music-master, "the tormentor of cat-gut"; David Peirson, her drunken butler; Ludowick Orramin, the Duke's footman; William Nicholls, the baker from Hampstead with his sackful of letters . . .

The Members of Parliament went home to bed to ponder upon Mrs. Clarke's astonishing progress from doubtful obscurity to the royal bed.

* The Royal Waggon Train lasted from 1799–1833, and was the equivalent of the Royal Army Service Corps – or Royal Corps of Transport as it is now called. As the name implies, the Royal Waggon Train was responsible for the transport of supplies for the army.

Chapter Two

MRS. CLARKE was born into that strata of society which Regency aristocrats summarily dismissed as "the lower orders". Without money or education, possessing only good looks and natural intelligence, she rose literally from the slums to become the mistress of a Royal Duke. At a time when class privilege was almost sacrosanct, and when the opportunities for social betterment were few, it was a miraculous, if precarious, achievement.

When asked about her early life she replied briefly and tetchily, often feigning forgetfulness or dismissing the question as an impertinent intrusion into her private affairs, but if she was silent about her origins, the gossip writers were not. She was the heaven-sent subject for lampoonists and purveyors of the smutty joke.

They embellished the known facts, adding colourful exaggerations of their own; they plagiarized shamelessly and, paying little more than lip-service to truth, they fanned the flames of public curiosity. They suffered no inhibitions; their yardstick being colour, titillation and profit. Inevitably many details of her life were invented or distorted.

Cautiously picking one's way through panegyric and calumny, it is hard to decide where fact and fiction begin and end. Yet the inventions and histrionics paint a vivid picture of Mrs. Clarke as she appeared to her contemporaries. She emerges as a good-time girl with boundless vitality and self-assurance; intelligent, witty, and reckless, who blossomed when the spotlight was on her but who wilted when ostracised by society. A girl who saw life as a game of chance and who boldly bid for the highest stakes.

Borrowing their facts from one another, most of her biographers assert that Mary Ann Thompson was born in Bowl and Pin Alley*

---

* Bowl and Pin Alley was a little to the north of where Breams Buildings now stand, running east to west joining Chancery Lane with Fleet Lane, and was roughly on the site of Nos. 15 to 25. In 1826 the name was changed to Bowl and Pin Gardens. It seems likely that there was either a public skittle alley here, or that it was the custom for people to play skittles in the alley itself, and that the name was a colloquialism derived from this habit.

off White's Alley, Chancery Lane, but, according to one "W. Clarke", her birthplace was Oxford and her parents moved to London whilst she was still an infant.

Bowl and Pin Alley was a tough environment for a child to grow up in and it undoubtedly played a prominent part in moulding the character of Mary Ann. Houses were divided into tenements, reached from a maze of alleys and yards leading off narrow streets, perpetually congested with barrows, drays and carts, and filled with "rubbish, dirt and nastiness of all sorts". As a result of the Window Tax, large numbers of windows had been bricked up. Many of the more humble dwellings had little natural light and were often without either water or sanitation. In the notorious district of "The Rookery" around St. Giles's High Street to the west, the slum conditions were infinitely worse, and crumbling houses sheltered poultry, pigs and people, indiscriminately.

Around Bowl and Pin Alley there were other perils of a more insidious sort. "The moral atmosphere," Elizabeth Taylor, a close friend of Mrs. Clarke in later life, suggests "was contaminated by the vices of some of the most abandoned prostitutes upon the pavé."

Mary Ann's father died whilst she was still a child, leaving her mother, one writer commented ambiguously, "to dispose of herself." This Mrs. Thompson successfully contrived to do, and before long she married again.

One account alleges that Mr. Thompson was killed in the American War of Independence whilst serving as a soldier. Mary Ann's brother, and later her son, both joined the Army and, if her father was in fact killed in action on some distant battlefield, it was an event that could have laid a strong hold upon the child's imagination. It could explain, perhaps, her compulsive interest in army affairs, and how she slipped so easily into meddling in military matters and the sale of commissions when she found herself the mistress of the Commander-in-Chief.

Robert Farquhar, Mary Ann's step-father, a Scotsman from Aberdeen, worked as a compositor for a printing firm in nearby Lincoln's Inn Fields, and before long the family left Bowl and Pin Alley and took lodgings not far away in Black Raven Passage, leading off Cursitor Street.

Although Robert Farquhar is said to have been "below the rank of Mr. Thompson", he was of a benevolent disposition and a conscientious substitute for the father Mary Ann had lost. He taught his step-daughter to read and write, and before long she was visiting him during working hours. Probably to keep her usefully employed and out of mischief, she was soon helping by reading copy for proof correction. To a girl with Mary Ann's quick sharp mind this helped enormously to increase her general knowledge, and particularly her understanding of the English language. It was an experience that she later put to practical use as she poured out with hasty fluency a voluminous quantity of articulate and pertinent letters.

The appearance of this high-spirited girl with her jaunty manners was a welcome diversion to the male staff of the printing works, and she is described evocatively as "a romp". From an early age she possessed that elusive, enigmatic quality that attracts men irresistibly and the eldest son of the manager of the printing works was probably the first to succumb to her charms.

At this point we come face to face with a riddle that will probably never be solved. Did Mary Ann receive any formal education, or did she rise entirely through her own exertions and abilities to enjoy a life of opulence and extravagance considered to be the prerogative of royalty and the wealthy aristocracy?

Miss Taylor in her biography answers the question by declaring that the young man, "wishing at the same time to encourage her merit, and to derive pleasure, and, perhaps, future assistance from the cultivation of her talents, placed this young lady, whom he fondly destined as his future wife, at a genteel boarding-school at Ham, in Essex." When Mary Ann returned home at the end of two years, however, there was an unfortunate sequel as she had "ideas very much altered from those which her benefactor had wished to have inspired."

If Miss Taylor is to be believed, these two years at one of the innumerable private boarding-schools then existing for the education of young ladies, could have provided precisely the influence that enabled Mary Ann so successfully to leave behind the working-class background into which she was born.

Yet is it credible that the young man would have been able to pay the school fees, and, even if he could, is it likely he would voluntarily separate himself for long periods from the young girl with whom he was very much in love? At a time when women were relegated to domestic duties and were almost completely subservient to their husbands, would the young man be so concerned with improving his future wife's education and manners as to send her to a boarding-school merely that she might "show herself off to the best advantage among his friends and the world, as a rare bit of fancy and fashion of his own taste"?

On balance the odds are against this educational excursion. It seems more probable that it was a romantic concoction on the part of either Mrs. Clarke or Elizabeth Taylor, striving to supply a reputable background when every detail of Mrs. Clarke's life was a topic for conjecture and speculation. Mrs. Clarke herself gives the impression of being self-educated; intelligent, quick to learn, sublimely confident of her own capabilities, and recklessly unafraid of any situation or its consequences.

"Miss Thompson's parents, although industrious, could not always supply by their industry those wants which became occasionally necessary", Elizabeth Taylor writes with grave solemnity. They possessed "neither plate nor jewels" and it was "the humbler appendages of obscurity, shifts and petticoats, etc., which first produced the supplies of necessity, and with these Miss Thompson was occasionally despatched for the relief of the family . . . to one of those magazines of ways and means which are distinguished by the appropriate emblem of three golden balls."

Mary Ann grew up with the knowledge that poverty was hard and odious, a stranglehold to be broken at whatever the cost, and using to the best effect her charm and powers of persuasion, she induced "the mercenary serpent of avarice" to lend more money than he normally would have done on the clothes she offered.

The situation has all the ingredients of a melodrama, and with delicate finesse Elizabeth Taylor proceeds to give the *coup de grâce* to Mary Ann's virginity. Whether the pawnbroker was actuated by love or lust she declines to distinguish, but he felt "so much of a sneaking inclination towards his young customer as to induce him to admit her occasionally into his private *cabinet,* a commodious back-parlour, where it is said the value of the specific articles offered as pledges did not always constitute the topic of conversation."

Elizabeth Taylor's twopenny-coloured interpretation of Mrs. Clarke's early life may in some respects be outrageously lacking in veracity, but she suggests evocatively the general tenor of those formative years. Poverty; life in an over-crowded, noisy London Alley; a step-father well disposed but lacking in authority; and Mary Ann herself, precocious, independent and high-spirited, a girl "whose sprightlier faculties were at an early period in a state of mutiny with the slow-paced drudgery of the needle".

In brief, Mary Ann was the type of girl who soon elects to pursue her own headstrong inclinations, and when she was fifteen she left home. The escape route she took was one that women have taken since time began – she eloped.

Joseph Clarke was the second son of a wealthy builder living in Angel Court, Snow Hill, and was apprenticed to a stone-mason with premises at the corner of Black Raven Passage and Cursitor Street, only a short distance from the Farquhar lodgings. From a chance meeting developed a mutual infatuation and before long the young couple "eloped from the confined air of an alley to enjoy the delights of love in the purer atmosphere of Pentonville."

When Joseph Clarke's father died he is alleged to have left a fortune of £80,000. There were at least four children in the family and, perhaps because Joseph was under age, or because he suspected some feckless streak in his son's character, his father prudently left him an annuity of £50, apparently payable weekly.

The Clarke boys appear to have been an irresponsible lot and one brother, who inherited £7,000 from his father, "shot himself in his chaise . . . one evening as he was returning home from town, in consequence of the embarrassment of his affairs."

From Pentonville the young couple moved to Charles Square, Hoxton. They were not yet married, but whether this was due to parental opposition or whether they were satisfied simply living together it is impossible to say. It is reported that two children were born before the Clarkes were at last married at St. Pancras Church on May 19th, 1792.

Mary Ann was under twenty-one and before the marriage took place it was necessary for her to obtain parental consent. On the previous day she and her step-father, Robert Farquhar, had signed the appropriate undertaking and this Marriage Allegation is now among the records held by the Guildhall Library, London. It is probable that to avoid any hitch in her wedding plans, Mary Ann persuaded Robert Farquhar to tell a white lie and pose as her natural father. What difference did it make if she ware married in the name of Farquhar instead of Thompson?

"Appeared personally", runs the Allegation, "Mary Ann Farquhar and made Oath that she is of the Parish of Saint Pancras in the County of Middlesex, a Spinster, a Minor of the age of Seventeen years and upwards but under the age of twenty-one years, by and with the consent of Robert Farquhar, the Natural and lawful Father of the said Minor, and intended to marry with Joseph Clarke of the Parish of Saint James, Clerkenwell, in the same County, a Bachelor, Aged above twenty-one years.'

The wedding ceremony was performed without fuss or formality, Robert Farquhar being the only relative present. To comply with the need for two witnesses, William Gabell, who was either the church cleaner or grave-digger, was co-opted, but as he could neither read nor write he marked the register with a cross.

Both the Marriage Allegation and Certificate were signed by Mary Ann in large, childish handwriting, and they show that at some later date she added an "e" to her second christian name, possibly believing that plain "Ann" stigmatised her plebeian background.

Joseph Clarke had by now completed his apprenticeship, and for the next year or two he did no work, the family living upon his annuity. It was possible at the end of the eighteenth century to live on a pound a week and many families eked out a semi-starvation existence on much less.

Writing at about this time, Charles Prescot, a weaver living in the north of England, declared bitterly that "a man's life is of no value". He worked sixteen hours a day for a weekly wage of twelve shillings, on which he supported his wife, and five children all under eight years of age. "It will take 2d. per week coals, and 1d. per week candles," he wrote. "My family live upon potatoes chiefly, and we have one pint of milk per day."

With one ominous exception the Clarkes were more fortunate. Joseph Clarke was a work-shy man of gregarious habits, and his spendthrift behaviour "kept the ingenuity of the wife eternally upon the rack to find the necessary supplies". It seems likely that Mrs. Clarke finally prevailed on her husband to lead a more purposeful life and set up in business on his own account. The family moved to Golden Square, Aldersgate, and, with a yard available for his tools and materials, Joseph Clarke began work as a stonemason.

Unfortunately he was as incapable of sustained effort as he always had been and "the parlour of the public-house now became the substitute for the counting-house, and the skittle ground a more congenial stage of action . . . than the stone yard".

The venture dragged on for three or four years until it ended inevitably in failure, bankruptcy – and another move.

At this point Mrs. Clarke apparently asserted her authority and, leaving the City life of noise and squalor, the family moved westwards to Craven Place, near Kensington Gravel Pits. Her main reason was probably to take her husband away from his familiar drinking haunts and the influence of friends as feckless as himself. There was also the assurance that with three young children to look after she would not be completely among strangers, as living two doors away was Elizabeth Taylor. The firm friendship that developed between them was cemented later by common family interests, because Mary Ann's sister married Miss Taylor's brother.

In hoping to wean her husband from a way of life which had brought their marriage almost to an end, Mary Ann was to be disillusioned. For a time Joseph Clarke lived with the family, coming and going erratically, but out of sight and mind for longer and longer periods. It became increasingly clear to Mrs. Clarke that she must now assume full responsibility for herself and her three children.

In describing this period Elizabeth Taylor blames not only the bottle and skittle ground for the breakdown of the marriage, but hints darkly at sexual excesses to exculpate Mrs. Clarke. "It might have been supposed that, with such a companion, so pre-eminently gifted both in mind and person, her husband could have no temptation for leaving the fair mountain of chaste delight to batten on the moor of mercenary prostitution. Such, however, is human frailty, such the paroxysms of intemperance and debauchery, that, from some discoveries not admitting of palliation, Mrs. Clarke formed the resolution of breaking a connection which, if longer continued, might have involved in distress or infamy twice the number of innocent individuals the family then consisted of."

Alone and penniless, Mrs. Clarke was at the cross-roads. Opportunities open to a woman in her predicament were few and servile. Domestic work was hard, endless, and badly paid and, to someone of her intelligence, it was an ignominious solution that she refused to contemplate. She was young and attractive and decided that the one hope of a better life for herself and her children lay in supplanting her husband with a lover of more ample means.

Mrs. Clarke's first venture into the realm of the kept women was not a success. The name of the baronet she enticed, a barrister by profession, and how she met him, is not disclosed, but taking her children with her, she lived with him for a time in Wiltshire. Springing to her friend's defence, Elizabeth Taylor declares that "as the baronet was obliged to pay close attention to his professional pursuits . . . it is probable that her paramour was oftener poring over parchment than feasting on the damask cheek of his fair protégé."

There was, in fact, a far more compelling reason for the brevity of this affair. Mrs. Clarke's eye was firmly fixed on the pecuniary advantage she was to gain from the liaison but discovered to her chagrin that the baronet and his money were not to be so easily parted. He refused to make the financial settlement that she at first expected and then demanded. Neither daunted nor dismayed, she decided to try her luck elsewhere, and the couple separated, although for a time the baronet continued to contribute to the support of her children.

Back in London again, Mrs. Clarke was to find the path she had chosen a precarious one. "The field of gallantry" was an anomalous sweepstake, a free-for-all without rhyme, reason or rules. Destitute and with her children dependent upon her, "she would fain have compromised with the legal baronet, and gone back to him, when a gudgeon came in her way; this was the late Sir Charles Milner, a coxcomb of the first water."

Slight, short, with lively blue eyes and sparkling vivacity, Mrs. Clarke was learning that to pick up a man was one thing, but that to hold him was an altogether tougher proposition. Sir Charles Milner soon slipped out of her grasp, only to be replaced by Sir James Brudenell. They had, says Elizabeth Taylor, "scarcely entered into a negotiation respecting the terms of their future connection (when) she made an attack upon his pocket to the amount of £200 for laces, etc." For Sir James Brudenell it was a straw in the wind indicating Mrs. Clarke's avaricious expectations, and he left her – with the bill – to her own devices.

Mrs. Clarke was furiously indignant, and the unpalatable fact stared her in the face that it was far easier to get into the beds of the aristocracy than to get money out of their pockets. It was a lesson she was to wrestle with again and again.

In terms of the experience gained on the road leading to the splendours of Gloucester Place, Mrs. Clarke's next encounter was an important one. It began on a note of false hope – and ended with her almost falling in love.

Going about her business, dressed in the first style of fashion, she met a young man "but too well calculated to find his way to the susceptible female heart." Believing Mrs. Clarke to be a woman of means, the young blade assiduously paid her court and took her to a hosier's shop to buy some "trifling articles" which she fancied.

Congratulating herself upon the capture of an attractive young aristocrat of congenial age and temperament, Mrs. Clarke was blissfully unaware that he was one of the young rakes, living on his wits, his luck, and other people. With both of them under the compulsion of a strong physical attraction, and the illusion of having made a wealthy connection, they arranged to meet one evening at Vauxhall Pleasure Gardens.

It seems likely that Elizabeth Taylor and Mrs. Clarke often laughed about this ludicrous charade of mistaken identities. "They met at Vauxhall", Elizabeth relates gleefully, "but finding more attraction in each other than in the amusements of the delightful spot they retired to the Royal Oak Tavern, where, it is said, an old press bed* supplied the place of Cupid's bower, and the lovers passed the night in all the ecstacies which the possession of a beloved object can bestow."

Mrs. Clarke's success with men depended largely upon her gaiety and scintillating conversation but, uninhibited and impetuous, she almost certainly regarded sex as an important part of the enjoyment of life. Sufficient proof is that although now aware that she was not the socialite she had at first pretended, the young buck lived with her for a time at a cottage in Bayswater.

From him Mrs. Clarke learned much about life in the upper echelons of society with all its snobbery and sophistry, and through him she met many men with a roving eye for a pretty face which helped them temporarily to forget the monotony and habit of conjugal ties.

At this point the pattern of Mrs. Clarke's life becomes obscured and devoid of detail. Her mother had separated from her second husband and went to live with her daughter in Tavistock Place. She helped to run the house and to care for her grandchildren,

---

* A press-bed was what we might today describe as a camp bed. It was made to fold up when not in use into the form of a press closed by a door or doors. The term was sometimes incorrectly applied to a box-bed, which did not fold up. James Boswell in his "Journal of a Tour of the Hebrides" writes that whilst at Aberdeen on 21st August, 1773, "I was to sleep in a little press-bed in Dr. Johnson's room. I had it wheeled out into the dining room." Elizabeth Taylor is making the point that Mrs. Clarke and her lover had to make do with a small, makeshift bed intended only for one person.

and for Mrs. Clarke it was probably a period of greater opportunity for promiscuity and short-lived affairs.

Exactly how she beguiled the Duke of York remains an enigma to which we may never know the answer. It was clearly impossible, as one writer naïvely remarked, "that she stepped directly out of the house of the stone-mason into that of the Commander-in-Chief", and equally inconceivable that she slipped from one bed to the other. To satisfy a public bursting with curiosity to know every salacious detail of the liaison, many colourful inventions were put out, each one as improbable as it was romantic.

Cyrus Redding insists that she applied to the Duke for a subscription towards the cost of publishing a poem which she had written called "Ianthe", but that when the Duke met her he decided that she had other talents of greater potentiality.

This and other legends were as specious as the one that she played Portia in "The Merchant of Venice" at the Haymarket Theatre, and "that if she had not had other game in view she might have made a good second-rate actress", but at least they provided value for money for the people eager to read the books rushed out to satisfy a public intoxicated by the spectacle of a royal scandal.

After Mrs. Clarke moved to Tavistock Place, Elizabeth still visited her, often staying the night, and when Mrs. Clarke became the mistress of the Duke the friendship continued. Knowing the Duke's predilection for female company, she frequently asked Miss Taylor to dine with them and the wine flowed freely and tongues were loosened. The dinner table conversations Miss Taylor heard, she remembered. She certainly knew the whole history of Mrs. Clarke's relationship with her lover, but with commendable integrity she withstood the pressure and temptation to divulge the more intimate details. When questioned, she declared that she had forgotten how long it was after the departure of Joseph Clarke before his wife became the mistress of the Duke of York.

All she would say was that Mrs. Clarke called on her one day and told her she was living in Park Lane, and although the real purpose of Mrs. Clarke's visit was undoubtedly to impart the exciting news of her skill and good fortune in decoying the Duke, Elizabeth Taylor was not prepared to reveal the details of their conversation for public ribaldry.

Mrs. Clarke was always eager to talk about any event or activity that came within her orbit and it is significant that about the beginning of her relationship with the Duke, she would say almost nothing. She conceded that he first took her "under his protection" in 1803 when he rented a furnished house for her in Park Lane and, confirming what everybody knew, she said she lived with him in Gloucester Place from 1803–1806.

It is generally supposed that the Duke was introduced to Mrs. Clarke by a mutual acquaintance, either in London or at one of the fashionable south coast resorts. Perhaps subconsciously compelled to say something on a question to which everyone wanted to know the answer, Elizabeth Taylor fell back upon an extraordinary generalisation. "His Royal Highness", she wrote, "found Mrs. Clarke literally a loose fish, an enterprising adventuress in the field of gallantry."

It seems probable that she was first introduced to him for an evening's diversion, to help him forget his Army duties, his money difficulties, and his frigid German wife living in seclusion at Oatlands near Weybridge, who asked no more than to be left in peace with her motley miscellany of dogs, monkeys and parrots.

Gay and scintillating, Mary Ann Clarke was all that the Duchess was not. A woman who loved life and who bubbled over with energy and enthusiasm, she was a lively antidote to the fusty protocol of the Royal Household and the daily routine at the Horse Guards. "Her whole air and deportment are untainted by affectation; in fact, she is nature in undress," commented one contemporary observer cryptically, and under the spell of her abandon to love and living, it is scarcely surprising that the Duke found his senses reeling.

Unlike his elder brother, the Duke of York was a man of habit and hard work and, as the conscientious Commander-in-Chief, he had outgrown the nightly carousals and sexual gambits that the Prince of Wales demanded to stir his jaded appetite. Not for him the hurly-burly of the *chaise-longue* when a comfortable four-poster and the witty Mary Ann were so easily available.

Established in the fashionable Gloucester Place house with twenty servants at her beck and call, watching her guests eating off the Duc de Berri's famous service of plate, and dazzled by their reflections in her pier glasses costing £400 to £500 (but not yet paid for), her early days in the teeming back streets of London became no more than a dim, unsubstantial memory.

The three-year reign of the egregious Mrs. Clarke had begun.

Chapter Three

Oh, the brave old Duke of York,
He had ten thousand men;
He marched them up to the top of the hill,
And he marched them down again.
And when they were up, they were up,
And when they were down, they were down,
And when they were only half way up,
They were neither up nor down.

Although few people may know about the Duke's amorous escapade with Mrs. Clarke, almost everyone remembers the nursery rhyme immortalising his preposterous military manoeuvre. Such is the irony of life that whereas the Mrs. Clarke débacle is historical fact, the nursery jingle, passed on from generation to generation, is only the fictitious taunt of an anonymous lampoonist.

The flat or mildly undulating countryside over which the Duke campaigned in Holland and Eastern France in 1793, 1794 and 1799, afforded him no opportunity to march his army either uphill or down. Unfortunately these expeditions brought only disappointment, defeat and disaster. The failure to capture Dunkirk, the victory of the French at Tourcoing ten miles from Lille, and, worst of all, the withdrawal from Holland in 1799, combined to shatter beyond redemption the Duke's military reputation.

It made no difference that he was badly served by the British Government, that he was let down by his Austrian allies, that it was the wrong time and the wrong place to launch an offensive against the French. The odium for these humiliating defeats was heaped squarely on the head of the Duke of York. "Glory after glory", sneered one of his contemporaries, "Dunkirk, Holland; defeat, retreat."

But it was the more subtle innuendo of the nursery rhyme that was to survive, damning the Duke as an incompetent and ludicrous military commander, burlesquing him as a figure of fun, as ineffectual as Humpty Dumpty and as absurd. It is a sad and summary dismissal of a man whose whole life was devoted to the army.

Frederick, Duke of York and Albany, was the second son of George III and Queen Charlotte. His father was known to be a brave and honest man, well characterised as "Farmer George", who became King in 1760 at the age of twenty-two, and, outliving most of his contemporaries, died at eighty-one, insane and sightless. "He feared nothing on earth, and he acted according to his convictions", wrote Leigh Hunt. "But unfortunately, his convictions were at the mercy of a will far greater than his understanding; and hence his courage became obstinacy, and his honesty the dupe of his inclinations."

George III's marriage to the seventeen-year-old Princess Charlotte of Mecklenberg-Strelitz was an admirable arrangement. They shared the same lofty standards of good and evil; they held the same inflexible convictions about religion, morality, etiquette and protocol; they recognised the same rigid demarcation between the lower orders, tradesmen and the aristocracy, with royalty a unique connecting link between heaven and earth.

Dumpy and despotic, Queen Charlotte was not the woman to excite either admiration or affection. "The English people did not like me much because I was not pretty", she confided to one of her Ladies-in-Waiting. "But the King was fond of driving a phaeton in those days and once he over-turned me in a turnip field, and the fall broke my nose. I think I was not quite so ugly after dat."

One wag unkindly dubbed her "The Old Beguine", and with her thrifty, meddlesome and inquisitive ways she was an inevitable target for the sallies of the caricaturists.

> The Queen loves plate – could she her silence hold?
> Was all *mock* splendour – or pure, solid gold?
> She could not ask, use spectacles, or lamp,
> She felt beneath the plates to find the stamp.

George, Prince of Wales, Prince Regent, and King from 1820–1830, was born in 1762. The birth of his brother, Frederick, Duke of York, took place on August 16th the following year at about ten o'clock in the morning. The Princess Dowager of Wales was present, several Lords of the Privy Council, and ladies "of elevated rank". There were a further thirteen children in the next twenty years and although the two youngest boys died in infancy there still remained a formidable family of six Princesses and seven Princes. One of these, Edward, Duke of Kent, four years younger than his brother Frederick, was to play a Machiavellian role in Mrs. Clarke's disclosures before the House of Commons many years later.

With only a year's difference in their ages, George and Frederick were brought up together and this close youthful companionship established a bond between them not shared by any of their brothers.

At Buckingham House* the two boys occupied a suite of rooms consisting of dining-room, breakfast-room, study, and sitting-room, and their bedroom looked out over extensive gardens. In the summer they lived at Kew House, previously the home of their paternal grandmother, the Princess Dowager of Wales. The grounds behind the house ran down to the banks of the Thames, and here they learned fencing and horsemanship, and played single-wicket cricket.†

The brothers received a classical education in Latin, Greek, French, Arithmetic and Geography, and when in later life their wild, extravagant behaviour was all too painfully apparent, their tutors complained that it had been impossible to teach them the value of money. Both the Prince of Wales and the Duke of York were easy-going spendthrifts by disposition, but it is obvious that neither their parents nor tutors possessed the common sense to realise the need to give these two young princes any help with money management, financial budgeting or economics. When Mrs. Clarke and the Duke of York came together many years later they were as recklessly improvident as one another, and it was almost inevitable that their relationship would end in disaster.

When the Duke of York was only seven months old the See of Osnaburg became vacant, which since the Treaty of Westphalia was alternatively Catholic and Lutheran. The nomination to the vacant Bishopric devolved by rotation upon George III in his

* Now Buckingham Palace. George III bought Buckingham House as a present for his wife, and it was commonly called "The Queen's House".

† Single-wicket cricket is still played, and every year one representative from each of the seventeen counties and six invited overseas players, take part in the Charrington Trophy single-wicket cricket competition, with the winner collecting an appreciable money prize.

capacity of Elector of Hanover, and he appointed his second son to this "secular dignity with an ecclesiastical designation".

The revenues of this Bishopric amounted to nearly £30,000 a year, a very attractive and tangible asset. As the income accumulated, the King purchased for his son the extensive estate of Allerton Mauleverer in Yorkshire for £100,000, but it was later sacrificed to the Duke's compulsive but unlucky gambling propensities.

When the Prince of Wales was seven and Frederick six, Queen Charlotte, always obsessed with ceremonial, was struck with the idea of presenting her children at their first drawing-room. The occasion was distinctly ludicrous. "It certainly could have entered into the head only of a German princess" commented Robert Huish acidly, "to place the children in such a ridiculous and truly anti-British situation." One of the caricaturists derided the occasion more humourously, depicting the Prince of Wales entering the room with his kite behind his back, the Bishop of Osnaburg riding his hobby-horse, Prince Henry spinning his top, and the Princess Royal behind a screen "receiving some very friendly assistance from her nurse". In the face of such ridicule these juvenile performances were abandoned, but from an early age the young princes were very much aware of their exalted position.

George III was a dutiful father, deeply concerned to provide his two eldest sons with the best possible upbringing and education to equip them for the state duties that lay ahead. His yardstick was strict discipline, Old Testament severity, and undeviating attention to their duties. It was a despotic regime unlikely to find favour with two high-spirited boys whose temperamental dispositions were at loggerheads with the devout, duty-prescribed horizons of their parents.

Intelligent, egotistical and vain, the Prince of Wales in particular revolted against his father's tyrannical expectations. From small beginnings the rift grew that was to divide and alienate father and son more deeply and disastrously as the years went by.

"Princess Sophia told me once," Amelia Murray recalled, "that she had seen her two eldest brothers, when they were boys of thirteen and fourteen, held by their arms to be flogged like dogs, with a long whip!"

"Was it any wonder," she reflected, "that the results proved anything but satisfactory?"

Since Princess Sophia was fifteen years younger than the Prince of Wales, Amelia Murray, who wrote her memoirs of the Court late in life, may have confused the identity of the Princess who told her this story, or perhaps the anecdote illustrating George III's severity was a well-known and frequently aired skeleton in the royal cupboard. It is at least fairly certain that Amelia Murray was not the kind of woman to invent such a bizarre episode merely to add colour to her reminiscences.

Good-natured, even-tempered, but less intelligent than his brother, Frederick made greater efforts to please his father. He behaved thoughtlessly, and sometimes badly, but he remained his father's favourite son, and his sins were quickly forgiven and attributed to the baneful influence of the Prince of Wales.

It was the Prince of Wales who took the lead in their amorous activities, and at the age of sixteen he fell under the spell of the petite, child-like actress Perdita Robinson, but Mrs. Papendiek, the wife of one of the pages at court, suggests that there were even earlier escapades, and laments the conduct of those who "introduced improper company when their Royal Highnesses supposed them to be at rest."

The Duke of York, with more plebian taste than his brother, succumbed to the charms of one of the dairy maids at Kew. There was, however, little time for the development of this youthful romance.

The Duke always took a keen interest in military matters. As a young boy he had idolised Frederick the Great of Prussia, and he transformed the gardens of Kew House into a miniature replica of the battlefields of the Seven Years' War, to fight again "with mimic skill and courage . . . the battles of Prague, of Schweidnitz and of Torgan".

The King decided that his son's military education would be best accomplished in Germany. On November 1st, 1780, at the age of seventeen, he was given the honorary appointment of Colonel, and on December 30th, accompanied by Colonel Grenville, he set out from Buckingham House for Hanover.

For the next six-and-a-half years the Duke remained in Germany. He conscientiously fulfilled his military duties, became an excellent shot, and an enthusiastic spectator at the grand-scale army manoeuvres. He also met his boyhood hero, the elderly Frederick, King of Prussia. There was time and opportunity, too, for off-duty pursuits of a more diverting sort.

At the German court at this time was a Baron Seltenheim, whom Huish roundly denigrates as "one of the most finished gentlemen, and also one of the most finished scoundrels of his age". "To this human shark", he wrote, "the young Frederick became the destined victim," and, unfettered by parental discipline, there was nothing to prevent him from indulging his innate propensities for wine, women and gambling.

He returned to England a tall, heavily built young man of twenty-four. He took his military duties seriously and was seen each day on parade, but the Archbishop of Canterbury complained that he did not come up to his expectations in his personal appearance. "It is like that of any other young officer you meet, neither *l'air noble* nor *militaire*. He stoops much, which I never saw in a German officer before, and therefore I wonder, because he has been living with German officers."

Writing to Lord Auckland, Mr. Storer revealed that the Duke's off-duty life was already a matter of curiosity and speculation. "The Duke of York's amours have been numerous hitherto," he reported. "I suppose before the winter is out he will have *une habitude*."

Mr. Storer's prophecy was not fulfilled. Although, like a large number of the young aristocrats and army officers of his age, the Duke indulged in numerous love-affairs, he was not yet ready to embark upon the sophisticated enterprise of a mistress supported in idleness and exorbitant luxury, the gleeful prey for the tittle-tattle of the gossip-mongers.

Four years later, at the age of twenty-eight, the Duke temporarily put an end to the speculations about his private life. In the evening of September 29th, 1791, he was married in Berlin to Princess Fredericka, the fair-haired, twenty-four-year-old daughter of the King of Prussia. The marriage ceremony was performed with the Duke and his bride sitting on a crimson velvet sofa under a crimson canopy, and when it was over the guests sat down to supper at six tables and ate off gold plate to the accompaniment of musicians playing in the galleries above. They returned to England immediately, and to conform to the Royal Marriage Act they were re-married at Buckingham House at nine o'clock at night on November 23rd.

The Duke and Duchess settled quietly at Oatlands, three miles from Weybridge. The original palace was destroyed by fire shortly after it was purchased by the Duke, and he re-built a sombre, square house situated in a thickly-wooded park. Here the Duchess slipped quietly into English country life, interesting herself in the welfare of her tenants and endowing the education of their children, attending Weybridge Church with unfailing regularity, and refusing to become embroiled in the scandals and acrimonious squabbles of the royal family.

The Duke had also a residence in Piccadilly, called the Albany after his second title, and in 1793 and 1794 he was abroad for long periods leading the British armies against those of revolutionary France.

Already his heavy drinking habits were attracting attention, and they inspired one lampoonist to launch a satirical attack –

My name is York,
I draw a cork
Much better than I fight,
The soldiers knew,
As well as you,
That what I say is right.

There was also other evidence of the Duke's pleasure-loving gambits, and the gossip-loving dandy, Captain Gronow, maintained that his cavalry officer friend, Captain Hesse, was the Duke's illegitimate son. As a boy, Captain Hesse lived at Oatlands with the Duke and Duchess, and at the age of seventeen he was given a commission in the 18th Hussars. He led a wild, turbulent life, ranging from a mild but indiscreet flirtation with Princess Charlotte, the daughter of the Prince of Wales, to an outrageous love-affair with the Queen of Naples so notorious that he was expelled from the city under an escort of gendarmes. He ended his life on the same dramatically romantic note, being killed in a duel by Count Leon, the illegitimate son of Napoleon.

At the beginning of the nineteenth century gambling for enormous stakes was like a disease with many of the aristocracy. George Harley Drummond, of the famous banking house, played whist only once at White's Club, and was ruined by losing £20,000 to Beau Brummell. Lord Robert Spencer lost the last shilling of the considerable fortune given to him by his brother, the Duke of Marlborough, but with courageous desperation teamed up with General Fitzpatrick, who was in the same plight, and together they borrowed sufficient money to keep a faro bank, a very popular card game with the club habitués at the time. The gamble succeeded, and his winnings of £100,000 Lord Spencer prudently invested in the purchase of the beautiful, wooded estate of Woolbeding near Midhurst, in Sussex.

The Duke played whist with more enthusiasm than skill and, although an indulgent Government had granted him on his marriage an annual income of £37,000, his gambling losses continually outstripped his resources. A constant companion at his dinner table was Count Montrond, a man with piercing blue eyes, sharp features, and completely bald. As "the most agreeable scoundrel and the greatest reprobate in France", he was a regrettable successor to the reprehensible Baron Seltenheim, and his presence at the whist table cost the Duke many thousands of pounds.

In his early life the Duke was also a keen real tennis enthusiast, one of the oldest of all ball games, played on a covered court, and he was an easy prey for the imposters who hung about to "pick up a flat". Ingratiating themselves with the Duke, they allowed him at first to win inconsiderable sums, but as the stakes rose the tables were turned and the Duke found himself deeply indebted. The keeper of the court was said to have been a privy to this chicanery and to have reaped a reward of £2,000 for his connivance.

In 1795 the Duke of York was appointed Commander-in-Chief of the British Army in succession to the seventy-nine-year-old Lord Amhurst, who for two years had been no more than a feeble figurehead, senile and inefficient, and his record as an administrator at home did much to atone for his failure as a commander on active service overseas. "At all events, he did *something*", one of his critics admitted grudgingly when he died, taking the opportunity also to fire a broadside at his elder brother who was now King. "He was not atrociously idle: he went to the office of a morning – he was somewhat clerkly, and did not at one and the same time, eat and drink the earnings of ninety-nine thousand weavers, and despise them."

The Duke had seen at first-hand in Holland and France the incompetence of the British officers, the badly fed, ill-clothed soldiers, and the appalling conditions under which they were expected to live and fight. At the Horse Guards he made sincere and strenuous efforts to effect long overdue improvements and, apart from his involvement with Mrs. Clarke which resulted in a break of two years in his appointment as Commander-in-Chief, it is for this work that he will be longest remembered.

As Commander-in-Chief, the Duke recognised that training and education were essential for every officer, and the military establishments that he inaugurated at Woolwich, Marlow and High Wycombe were the early beginnings to provide much needed officer-training. The military school at Marlow was for cadets between the ages of thirteen and sixteen and later became the Royal Military College of Sandhurst.

By 1800, after nine years of childless marriage, the Duke and Duchess were leading their own independent and separate lives. There was no open rupture as between the Prince of Wales and Caroline of Brunswick; no recriminations, angry words and public scandals. Amiable and tolerant, and probably caring little so long as nothing disturbed her peaceful routine at Oatlands, the Duchess lavished her affections upon a large collection of dogs, parrots and monkeys. She was delighted when anyone gave her a new pet, and Huish complained of her apartments "resembling a dog-kennel rather than the abode of a British Princess".

English lapdogs, French barbettes and Dutch pugs were her favourite breeds, and at all hours of the day and night she wandered through the grounds at Oatlands surrounded by a noisy pack of forty or more dogs. In the park was a dog cemetery, and the Duchess erected little headstones marking the spot where her favourites lay buried.

In London, the Duke pursued his own life of gaiety and pleasure, and at Oatlands was only a week-end guest, arriving with his friends. Dinner was a protracted ritual, beginning at eight and lasting till eleven. "In about a quarter-of-an-hour after we leave the dining-room," wrote Charles Greville, "the Duke sits down to play at whist, and never stirs from the table as long as anybody will play with him. When anybody gives any hint of being tired he will leave off, but if he sees no signs of weariness in others he will never stop himself. He is equally well amused whether the play is high or low, but the stake he prefers is fives and ponies." (£5 points and £25 on the rubber.) The Duchess generally played a quieter and more modest game of half-crown whist in another part of the room.

Both the Duke and Duchess were highly amused by jokes and stories "full of coarseness and indelicacy . . . which would shock a very nice person", Grenville reported with pained pomposity. The Duchess's mind, Grenville said, was not perhaps the most pure, but he admitted that her conversation was never polluted with anything the least indelicate or unbecoming.

When the Duke met Mrs. Clarke he was in his fortieth year, and "a fool at forty is a fool indeed," commented one of his biographers slyly. Although once considered to be handsome, his excessive appetite and heavy drinking had taken their inevitable toll. He was fat and corpulent, or, as another writer expressed it with more finesse, "his form had lost its symmetry." His heavy, florid features resembled his father's more closely than any of his brothers, and his indistinct and guttural speech added nothing to his charm.

Mrs. Clarke was all that the Duke was not. Twelve years younger, small and slim, she bubbled over with vivacity, and her zest for life ran riot even in that riotous age. She had attained the pinnacle of achievement in her dubious life, and now gave full rein to her reckless ambitions. With neither chart nor compass, and following only her own headstrong inclinations to live a life of luxury and to mix in the highest circles of society, she led the Duke on a wild Bacchanalian excursion.

The Duke was infatuated with Mrs. Clarke's physical attractions, her gaiety, and her laughter echoing round the drawing-room of Gloucester Place. She was the perfect antidote to the all-male company and official duties at the Horse Guards, to the life at Oatlands, and to the eccentricities of the Duke's German-born wife.

Nothing was sacred and when the affair became public property the innumerable versifiers busily poked fun at the Duke's over-credulous passion for the artful Mary Ann Clarke.

To gaze and kindle at thy charms,
And life to spend in thy fond arms;
And if it would not be too heavy,
I there would always hold my levee.

Chapter Four

A VERY MARKED difference in the characters of the Prince of Wales and the Duke of York was their attitude towards their wives, their mistresses and their extra-marital affairs.

The life of the Prince of Wales was blighted by the idleness imposed upon him by his father's inflexible determination to keep him safely in cold-storage waiting for a throne that he had no intention of vacating – and no one was less amenable to cold-storage than the exuberant, pleasure-loving Prince of Wales.

His marriage to Caroline of Brunswick was a bizarre admixture of charade, public spectacle and free-for-all. He was so helplessly drunk after their wedding, Caroline reported, that he "passed the greatest part of his bridal-night under the grate, where he fell and where I left him."

And no one knew where his extra-marital activities began and ended: from the pretty, child-like actress, Perdita Robinson, to the petite, perfidious Lady Jersey; from the statuesque, twice-widowed Roman Catholic Mrs. Fitzherbert, to the designing, forty-seven-year-old Lady Hertford; from Mrs. Crouch to Mrs. Billington; and, aided and abetted by the backstairs pimping of Colonel M'Mahon, it was anybody's guess how many more had romped briefly in the royal four-poster.

The Duke of York was a man of less concupiscence and greater conventionality. He invested his relationships with a succession of mistresses with an aura of permanence and respectability, regarding their establishments as a second and more congenial home. Perhaps, like many other men, he needed also the illusion of loving and being loved to arouse his sexual desire.

"I think Mrs. Clarke had a very good opportunity of understanding His Royal Highness's character," wrote Leigh Hunt, "and it was not the least memorable of her observations on him when she said that were he compelled to live at Oatlands he would cut his throat."

The Duke was completely captivated by the charm and sparkling vivacity of Mary Ann Clarke, and her world took on a new and opulent dimension. The furnished house in Park Lane, which she had reported so impressively on her visit to Elizabeth Taylor, was only temporary accommodation, and a few months later in 1803 she moved to No. 18 Gloucester Place, a four-storied house in a broad thoroughfare running northwards from Portman Square to Baker Street.

As a house-warming present the Duke gave Mrs. Clarke £500, which was soon spent on "some little necessary things in plate and linen". There were also other equally necessary but less trifling items: the chandeliers, the grates, and the fitted mirrors reflecting the dazzling attractions of Mrs. Clarke's well-turned arms, her delicate colouring, and her lively blue eyes "beaming with the most irresistible archness."

There was independent testimony, too, to the impressive furniture which she bought from Summers and Rose in Bond Street, already a shopping centre of fashion and repute, and from Francis Wright, an upholsterer with a warehouse in Rathbone Place at the eastern end of Oxford Street.

As well as the furniture and fittings, there was also the important business of recruiting a suitable retinue of servants to staff the establishment she had so confidently launched.

The first to join her, as housekeeper, personal maid and general confidante, was Martha Favery, who later gave evidence that she first went as a servant to Mrs. Clarke six weeks after her marriage, and had been with her on and off ever since.

The services of Martha Favery were quickly augmented by a butler, two footmen in uniform, a house-maid, a laundry-maid, a kitchen-maid, "a little girl who worked at her needle", and, once a week, a charwoman to do the heavy cleaning. The servants, including a coachman, ostler and groom, outnumbered by two to one the household consisting of the Duke, Mrs. Clarke and her three children, and it is difficult to imagine that they were all usefully occupied – but what was that to Mrs. Clarke compared with the impression of style and grandeur imprinted upon her visitors and neighbours?

The Duke's heavy drinking and hearty appetite played a large part in his enjoyment of life, and Mrs. Clarke took considerable trouble to satisfy his gourmand habits by providing the elaborate dinners to which he was accustomed. Two, and sometimes three, male cooks were employed and each was paid a guinea a day. It was a high rate when carpenters, bricklayers and masons were supporting large families on an average weekly wage of eighteen shillings, but Mrs. Clarke explained that her cooks "stayed a very short time with me, anyone. His Royal Highness is very difficult."

Mrs. Favery elaborated the point. "There were always very elegant dinners went up," she said, "and what they could not do came from the pastry cooks . . . If there was any dinner found fault with by His Royal Highness she would have another."

There were no lavish parties or large-scale entertaining at Gloucester Place, but small intimate dinners with Mrs. Clarke, pertly pretty, and two or three times a week Elizabeth Taylor added an additional touch of feminine charm.

"His Royal Highness did not mind what he said before Miss Taylor," declared Mrs. Clarke blithely. "He was very fond of her."

But it was probably the three children and the easy, homely atmosphere which contributed most to the Duke's enjoyment. In particular, her son George was firmly entrenched in the Duke's affections, a changeling substitute for the legitimate son he would never have.

An expensively furnished house, a full complement of servants, and, to complete the picture of high society, Mrs. Clarke's elegant dinners served on equally elegant plate. Here she had a stroke of good fortune. From Birketts, the jewellers, she obtained a magnificent and extensive service, and the fact that it had once belonged to the exiled Duc de Berri was the hall-mark adding style and status to the dining room at Gloucester Place. Like a child with a new toy, she was enchanted with the chased silver epergne – the large centre ornament with branches – the silver salvers, the soup plates with fluted edges, and the silver teapot with ivory handle. No. 18 Gloucester Place was an establishment fit for a Duke, the King's favourite son, the Commander-in-Chief of the Army – and over it all with brains and beauty presided Mrs. Clarke.

The Duke gave her a landau, a most necessary acquisition for her shopping expeditions, the afternoon drives through Hyde Park and Kensington Gardens, and her visits to the theatre, but there soon arose an urgent reason for the purchase of a second carriage.

The Duke still spent his weekends at Oatlands, and well aware of his philandering ways, and his susceptibility to the influence of friends and advisers urging him to end their association, Mrs.

Clarke was quick to sense the danger of being out of sight and mind from Saturday morning until Monday night. The Duke acquired a house for her conveniently close to Oatlands, and to the splendours of her London residence was now added a rural retreat at Weybridge in Surrey.*

A groom, gardener, and two maids were permanently installed, and with her from London on the regular weekend migration Mrs. Clarke was accompanied by four or five extra servants. The landau was hopelessly inadequate, and as Mrs. Clarke bowled along ahead the servants followed in a second carriage that she herself had purchased.

One Sunday curiosity prompted her to attend a service in Weybridge Church when the Duchess of York was present. Tolerant as she was, the Duchess protested to the vicar at Mrs. Clarke's effrontery, and no doubt the Duke informed her in far stronger language that Weybridge Church was strictly out of bounds.

Holding an ambivalent position on the staff as footboy, and also in Mrs. Clarke's affections, was an eighteen-year-old orphan, Samuel Carter. "He was not well educated till he came to me," she declared. "He used to go to school while he was in my service, every leisure hour," and undoubtedly Carter's superior education was a useful gambit when Mrs. Clarke later persuaded the Duke to give him a commission in the 16th Foot Regiment.

The Duke's association with Mrs. Clarke was no hole-in-the-corner affair of brief clandestine visits and sexual satisfaction. "I was in the habit of seeing His Royal Highness every day, except he was in the country", Mrs. Clarke maintained, "and that happened perhaps only for a week or ten days in one year". The Commander-in-Chief was away all day, attending to his duties at the Horse Guards, and if her nights belonged to the Duke, her days were her own.

---

* It has not been possible to identify the house occupied by Mrs. Clarke, and the Surrey land tax records contain no details of any property in her name. "With regard to Weybridge", the Duke of York wrote to her after their separation, "I think that you had better remove your furniture, and then direct the person employed to take the house to give it up again", indicating that it was rented accommodation, and Mrs. Clarke a sub-tenant. It has been suggested that she might have lived in York Cottage, Oatlands Drive, in the Duke's own Park, but this would certainly have been too close to the Duchess for comfort, and was in any case not built until after the Park was sold in 1846.

Like many women of physical charm and innate intelligence who have risen from humble beginnings to positions of prominence, Mrs. Clarke pursued a chaotic course of potted culture between her callers and her correspondence.

Among the men who regularly found their way to Gloucester Place was Dominigo Corri, the music master, whose varied talents were to be exercised later in unsuspected directions. Neither did Mrs. Clarke's musical aspirations end with Dominigo Corri. "Instead of a 60 guinea harp let it be 100", she wrote to a friend, adding with rapacious cajolery, "as I have told him that you were going to present me with one, therefore it must be very elegant."

Painting on velvet was a fashionable pastime for ladies with time on their hands and artistic pretensions, and their pictures, framed and hung round their drawing-rooms, elicited approbation and emulation. To instruct Mrs. Clarke came Benjamin Town, who taught, so he said, landscapes, flowers, figures and fruit. He was a man of as many parts and potentialities as the pawky Mr. Corri, and more was to be heard about him before he disappeared into the obscurity from which he had been momentarily raised by his association with Mrs. Clarke.

Beside Elizabeth Taylor, her most frequent visitors were three men of very different professions and purpose, but all found themselves caught in the net as the House of Commons probed deeper into the private life of Mrs. Clarke.

Dr. Andrew Thynne attended Mrs. Clarke professionally for several years. He was disparagingly dubbed "the celebrated accoucheur", but Mrs. Clarke was not the woman to blight her life of royal protection by an unwanted pregnancy, and summoning him to minister to her mild indispositions merely added a gratifying veneer of privilege and position. If she made no calls upon the special talents of Dr. Thynne, his request to her to use her influence with the Duke of York to expedite the exchange between Lieut.-Colonel Brooke and Lieut.-Colonel Knight was to have painful repercussions. He was the first witness called to give evidence in the House of Commons.

Another visitor with a very different purpose was the Duke's German-born footman, Ludowick Orramin. He arrived each morning at eight, bringing with him the Duke's neatly pressed uniform, and soon after the Commander-in-Chief stepped smartly from Mrs. Clarke's elegantly furnished home to the parade ground and his duties at the Horse Guards.

Ludowick had waited on the Duke for eighteen years and was the only servant permitted to visit his off-beat establishment. "I had an order from His Royal Highness", Ludowick explained, "that I was to bring these things, and no other servant, and no other dared to do it." And so it was Ludowick who received "the prompt message" to take one of the Duke's favourite dogs to Gloucester Place for Mrs. Clarke to see, and who carried the Duke's notes to her from the Horse Guards. Time was to prove Ludowick a man of loyalty and circumspection.

But doctor and servant played only a minor part in the routine life of Mrs. Clarke. It was William Dowler, a long standing admirer, who became the most favoured guest, sharing her secrets, her intrigues, and, from time to time, her bed.

Dowler's father was a man of means and position, a wine and general merchant and a councillor of the City of London, and when he retired to the country his son went with him, supported in idleness by his father's generosity. Perhaps bored by a life of leisure, or perhaps beguiled by the enticement of speculation and profit, Dowler returned to London, set up in business as a stockbroker, and succumbed to the fascinating Mrs. Clarke. Both these ventures were to have unhappy consequences.

Dowler's father constantly cautioned his son that brokerage was "a very dangerous and hazardous occupation", and strongly urged him to quit "The Alley". Despite these warnings Dowler persisted. Shortly after the resumption of war with Napoleonic France on May 16th, 1803, he ran into financial difficulties and the enterprise ended as his father had predicted.

Foot loose but not fancy free, Dowler frequently visited Gloucester Place, drawn as irresistibly as the moth to the flame by the mock splendour, the pseudo-aristocratic graces, but above all by the vivacity and physical attraction of Mrs. Clarke. Was he – the piquant question was on every lip – also her lover, adding the jibe of cuckold to the abuses already heaped on the head of the Duke of York? After his failure on the Stock Exchange, Dowler was again dependent upon his father, and at Mrs. Clarke's instigation he now applied for a Government post as commissary of stores and provisions. "It was suggested to me", Dowler remarked primly, "that the commissariat was an eligible and gentlemanly employment, and not an inactive one".

His first appointment was in the Colchester/Sudbury area fifty miles north-east of London on the borders of Essex and Suffolk, and in 1806 he was sent overseas with an army expedition to Buenos Aires. Distance did not diminish Dowler's affection for Mrs. Clarke, and the disclosure that she had surreptitiously spent the night with him at his hotel when he returned to London whilst the inquiry in the House of Commons was in progress added further salacious gossip to an already abundant crop.

This débâcle, however, lay ahead, and for the moment her days slipped by in the heady pursuit of gaiety and pleasure: a day at the races and weekends at Weybridge; boxes at the theatre and outings to Vauxhall Pleasure Gardens; hot, sunny days at the Royal Hotel, Margate – music lessons, velvet painting, and trips to Worthing.

It was the life that Mary Ann had always craved for, the brief halcyon days of wine and roses, but above her, like a black cloud threatening the idyllic serenity of a summer day, her wild expenditure and soaring debts menaced the whole structure of her insubstantial life.

"I am so dreadfully distressed I know not which way to turn myself", she wrote distractedly to Captain Sandon, who was a frequent visitor to Gloucester Place.

In the House of Commons five years later, Mr. Simeon asked how much she was indebted at the end of her first six months in Gloucester Place. "I really cannot say," Mrs. Clarke answered simply, "I was always frightened to look at it."

Chapter Five

THE PARTING of the ways in May, 1806, was a traumatic if clearly predictable event in the lives of the Duke of York and Mrs. Clarke. During their two and a half years together, the Duke had discovered that living with Mrs. Clarke was a turbulent experience of constantly recurring crises, and her reckless extravagance was a permanent source of embarrassment. In the summer of 1805, a man named Turner served her with a summons for debt and, probably anticipating that to avoid payment she would plead her coverture as a married woman, he spiked her guns by notifying the Duke that he proposed to subpoena him to give evidence on his behalf.

The ruse was successful. The debt was paid to avoid the public scandal it would have engendered had the case come to court, and in the privacy of Gloucester Place the Duke undoubtedly made it clear to Mrs. Clarke that he was not amused at her immoderate behaviour.

A further invidious incident occurred in the autumn that year when Joseph Clarke appeared unexpectedly at Gloucester Place and created consternation and alarm by threatening to sue the Duke for crim. con.* Mrs. Clarke had dealt with her drunken husband before and, plying him with money, she persuaded him to return to his friends and companions in the public houses of Hoxton, where his threats and imprecations evaporated in an alcoholic haze.

William Adam and Colonel Gordon repeatedly urged the Duke to dismiss Mrs. Clarke, and he at last agreed to their suggestion that his attorney, Thomas Lowten, should undertake a private investigation and report fully on her husband, her family, and her

* Criminal Conversation. Down to the enactment of the Matrimonial Causes Act, 1857, the common law action for criminal conversation (known as crim. con.) lay at the suit of a husband to recover damages against an adulterer.

Page 214 (The Year 1792)

No. 673 } Joseph Clarke of the Parish of St James, Clerkenwell, in the County of Middlesex, Bachelor & Mary Ann Farquhar of this Parish, a Minor, Spinster, by the Consent of her Father were Married in this Church by Licence this Nineteenth Day of May in the Year One Thousand Seven Hundred and Ninety two By me, Edwd Sawyer, Minister

This Marriage was solemnized between Us { Mary Ann Farquhar
Joseph Clarke

In the Presence of { R Farquhar
The Mark X of Willm Gaball

Entry in the St. Pancras Church Register of the marriage of Joseph Clarke and Mary Ann Farquhar on May 19th, 1792.

The Duke of York, Commander-in-Chief of the British Army. From the painting by D. Wilkie, 1823.

Colonel Wardle, Mrs. Clarke's "Mushroom Patriot", at the height of his popularity.
From the painting by A. W. Davis, 1809.

A glazed Staffordshire jug with a portrait of Mrs. Clarke's friend, Miss Taylor, whose evidence in the House of Commons produced an outburst of hilarity.

past. Although the report submitted early in May, 1806, contained no evidence or allegation that Mrs. Clarke was trafficking in army commissions, it made it clear that it was likely that her wild expenditure and intemperate way of life might sooner or later involve the Duke in a public scandal.

The Duke was not convinced but William Adam persisted and, probably swayed by his adviser's insistence that by continuing the liaison he might well forfeit his appointment as Commander-in-Chief, the Duke, with misgivings and regret, reluctantly agreed to end the affair.

Perhaps nagged by an uneasy conscience at discarding Mrs. Clarke so peremptorily, or possibly afraid of her sharp tongue and marked felicity for home truths, the Duke shirked the direct confrontation and asked William Adam to convey his decision in a personal interview. It was a brief that William Adam would have preferred to decline but bravely declared that he felt "it to be a duty, as I had commenced the transaction which was to lead to this, not to flinch from any personal inconvenience, or any unpleasantness which might arise at the time or in the future, to make the communication".

The Duke wrote Mrs. Clarke a short letter announcing the visit of his legal adviser, but even had the thought of being pensioned off passed through her mind she can scarcely have anticipated the arrogant proviso accompanying it.

"The Duke thought it his duty, if her conduct was correct", William Adam informed her, "to give her an annuity of £400, to be paid quarterly. That he could enter into no obligation in writing, by bond or otherwise, that it must rest entirely upon his word, to be performed according to her behaviour, and that he might, therefore, have it in his power to withdraw the annuity in case her behaviour was such as to make him consider that it was unfit it should be paid."

With commendable restraint Mrs. Clarke held her tongue. Sublimely convinced of her powers of persuasion and charm, she held firmly to the idea that in spite of William Adam she would see the Duke again and bring him back to Gloucester Place and her seductive embraces.

In the evening of the day of her interview with Mr. Adam, Mrs. Clarke expected the Duke for dinner as usual. After her summary dismissal that morning she can scarcely have anticipated his presence as a matter of course, and as she was constantly dashing off letters in every direction it is probable that after Mr. Adam's departure she underpinned her expectations with her pen.

It must have been a fidgety, irascible Mrs. Clarke waiting impatiently as the hands of the clock moved slowly towards the hour for dinner. Slight, short, and fully alive to making the most of her physical charms, she would certainly have chosen with particular care her high-waisted gown, with the skirt hanging loosely to the ground, and was undoubtedly wearing the heavy make-up so much more fashionable at the beginning of the nineteenth century than it is today.

She knew that the Duke was at his house in Portman Square only a short distance away. "I waited dinner for His Royal Highness . . . till ten o'clock," she said, "and sent down several times to Portman Square to know whether he dined with me or not. They said they fancied he dined with me, as he had ordered no dinner."

Between eight and nine, Charles Greenwood, the Army agent, made his appearance in Portman Square. He and the Duke sat down to their dinner and their wine, and later that evening Mrs. Clarke received a letter.

"You must recollect the occasion which obliged me, above seven months ago, to employ my Solicitor in a suit with which I was then threatened on your account; the result of those enquiries first gave me reason to form an unfavourable opinion of your Conduct; you cannot therefore accuse me of rashly or hastily deciding against you: but after the proofs which have at last been brought forward to me, and which it is impossible for you to controvert, I owe it to my own Character and Situation to abide by the resolution which I have taken, and from which it is impossible for me to recede. An interview between us must be a painful task to both, and can be of no possible advantage to you; I therefore must decline it."

There was no question that the letter Mrs. Clarke received was in the Duke's handwriting, but whether it was composed by him remained a matter of dispute.

"It was written by the Duke of York," Greenwood deposed, "and copied by me."

"It was written by Mr. Greenwood," Mrs. Clarke contradicted him. "His Royal Highness copied it, and sent it instead of coming for dinner . . . His Royal Highness's servant told it to my servants."

The Duke's letter made it painfully plain to Mrs. Clarke that his mind was made up, and she knew that unless she could prevail upon him in person he would never be returning to Gloucester

Place. If the mountain wouldn't come to Mohammed, she decided, Mohammed would go to the mountain.

Either mounting a watching brief herself in Portman Square, or entrusting the task to a servant, she waited for Greenwood's departure, and then by stealth, charm or confidence trick gained admission to the Duke's house. His account of their bizarre encounter in the late hours of an early spring night was never heard, but, as usual, Mrs. Clarke had her own version to disseminate.

"I saw His Royal Highness afterwards in his own house that same night," she said, "but he ran away from me" – a malicious thrust at the manliness and valour of the Commander-in-Chief of the British Army!

Having failed in person to win him back, Mrs. Clarke now pursued her capricious lover with her pen. She had, she said, frequently received letters from him after their separation, which "always consisted of short notes in answer to some request of mine in some letter", adding sanctimoniously, with a neat choice of words, "but they are not civil ones since I left him." To confound the sceptical who believed that this was merely one more glib assertion to add to all the others she produced four for public digestion.

"If it could be of the least advantage to either of us, I should not hesitate in complying with your wish to see me; but as a Meeting must, I should think, be painful to both of us, under the present circumstances, I must decline it."

Mrs. Clarke,
No. 18 Gloucester Place,
Portman Square.

"I enter fully into your sentiments concerning your children, but cannot undertake what I am not sure of performing . . . ."

Mrs. Clarke,
No. 18 Gloucester Place,
Portman Square.

"Without being informed to what amount you may wish for assistance, it is impossible for me to say how far it is in my power to be of use to you."

Mrs. Clarke,
No. 9 Old Burlington Street.

"It is totally out of my power to be able to give you the assistance which you seem to expect."

Mrs. Clarke,
Southampton.

It was clear at last to Mrs. Clarke that the Duke would not be returning, and having lost her lucrative four-star meal ticket there was nothing left but to salvage what she could from the wreckage of his defection.

Her financial predicament was critical. She admitted to having debts at the break-up of "something under £2,000", and losing no time she sent details of them to the Duke the day after her dismissal, but confided that she "found them to be more upon examination".

No. 18 Gloucester Place had been bought by the Duke in the heyday of his passion for Mrs. Clarke, and grasping at it as the most valuable asset in sight she wrote asking him to give her the lease so that she might sell the house and her possessions, and pay her debts. The Duke agreed, probably relieved to see the end of a ménage that was now only an embarrassment.

There was excitement and curiosity at the sale of the booty accumulated by Mrs. Clarke during her three-year occupation as mistress of the Commander-in-Chief of the Army, and one querulous contemporary wrote that "The most splendid assembly of furniture, plate, etc., was offered to the public that perhaps ever came under the hammer."

"We are still more grieved to add," he continued "that . . . amongst other articles which came to the hammer was a miniature of the Queen, set around with diamonds. By whose hand did she receive it?" he asked rhetorically.

Her wine glasses were bought by Mrs. Fitzherbert's brother at a guinea each, and one pundit, aghast at her prodigality, complained that they were "such in size as individuals use at dinner." No wonder the Duke scolded Mrs. Clarke that the wine went too quickly!

After selling Gloucester Place, Mrs. Clarke took stock of her position. "The whole," she said, "sold for £4,400," but claimed that before she could appropriate any money herself it had all gone, paid out to her innumerable creditors. "Some short time before I had borrowed different sums of money of my lawyer, to the amount of £1,200 to £1,400 . . . I fancy the taxes for a twelvemonth were not paid . . . £700 was due to Mr. Parker for trinkets which were got from him to be sold in the sale . . . there was £400 to £500 to Mr. Harry Phillips for his commission . . . and I took £700 on account to pay the poor trades-people and the servants."

"I had no balance coming to me", she declared, an implied criticism of the plight in which the Duke had left her, but somewhere in her calculations she overlooked more than £1,000 – and a woman of Mrs. Clarke's rapacity was scarcely likely to allow herself to be left completely penniless as a sequel to the sacrifices that she felt she had been called upon to make.

The exact date when Mrs. Clarke left 18 (now No. 62) Gloucester Place is not clear. She last paid rates for the Christmas quarter of 1806, which suggests that she left either late in 1806 or early in 1807.

Still owing money, and far more vulnerable to the importunities of her creditors now that she was no longer living under royal protection, she decided that the time had come to carry out a strategic withdrawal and leave them to their own devices. Once again the lampoonists followed her activities with epigrammatic wit –

> So Fie, Fie took four hundred pounds a year,
> Cut town – all agencies – and left her dear.

In reality her departure was a little less precipitate. "I had nothing even to take me out of town," she blandly asserted, and with characteristic predictability wrote to the Duke informing him of this sorry state of affairs.

"He promised to give me two hundred pounds for my journey but Mr. Adam objected to that to my lawyer and said a hundred pounds was plenty, but the Duke overruled it and sent me two sometime afterwards," she divulged, undoubtedly as pleased at having put Mr. Adam in his place as she was with the money.

Two of the Duke's letters to Mrs. Clarke after the separation are addressed to Old Burlington Street and Southampton. There is no other reference to these two addresses and in all probability after leaving Gloucester Place she retired for a few weeks to furnished rooms in Old Burlington Street behind the Royal Academy in Piccadilly, and upon receiving the two hundred pounds she packed her possessions and left London for Southampton. Apart from the Duke's letter, there is no evidence of her stay in Southampton and it was probably brief.

For her provincial début, Mrs. Clarke decided to spend the summer of 1807 at Exmouth, an unpretentious seaside resort on the estuary of the river Exe, with excellent sands and bathing for the children, and conveniently remote from her creditors in London.

In a still far from forgotten pamphlet on the "Memorials of Exmouth" published in 1883, the Rev. William Everitt quotes the evangelical author of "Experiences of a Gaol Chaplain" as recalling Mrs. Clarke's sojourn there in 1804.

These three volumes of autobiographical reminiscences published in 1847 reveal that it was not, in fact, the Gaol Chaplain who remembered Mrs. Clarke at Exmouth, but one of the prison inmates he interviewed, a white-haired, blue-eyed octogenarian, who nearly forty years before had been secretary and steward to the Rev. George Henry Glasse, the rector of Hanwell, whose connection with Mrs. Clarke had had calamitous consequences.

"It was my duty more than once to wait the leisure of the royal favourite", the vicar's old manservant related, "and I well remember the splendour in which this lively, vain, extravagant, and after all, not particularly handsome woman lived. But I recollected her long, long before she had attracted the notice of the Duke of York. I remembered her at Exmouth, when she resided at Manchester House, in those days a noble dwelling, adjoining that belonging to Mr. Russell, the Exeter banker, and when she had neither bishoprics, commissions, nor clerkships in the ordnance to dispose of to the highest bidder."

Unfortunately it has not been possible to confirm Mrs. Clarke's occupation of Manchester House as the rate books held by Exmouth Urban District Council only go back to 1854, but as her movements are fully authenticated from October 1807, the summer of that year is the only period after the separation when it was possible for her to have been living in Exmouth.

Manchester House is still standing, and the visitor to Exmouth will find it in Imperial Road, opposite the bus station and the recreation ground. Recently converted into suites of offices, occupied by solicitors, builders, and the local Conservative Agent, it is a long time since the house echoed Mrs. Clarke's light, attractive voice, and the laughter and cries of her three young children.

A most illuminating account confirming that Mrs. Clarke's visit to Exmouth took place after her dismissal by the Duke and before the House of Commons inquiry, appeared more than twenty years later in "The Court Journal". It was written under the intriguing *nom de plume* of "Cousin Alice", and lugubriously entitled "The Lucubrations of a Lady of Rank".

"By the way, there was a lady much about the same time at Exmouth, who subsequently made a pretty considerable stir in St. Stephen's Chapel – Mrs. Mary Anne Clarke. Many a walk have we had on the Warren together, and many a hearty laugh (for her drollery was irresistible) have I enjoyed at her ready repartee. She was rather pretty, but her face wanted expression; not altogther unlike the late Mrs. Long-Wellesley, fair-complexioned, with a lively, laughing eye. I don't pretend to defend her; but a more generous, kind-hearted creature I never met with. She did not wait to be told of distress; she sought it out and relieved it. I am speaking of a period antecedent to "the investigation" when she was living in the greatest privacy, and her connection with royalty was unknown. But the immense quantity of letters she daily received, the greater proportion franked, led speedily to a suspicion that she was other than she pretended, and I shortly after learned the truth from Lady Nelson."*

Mrs. Clarke lived in a man's world, and what they said and wrote about her was prejudiced by their politics, their sense of outraged propriety, or their partiality for her physical attractions, and this glimpse of her through the eyes of a woman is of particular interest.

---

* Lady Nelson, the widow of Vice-Admiral Nelson, lived for many years in Exmouth until her death in 1831.

Chapter Six

IT WAS PLAINLY evident to those closely connected with the Duke that a growing number of people were as critical of his conduct as Commander-in-Chief during the past two years as they were of his private philandering, and the build-up of their strictures, protests, and scurrilous lampoons were the straws in the wind for the sensational dénouement that lay ahead. In Exmouth Mrs. Clarke undoubtedly followed the Duke's discomfiture with smug satisfaction.

The case of the Hon. Cochrane Johnstone, an ex-Colonel of the 8th West India Regiment and one-time Governor of the Island of Dominica, had been a source of controversy and contention for several years.

Cochrane Johnstone's resentment stemmed from his exclusion without any explanation when a promotion of Colonels to Major-Generals took place in October, 1803. He wrote to the Duke of York asking "to know the cause of a punishment so severe and unexpected", and was informed that "it is an inevitable rule of the services not to include in any general promotion an officer . . . against whom there existed charges, the merit of which has not been decided."

Cochrane Johnstone at once demanded particulars of the charges about which he knew nothing and in May, 1804, he received a reply stating that the Commander-in-Chief had called on Colonel Gordon, his military secretary, "to state whether he meant to bring forward any charges at all."

In March the following year the Colonel proceeded to Canterbury, where his trial was to take place, when "all of a sudden" it was removed to Chelsea. The case dragged on and although Cochrane Johnstone was eventually acquitted he resigned from the army in disgust.

On March 10th, 1807, Samuel Whitbread revived the criticism of the Commander-in-Chief for partiality and inefficiency when he presented a Petition in the House of Commons in which Cochrane Johnstone again protested that although he had served more than twenty years in the army, thirteen of them overseas "under circumstances of great fatigue and danger", he had been most unfairly victimised in his bid for promotion more than three years earlier.

Two months later the attack on the Duke switched from the House of Commons to the public prints. "The New Military Road to York by way of Frome", by Williams in May, 1807, depicted Frome, an agent for army commissions, as a turnpike keeper accepting bribes from spruce young officers, whilst shabbily dressed and crippled veterans were forced to trudge the old road because they could not afford the money demanded. Frome later asserted that the caricature had been shown to George III, who was so incensed that he immediately sent for the Duke of York and ordered him to close the agent's office.

The following month Blackwood & Company channelled the charges of corruption to the doorstep of the Commander-in-Chief himself. "Military Leap Frog – or Hints to Young Gentlemen" the print proclaimed, portraying three smartly-dressed young officers on a country road leaping towards Mrs. Clarke over the backs of war-crippled veterans with amputated limbs and hobbling along on crutches and sticks.

"Throw in your 700 (pounds) here and I'll give you a Majority", coaxes Mrs. Clarke in high-waisted gown with short sleeves and straw hat trimmed with ribbons. "I am the Principal Clark."

A jaunty civilian solicits a further bribe. "Throw in your purse of 300 pounds and you will jump the quicker."

The insinuation that Mrs. Clarke was still trafficking in army commissions was, in fact, more than a year out of date and at the time the print was published in June, 1807, she was living in Exmouth with her three children. As if to put the record straight, Williams followed with a caricature of Mrs. Clarke's fall from favour.

"The Discarded Clark, or Eve driven out of Paradice" (sic) made public the high drama enacted in the drawing-room of Gloucester Place when William Adam presented Mrs. Clarke with her marching orders.

The part played by the Duke's legal adviser was emphasised by a quotation from "Coriolanus" – "Thou hast a grim appearance and thy face a command in it" – whilst the adaptation of a line from "Paradise Lost" slyly hinted that one of Mrs. Clarke's principal denigrators, the army agent, Greenwood, was also involved. "Thro' the Greenwood she took her lonely way and all the world before her", ran the inscription on the scroll at Mrs. Clarke's feet as she was driven from the Paradise of her Commission Warehouse in Gloucester Place, although the lithographer was misinformed about its having been "removed to Charing Cross".

What the Hon. Cochrane Johnstone and the lampoonists had begun the phamphleteers continued with tracts of almost staggering calumny.

In these venal times many men pursued unchecked a riotous course of hedonistic revelry and sexual satisfaction, but the suspicion of departure from the paths of virtue or decorum on the part of a woman was sufficient "to swell the very air with detraction, slander and ignominy, to blast with one poisoned breath both her honour and her repose."

Mrs. Clarke had elected with cool premeditation the vicarious life of the kept woman. However vitriolic her denigration, she was scarcely likely to have suffered either mortification or insomnia, and probably grasped with calculating audacity the advantages to be gained from being projected with such vehemence into the forefront of the assault upon her renegade lover.

One of the first tracts to be published in 1807 was pompously entitled "Mentoriana or A Letter of Admonition and Remonstrance to His Royal Highness the Duke of York relative to Corruption, Oppression, Cowardly Revenge, Agency Monopoly, Meretricious Influence and other Subjects connected with the Army", and quickly went into a third edition.

"Let me, therefore, entreat your Royal Highness never to entrust your honour to the keeping of a strumpet," was the censorious advice of the anonymous author. "Avoid her as the serpent of Ceylon, whose embrace is mortal, for the venom of his tooth is not more fatal than the honey of her lip. Reflect on the indelible disgrace, the lasting infamy, that would be the consequence of having it supposed that the Duke of York, the son of the British Monarch, the Commander-in-Chief of the British forces, was governed by an abandoned woman: and that promotion in (the) army was only attainable by the bribery of an avaricious and infamous concubine."

Perhaps incited by the intrepid example of others, "An Englishman" now took up his pen to write "A Letter to His Royal Highness, or A Delicate Inquiry into the doubt whether he be more favoured by Mars or Venus", in which he found no evidence of special dispensation for the British Commander-in-Chief from the Roman god of war.

"Glory after glory," he sneered. "Dunkirk, Holland; defeat, retreat..."

The author next turned his attention to the Duke's domestic affairs. "Tradition represents you as preserving the dignity of your rank," he reminded him, "never descending to the dirty delight of low sordid company . . . . In your retreat from such society, where you sought and found repair, I presume not to say Oatlands was too remote; Gloucester Place was perhaps adjacent."

Tearing Mrs. Clarke's character to shreds, the pamphleteer decided that the goddess of love had been equally negilgent. "With respect to C . . . . ke, I must be explicit: – this artful, vain, flippant, mercenary yet prodigal giglet, by one common seal, affixes shameless depravity on two hearts, and stultifies two heads."

"Such a couple of personages came together; all the costly luxuries of life were suddenly poured down upon her: a stately mansion was superbly furnished, an expensive side-board of plate (the poor Duke de B . . . 's was purchased at £3,000), diamonds glittered at every point, and the richest jewels and drapery adorned her person. A vast retinue of servants, splendid equipage, royal liveries, and high-priced horses, rattling through the streets with a dangerous velocity, threatening the safety of the passengers, and provoking inquiries, which terminate for the present only in exposing the thoughtless profligacy of the man, and the audacious licentiousness of the woman."

* * *

The days became shorter and the nights grew cooler at Exmouth and, confronted with the gloomy prospect of spending the winter in seclusion there, Mrs. Clarke made up her mind to return to London. Behind her decision lay also a very practical motive.

The payment of the annuity promised by the Duke had fallen ominously into areas, and she knew that only by employing her talents of persuasion and personal pressure at much closer quarters was she likely to obtain the money which was now her only source of income. She also knew that in returning to London she was running a considerable risk.

Having left behind many irate creditors, and now having neither money nor protection, she could scarcely hope to escape the privations of a debtors' prison should they pick up her trail again. It was a hazardous gamble that would have deterred a woman of weaker resolution.

Knowing she could not hope to live anonymously for long in central London, she tempered boldness with discretion, and in October 1807 took lodgings with William Nicholls in Hampstead,* a village high above London six miles to the north west.

Mrs. Clarke moved in, together with her brother, Captain Thompson, and a French girl called Josephine, and before long her three children were also installed. Her household of six appropriated "four or five bed-chambers", and appears to have been larger than William Nicholls had bargained for, as he complained rather testily that "she occupied the whole house almost".

Mrs. Clarke now made a concerted effort to obtain the money which the Duke had so glibly promised. "I have written repeatedly," she chided William Adam, "but of no avail." Realising at last the need for punitive action she sat down with her memories, her letters and her pen.

Searching for the Duke's love-letters in an old trunk crammed with a mass of papers from Gloucester Place, she threw out a miscellaneous pile of letters which were then no more than an invidious reminder of better days. She sent them downstairs for lighting the fire, and the maid put them in the closet.

Here they were discovered by William Nicholls. Fully alive to the treasure trove of scandal which had fallen so unexpectedly into

---

* Mrs. Clarke's address is given simply as "opposite New End", but a search of the Hampstead rate books for 1807 and 1808 by the Librarian for the Borough of Camden has discovered a William Nicholls living in Heath Street, part of which is opposite New End. As one of the overseers of the poor, William Nicholls was a man of some local standing, and during the years 1806–1809 his name frequently appears in the Manor Minute Book, a contemporary record of the buying and selling of property owned by the Lord of the Manor.

At a distance of more than a hundred and fifty years it is difficult to be certain that William Nicholls of Heath Street is the man with whom Mrs. Clarke lodged on her return from Exmouth, particularly as when giving evidence in the House of Commons, Nicholls described himself as a baker, a fact not mentioned in the Hampstead records. Yet, on balance, it is highly probable, as no other householder or housekeeper of the same name is listed in the rate books for this area, and Nicholls emerges as an educated man of forceful character, well able to oversee the poor and engage in property deals.

his hands, they were, he shrewdly decided, "too curious for the fire".

In June, 1808, Mrs. Clarke left Hampstead for 11 Holles Street, a short thoroughfare linking Oxford Street with Cavendish Square. Penniless and her annuity still unpaid, she now owed William Nicholls eight months' rent.

"I applied to Mrs. Clarke in town, to ask her to pay me my bill," he said, "when she was not to be seen. I told the housekeeper, unless she settled the account with me, I should dispose of some instruments of music that were left in part to satisfy me."

Mrs. Clarke was a staunch believer in the stratagem of attack, and that evening William Nicholls received a letter threatening him that she knew that he had forged a Will, and words to the effect that she had evidence to hang him.

William Nicholls took the letter to a lawyer but there the matter ended. "I thought she owed me enough money already", he remarked laconically, "and I did not like to throw good money after bad."

Although freely admitting that at this time she was "without a single guinea in the world", Mrs. Clarke was sublimely confident of the irresistible power of her physical attractions, and on leaving Hampstead she decided to make another bid for a life of affluence and éclat.

During her days of prosperity, Francis Wright, an upholsterer of Rathbone Place, St. Giles's Circus, had taken "many thousands of her money", and she still owed him £500. Her patronage had once provided Wright with a handsome living and she now persuaded him that if he would help her to obtain an unfurnished house, she would have no difficulty in decoying some wealthy aristocrat, who in return for her favours by night could easily be cajoled into paying for her furniture by day.

Her need for accommodation was urgent, and as a stop-gap arrangement Francis Wright had rented for her from Simeon Bull the furnished house in Holles Street. Concealing Mrs. Clarke's true identity he introduced her to the house agent under her mother's name of Farquhar.

Mrs. Clarke's financial fortunes were at a desperately low ebb but she had one trump card still to play. There was also a very auspicious precedent for the success of her machinations.

As a hot-headed boy of eighteen, the Prince of Wales had fallen in love with the lovely child-like actress, Perdita Robinson, and the passion that enslaved him by night he poured out in "a multitude of letters" by day. When the flame of his infatuation flickered and died two years later he left Perdita "little less than frantic, deeply involved in debt, persecuted by my enemies, and perpetually reproached by my relations".

Distractedly turning her love-letters to good account she had threatened the King that unless he bought them from her she would publish them for the world to read. Shocked and alarmed, George III agreed to pay £5,000 "to get my son out of this shameful scrape". In addition Perdita received an annuity of £600, which on her death was to revert to her daughter in an amount of £200.

What Perdita Robinson had accomplished twenty-five years earlier, Mrs. Clarke was confident she could repeat now. Taking up her pen she presented William Adam with an ultimatum in a letter as remarkable for its fluency as it was for its audacity.

"Sir;

On the 11th of May 1806 you waited on me, by the desire of his royal highness the Duke of York to state his intention of allowing me an Annuity of £400 per annum. His royal highness, by his promise, is now indebted to me £500 . . . His conduct towards me has been so devoid of principle, feeling, and honour; and as his promises are not to be depended on, though even given by you; I have come to the determination of making my intentions known to you, for the consideration of his royal highness; and thus it is – I solicit him to make the Annuity secure for my life, and to pay me the arrears immediately, as my necessities are very pressing (this he knows). If he refuses to do this, I have no other mode for my immediate wants, than to publish every circumstance ever communicated to me by him and everything which has come under my knowledge during our intimacy, with all his letters; those things amount to something serious; He is more within my power than may be imagined. Yet I wish for his sake and my own, that he will make my request good, as I know full well I should suffer much in exposing him in my own mind; yet before I do anything publicly, I will send to every one of his royal highness's family, a copy of what I mean to publish. Had he only have been a little punctual, this request had never been made. One thing more: should he throw up his protection to my boy (for which I thank him much for the past) I hope he will place him on the foundation of the Charterhouse or any other public school: the child is not accountable for my conduct. You will please then, Sir, to state this communication to the Duke of York; and on Wednesday I will send to your house, to know what may be his royal highness's intention; which you will please to signify by a letter to

Your most obedient, humble servant,
M. A. Clarke

Sunday morning,
June 19.

His royal highness must feel, that his conduct on a late affair deserves all this from me, and more.

William Adam, Esq.,
Bloomsbury Square.
Private.

Indorsed: Mrs. Clarke,
19 June 1808

William Adam showed the letter to the Duke, the Duke read it and handed it back to him. It seems likely that the Duke had never intended to fulfil his promise to pay Mrs. Clarke the annuity of £400 a year, or, perhaps overburdened with debt, he simply did not have the money, but precisely what passed between the two men was never disclosed.

"His Royal Highness expressed himself as not at all apprehensive respecting anything which could be published," said William Adam, a model of rectitude and circumspection.

A week later Mrs. Clarke wrote again.

11 Holles Street,
Cavendish Square.

"Sir;

On Wednesday, finding that there was not any answer to my letter, I am led to inquire (whether) his royal highness the Duke of York, thinks proper not to make good his promises given by you, and that you encourage him in it. I have employed myself since, in committing to paper every circumstance within my recollection during the intimacy of his royal highness and myself. The fifty or sixty letters of his royal highness will give weight and truth to the whole. On Tuesday I have promised to give these up, if I hear nothing further after this last notice; and when once given out of my own possession, it will be impossible to recall. It is to gentlemen, and not any publisher, they will be committed; and those gentlemen are just as obstinate as his royal highness, and more independent: they are acquaintances of yours; and to relieve my wants, in pique to others, will do what the Duke will not: however, he has it all within his own power, and so he may act as he pleases.

I am, Sir, your most obedient,
M. A. Clarke.

Saturday morning.
William Adam, Esq.,
Bloomsbury Square.

William Adam did not reply to these threats, and Mrs. Clarke's rancour grew.

Simeon Bull quickly discovered that his tenant in Holles Street was none other than the notorious Mrs. Clarke, and he angrily denounced Francis Wright for his treachery. "How dare you deceive me and bring that strumpet into my house," he thundered.

At the end of a month Simeon Bull heaved a sigh of relief when Mrs. Clarke was taken from his house by a Sheriff's officer, leaving Francis Wright to pay the rent. How she escaped from the clutches of the law remains a mystery, but at the end of July she bobbed up again, comfortably installed in a house belonging to Francis Wright at 14 Bedford Place, Russell Square.

"As I have removed from Holles Street to this place," she urbanely informed Captain Sandon, "to save you the trouble of calling there, these few lines are now addressed to you. I am now with my mother, and, I fear, for the rest of the summer."

Chapter Seven

THE HUNT was up. Thomas Hague, an experienced commentator and versifier, now entered the field to add to the story of Mrs. Clarke's fall from favour. He brought into view also the army agent, Charles Greenwood, whom he suspected as the instigator of her dismissal.

> 'Twas Greenwood christen'd her a rank fie! fie!
> He prov'd her agencies were gross and base,
> And might endanger his great patron's place.
> She heard – refus'd – or granted all petitions,
> *Gave* rank – promotion – and bestow'd commissions;
> Expensive – selfish – cunning – daring too –
> What could a *fool*, with *such* a woman do?

Taking a swipe at Greenwood's sexual activities, Thomas Hague provocatively suggested that, drunk and impotent by night, the Duke's confederate had his own artful stratagem for slaking his sexual desires by day.

"Charley is a great agent among men, and a tidey little factor among women. His *modus operandi* is peculiar – his carriage is ordered to convey the favourite nymph to Audley Square by seven in the morning. Arrived, she is conducted to the chamber of the mogul agent – there the society for the suppression of vice cannot enter."

Thomas Hague also made public in 1808 the fact that the Duke had defaulted in his payments of the annuity that he had promised Mrs. Clarke. He spread the information merely to bespatter the Duke's character, but the seed was sown that in any attempt to remove the Commander-in-Chief from his post at the Horse Guards, Mrs. Clarke might prove a useful ally.

"Mr. Hague presents his compliments to His Royal Highness the Duke of York", he wrote with tongue in cheek, "and begs to inform him that Mrs. Clarke has been compelled to return to town for the purpose of obtaining payment of the long arrears due upon the pension contracted for and agreed upon by the other agent in Craig's Court. Mr. Hague must observe that the Convention by which it was stipulated that she should evacuate London, differs from that at Cintra – the French were permitted to go away with the public altars, the spoils of the church, the plunder of a nation, and the robbery of individuals; but, here, Mrs. Clarke disposed of the whole of her furniture, plate, linen and china for the benefit of her creditors. Mr. Hague finds upon enquiry that her principals (sic) were thus just, and her conduct thus honest, which is the more extraordinary when it shall be remembered with whom she had been associated."

These were the years when society was convulsed by paroxysms of dissipation and scandal, and a corps of commentators poured ridicule and obloquy upon the heads of the protagonists. Today, when the most muted criticisms of the royal family provokes a furore of indignation, one reads with astonishment the scandal published almost daily only a century and a half ago.

The Duke of York was an obvious Aunt Sally for the scorn of his contemporaries, and adding variety to the mounting taunts, a "Serio-Comic Satire" now appeared on "The Miss-Led General", introduced with the quip that "For many years he drove a kind of broking-trade in love."

As the author deftly perceived, a burlesque of the Duke's amorous activities could scarely fail to whet the reader's appetite. ". . . as we have seen that our general was always beaten in the field," he wrote, "why – he was no more able to withstand the fire in the *boudoir*, which enfiladed him, and took him in every position – back, front, side, standing, sitting or lying."

Neither did the Duke's German-born wife escape the author's riotous fantasy. "If the direful note of preparation for war had not already made all the welkin resound, yet Madam Frederica would have smelt a rat from her husband's perturbed sleep. For sometime she might as well have been a stranger to his bed, as he answered all her caresses only with a pish – trifles – and nonsense. 'It ish you, yourself, dat is nonsense', exclaimed the Lady Frederica one morning, unable to bear this neglect any longer. 'You kick and gallop, and snort and whip and spur, in your sleep, as if you were mounted upon some great Flanders mare at a review; and den you cry out about breast-works and breaches, mines and trenches –

attacking, assaulting, battering, mounting, driving in, sallies, retreats and burying under the works. Vat is de use of all dis great talking and little doing?' "

Sometime during August or September, Mrs. Clarke spotted an advertisement for an unfurnished house to let in Westbourne Place*, Sloane Square, and as directed she called at once upon Joseph Curt, a coffee-house keeper in Coventry Street. "You must give me some references as to your respectability," he informed her. "You tell me you are a lady of character, and by your appearance I should judge so; nevertheless, there are many imposters nowadays. I should wish a reference."

"Oh, there will be no difficulty on that head," Mrs. Clarke replied smoothly, still posing as Mrs. Farquhar, and referred him to Francis Wright.

Joseph Curt hurried round immediately to Rathbone Place and found Francis Wright in his counting-house. "I requested him to be candid with me," he said, "as one tradesman should be with another, on such an occasion."

"Mrs. Farquhar is a very respectable woman," Francis Wright glibly reassured him," . . . if I had fifty houses to dispose of Mrs. Farquhar should have the choice of them all."

When Joseph Curt called at 14 Bedford Place with the agreement for Mrs. Clarke to complete he was surprised to find the house so elegantly furnished, and observed conversationally that most of the furniture would do very well for her new home in Westbourne Place.

"Oh no! It is quite too old-fashioned for me," Mrs. Clarke informed him, remembering no doubt her compact with Francis Wright. "I shall take only the drawers and the beds."

While waiting for the lease to be executed, she was forced to take temporary refuge in Hampstead. She disarmingly admits in her own account that her financial difficulties "obliged me to conceal myself at different times under the roof of a Mrs. Andrews at Hampstead, a very worthy woman, who has been twenty years a resident in that village."

Here at the end of September she was tracked down by Pierre M'Callum, who told of being directed "to call on Mr. Andrews . . .

* Westbourne Place was a short residential road running north-east from Sloane Square to Eaton Square, and was re-named Cliveden Place in 1890.

who resides in a yellow cottage on Haverstock Hill, where I might hear of the celebrated harlot."

Of all the men with whom Mrs. Clarke came into contact, Pierre M'Callum is one of the most offensive, and he wrote with obvious malice and little truth of Mrs. Clarke being "forced to chum with Mrs. Andrews in a wretched hovel behind the cottage, into which Mrs. Andrews retired at times when the cottage was let. From Mrs. Andrews I learn that she was indebted to her from day to day for a scanty subsistence, which they divided between them."

Mistaking M'Callum for a bailiff, Mrs. Andrews refused to tell him where Mrs. Clarke was then living, but she delivered to Bedford Place the letters that M'Callum entrusted to her. These were sent on to Mrs. Clarke at 2 Westbourne Place, where she had taken up residence, the lease having been executed on Novmber 9th. She replied on November 16th, agreeing to see him.

"Although Mrs. Clarke has not the honour of recollecting Mr. M'Callum, she will be at home to him tomorrow morning before twelve, if he sends up his name; should he not get this in time, the next day same time."

M'Callum was Colonel Wardle's go-between, a man of sallow complexion, dark hair, badly dressed and "rough in his manner of speaking". "A very awkward figure," said Dominigo Corri, the music master. "I would call him rather an ugly man."

Born in Argyll, M'Callum was one those unfortunate people obsessed by grievances both real and imaginary. Whilst serving in the West Indies, the Governor of Trinidad, Sir Thomas Picton, had imprisoned him in a dungeon and this coercive treatment still rankled.* Upon returning to England, M'Callum's bitter resentment boiled over in a pamphlet innocuously entitled "Travels in Trinidad."

He also directed his attention to hunting out abuses and corruption in the army and his acquaintance with Colonel Wardle began when the latter instigated a Parliamentary inquiry into the

---

* These were days of rude justice and savage punishment, and among other ugly incidents during Sir Thomas Picton's administration was the "Picketing" of a fourteen-year-old Spanish girl, Louisa Calderon, to compel her to confess the name of her lover suspected of committing a theft. "Picketing" was a particularly vicious military punishment inflicted by suspending the victim by one arm, with the whole weight of the body resting on a bare foot impaled on a sharpened peg stuck in the ground.

supply of great-coats, which, it was claimed, saved the country £100,000 a year.

M'Callum told Mrs. Clarke that he was writing a pamphlet denouncing "The Duke of Kent's Shameful Persecution since his recall from Gibraltar" – a blistering broadside upon the character of the Duke of York as Commander-in-Chief. In fact, the real purpose of M'Callum's visit was to arrange a meeting between Mrs. Clarke and Colonel Wardle.

It was agreed that Wardle should call on Mrs. Clarke next day who, she reported, "after the customary ceremonies of reciprocal civilities, seated himself and continued with me from one till my dinner time, about six o'clock."

Forty-six-year-old Gwyllym Lloyd Wardle, who later was to lead the attack on the Duke of York in the House of Commons, was a man, remarked one contemptuous critic, "of mean capacity and meaner disposition". An old Harrovian, he had graduated via Cambridge University to the rank of Lieutenant-Colonel in "The Ancient British Light Dragoons," popularly known as "Wynn's Lambs" after their commander, Sir Watkin Williams-Wynn. Before they disbanded, following the short-lived Peace of Amiens in 1803, Wardle took part in suppressing the Irish uprising and is said to have fought at Vinegar Hill.

At the age of thirty he married a Miss Parry from Wrenfaur in Cornwall, a marriage blessed not only by seven children but also by his wife's wealth, which included a valuable estate in Caernarvonshire. "Mr. Wardle, therefore, who was not very rich before," blithely commented his biographer, "had now, as it were, crowned his happiness by a double throw – he had obtained an amiable wife and a competent fortune in one cast!"

In 1807 Wardle was elected Member of Parliament for Okehampton in Devon, but until his spectacular rise to public popularity for his part in the inquiry into the Duke of York's conduct, his reputation as a convivial companion and ardent sportsman completely overshadowed his pursuit of a political career.

There had been much critical comment about the expense of the Martello Towers and their efficacy as a defence against Napoleon's threatened invasion and, before bringing the matter up in Parliament, Wardle had arranged with Major Thomas Dodd, military secretary to the Duke of Kent, and James Glennie, an ex-Artillery officer, to make a first-hand inspection of these controversial military innovations. With the help of Mrs. Clarke, Wardle decided he could launch an attack, not only upon the incompetence of the army in general, but on the corruption of the Commander-in-Chief in particular, and could profitably combine a tour of the Martello Towers with a leisurely interrogation of Mrs. Clarke.

During her three-year intimacy with the Duke, Mary Ann had learned much about politics and politicians, but she had her reservations about throwing in her lot with Colonel Wardle.

"I was rather fearful of doing what he wanted of me with him alone," she admitted afterwards, "because he was not much known in Parliament."

Whatever scruples she had were overcome when Wardle confided that his real purpose was to serve the Duke of Kent by routing out the Duke of York from his office as Commander-in-Chief. If she had lost the love and protection of one of the King's sons, she decided that here was the opportunity of gaining the financial support of another. In addition, the publicity to be obtained by participating in the attack on the Duke of York would provide a valuable puff for her memoirs.

Two days later, to convince her of his good faith, Wardle, she alleged, brought a letter written to him by Major Dodd, but the authenticity of it remains a matter for speculation.

"I have no hesitation in believing that her co-operation will be more material than that of any other human being," wrote Major Dodd on November 21st, 1808, according to Mrs. Clarke. "God knows she has been infamously and barbarously treated by an illustrious great beast; but she may now have an opportunity of redressing her wrongs; and by serving a generous public, most essentially to benefit herself."

Of all the people embroiled in the conspiracy against the Duke of York, the part played by the Duke of Kent is the most ambivalent. In private life he was an amiable and inoffensive man, and is perhaps best remembered for fulfilling his royal duties by discarding Madame de St. Laurent, his mistress for twenty-seven years, to marry in 1818 the Princess of Leiningen, thus securing the succession to the English throne with the birth of Princess Victoria when in his fifty-second year.

"The Duke's affection for his old French lady," Mrs. Clarke remarked, "whom he lamented he could not marry, was a proof of his steady disposition and domestic good qualities, added to which he regularly went to church and was never seen inebriated – a habit he always endeavoured to check in those over whom he had any influence."

It was this almost obsessional abhorrence of drink and drunkenness that led to his undoing, and as a military commander the Duke of Kent was little less than a monster.

In 1802 he was appointed Governor-General of Gibraltar, eleven years after he had been removed from the fortress for his callous and repressive discipline. Almost his first order on re-reaching Gibraltar was to put out of bounds all except three of the ninety wine houses which proliferated on that rocky island fortress.

"No non-commissioned officer, drummer or private whatever is permitted at any time to enter a wine house, tavern, or house of any retailer or vendor (sic) of wine or spiritous liquors – they are to confine themselves either to the canteen of their own regiment, or to three houses licensed to sell malt liquor only . . . any disobedience will meet with the most exemplary punishment."

The final straw was the Duke's order forbidding drunkenness and festivity on Christmas Day 1802. It was received by the garrison with bitter resentment, and on Christmas Eve one battalion broke out of barracks. Three days later there was a more serious insurrection assuming mutinous proportions and order was restored only in the early morning after five soldiers had been killed and many others wounded.

The consequences were deplorable. Three men were executed, others flogged – and from London came the order for the Duke of Kent to return home.

The army was the Duke's one dedicated interest in an otherwise arid life, and for five years he was offered no military appointment or command of any sort. It was common tea-table and tap-room talk that he held his brother, the Commander-in-Chief, responsible for this intolerable state of affairs.

At the beginning of 1808, the Duke of Kent wrote to the King asking to be allowed to return to Gibraltar as Governor-General, and his chagrin knew no bounds when he received a reply from the Duke of York, to whom he had sent a copy of his letter, recalling the "unfortunate events . . . which have already, and must ever preclude the confidential servants of the King from advising His Majesty to permit you to resume your station there."

The Duke of Kent seethed with indignation, and many people, including the Prince of Wales, firmly believed that he supported the attack upon the Duke of York in the House of Commons.

The role of Major Dodd was less equivocal. As private secretary to an unwanted and out-of-work military commander his future was bleak indeed, although he endeavoured with little success to persuade Mrs. Clarke that he despised any idea of reward "if the Duke of Kent should be so fortunate as to remove his royal brother from the command of the army, and be able to slip into this station." If this was so, the part he played in the preparation of the case against the Duke of York can be attributed only to motives of jealousy and revenge.

Colonel Wardle, having arranged with Major Dodd and Captain James Glennie to carry out an investigation of the south coast defences, agreed it would take time and patience to elicit from Mrs. Clarke all the details of the trafficking in commissions that went on at Gloucester Place during her life with His Royal Highness, and that the journey down there would give them an excellent opportunity for a leisurely interrogation. He suggested she should accompany them on the four-day excursion.

Brimming over with glee at this unexpected revival of her flickering fortunes, Mrs. Clarke gaily accepted, but before she could go, she informed Wardle, he would have to give her £100 to pay her butcher and baker – a sharp reminder of her financial expectations.

Wardle intended they should drive straight to Hythe, one of the Cinque ports on the East Kent coast nearly seventy miles away. Next morning he was distinctly upset when, on arriving at Westbourne Place, he found Mrs. Clarke unable to depart, as the young woman who was going to accompany her had failed to turn up.

Nearly an hour elapsed with no sign of the maid, so Wardle and Mrs. Clarke decided to go round to Charles Street, Mayfair, where she could be introduced to Major Dodd and Captain Glennie. A further hour passed in conversation before they finally decided to wait no longer for the maid. The delayed start made it impossible to reach Hythe that night, and the party broke their journey at the Medway town of Maidstone. The next day, on a fine and frosty morning, Wardle and his friends began their inspection of the invasion defences.

The Martello Towers, strung out along the south coast, were about 40 feet high, each one mounted two or three guns, and they were only accessible to the garrison by means of a ladder leading to a door about 20-feet from the ground. A similar tower built on

Mortella, a cape in Corsica, had played a prominent part in resisting a combined land and sea attack by the British in support of Corsican insurgents during the French revolutionary wars of 1794.

James Glennie was a self-styled expert on military defence who had written a book on the Dock Yard fortifications, and as the party carried out their tour of inspection "he took minutes of every particular relating to the construction of these military works," Mrs. Clarke related, "all of which he surveyed with a geometrical accuracy and a malicious satisfaction." As they proceeded they came upon a number of workmen repairing the foundations of one of the Towers, and Glennie sharply criticised the coastal defences "as an ineffective obstruction to the landing of the enemy, and consequently an unnecessary expense to the country."

That night at Hythe the party sat down to dinner, and "when the cloth was removed and the wine in circulation," reported Mrs. Clarke, "I was gradually raised into great mirth, as it became the task of Mr. Glennie and Major Dodd to make Colonel Wardle understand the true principle of the Martello Towers, and what ought to have been the construction of the military canal; and in what points they were defective and useless as a defence of this part of the coast.

"The task of teaching a dull child the first elements of a language or science is nothing compared with the trouble and whimsical difficulties that attended Glennie and Dodd's explanation and illustration of the subject, upon which the immaculate Patriot was to make a luminous speech in the House of Commons.

"Heaven only knows how he at last got (it) into his head for oral description in Parliament," she prattled on, "for on the day of which I am speaking it appeared to require a hammer to beat in the difference between an octagon and a triangle."

If Wardle was slow to grasp the defects and deficiencies of the Martello Towers, he bubbled over with excitement and perspicacity as the wine flowed freely and Mrs. Clarke reminisced about her life with the Duke of York, and repeated what she had heard about the Royal family. James Glennie again took out his notebook as she chattered on all about "making baronets and peers, and carving out districts for generals."

At the end of four days the party returned to London. Wardle was elated at the success of the trip and with the prospects of the attack he proposed to launch in Parliament upon the conduct of the Duke of York, whilst Mrs. Clarke confidently contemplated the return of days and nights of plenty and popularity.

* * *

The offensive against the Duke continued and culminated in a dramatic "Appeal to the Public and A Farewell Address to the Army" by Denis Hogan, an acting major who had resigned his commission "in consequence of the treatment he experienced from the Duke of York, and the system in the Army respecting Promotions". Priced at 2/6d., the pamphlet rapidly ran through nine editions, and the publishers assured a feverish public that a second copy had been composed, "and four presses are at work without intermission".

Major Hogan was a furious but honest Irishman who had served in the army for seventeen years, but in spite of repeated applications and promises he had seen forty captains promoted over his head, all of them his junior in rank, and many of whom were not in the army when he was a captain.

Provoked beyond endurance at being told for the sixth time that he had been noted for promotion and would be "duly considered as favourable opportunities offered", he challenged the Commander-in-Chief in his office at the Horse Guards, and told him forcibly of his maltreatment and disgust.

"My applications for promotion have been made in the manner prescribed by the practice of the army, and by the king's regulations; unfortunately without success. Other ways, please your Royal Highness, have been recommended to me . . . but I would feel it unworthy of me, as a British officer and a man, to owe the king's commission to low intrigue or petticoat influence".

If Major Hogan naïvely "expected the instantaneous expression of his Royal Highness's gratitude for such a candid declaration", he was quickly disillusioned. The Duke was nonplussed, he said nothing, and Major Hogan was told by his friends that he had given offence and was unlikely ever to be promoted.

Resigning from the army, Major Hogan continued his diatribe in writing. "It has been observed to me, by connoisseurs, that I should have no reason to complain if I had proceeded in the proper way to seek promotion. But what is meant by the proper way? I applied to the Duke of York because he was Commander-in-Chief . . . But if any other person had been the substitute of the

Duke of York, I should have made my application to that person.

"If a Cooke, a Creswell, a Clarke, a Sinclair, or a Carey", declared the reckless Major, trotting out a list of the Duke's better known mistress, "or any other name had been invested by His Majesty with the office of Commander-in-Chief, to that person I should have applied. Nay, if it had pleased His Majesty to confer upon a female the direct command of the army, I should have done my duty in applying to the legal depository of power".

On August 26th an advertisement appeared publicising Major Hogan's forthcoming pamphlet, and that evening "a lady in a dashing barouche" called at the newspaper office asking for his address. The following evening at dusk she handed to one of the waiters at Frank's Coffee House at 3 Brook Street a letter for Major Hogan containing four £100 bank notes.

"Sir,

The enclosed will answer for the deficit of which you complain, and which was not allowed you through mere oversight. I hope this will prevent the publication of your intended pamphlet; and, if it does, you may rely on a better situation than the one you had. When I find that you have given up all your secrets from public view, which would hurt you with all the royal family, I shall make myself known to you, and shall be happy in your future acquaintance and friendship; by which, I promise you, you will reap much benefit. If you will recall the advertisement, you shall hear from me, and your claims shall be rewarded as they deserve".

The Major was not to be so easily deterred, and announced that the money would be returned if the numbers of the notes were sent to 14 Angel Court, Throgmorton Street.

There was wild speculation as to the identity of the lady in the dashing barouche, and many people were convinced that it was none other than the ubiquitous Mrs. Clarke. She, however, had her own improbable explanation, given at a later date.

'The barouche lady, Colonel Wardle acknowledged to me, was no other than his *dear wife*", she wrote with wry humour, "but there was no harm in such an act, it was merely a little generalship, which sheds a lustre on modern patriotism."

The government could not allow such outspoken charges of corruption against the Commander-in-Chief to go unchallenged, and the publisher, Mr. Finnerty, was served with a summons for libel. Major Hogan's testimony was of vital importance but before the case was heard he had sailed for America "upon some business relating to the concerns of his family", and was not expected back until the following March.

The government took action also against 'The Examiner' for its comments on these disclosures, "of a nature that was to be expected from its ardour in the cause of Reform". The government, declared its editor and co-founder, Leigh Hunt, cared nothing for the distinction made by his paper between the rights of domestic privacy and the claim to indulgence set up by traffickers in public corruption.

Before the case against 'The Examiner' came to court, however, Colonel Wardle had publicly indicted the Duke before the world at the bar of the House. "The prosecution against the paper was dropped, and the whole attention of the country was drawn to the strange spectacle of a laughing, impudent woman, brought to the bar of the House of Commons, and forcing them to laugh in their turn at the effrontery of her answers."

Chapter Eight

The inquiry investigating the conduct of the Duke of York as Commander-in-Chief faced one insuperable obstacle. As a peer, he could not be called to the House of Commons to explain, repudiate or refute the allegations made by Colonel Wardle, and his absence was the ineluctable impediment, vitiating the entire proceedings. It was a dilemma from which the Committee could never escape.

If the Duke was excluded from the proceedings, Mrs. Clarke enjoyed no such immunity. Gaily admitting to having accepted bribes for using her influence with the Commander-in-Chief to obtain army commissions or coveted appointments, it was inevitable that she should be the butt of the investigation. It was a very different proposition to prove that the Duke had connived in these nefarious practices, or had profited from her illicit money-making gambits.

Although time had tempered Mrs. Clarke's wrath at being discarded by him and supplanted by Mrs. Carey, his betrayal still rankled. There was also another more insidious reason why it was to her advantage for the Duke to be ousted from his post at the Horse Guards.

As Mrs. Clarke dexterously exerted her energies to implicate the Duke in her chicanery, Government supporters exerted theirs to denigrate her credibility, to contaminate her character, to prove her word as worthless as her way of life, and the investigation which began as an inquiry into the conduct of the Duke of York eventually degenerated into the trial of Mary Ann Clarke.

Her wild expenditure and indiscriminate debts were of two-fold importance, exposing not only her profligate habits and duplicity, but providing also evidence of the money she derived from her traffic in commissions. Both these unedifying traits were pursued with energetic thoroughness.

Mrs. Clarke had always led a tempestuous life, moderated neither by caution nor apprehension. Having embarked upon the pursuit of the kept woman she was fully prepared to concede her part of the bargain by night, but insistently demanded in return a life of affluent pretension by day. Before meeting the Duke she had lived with several men, "all of whom complain of her extravagance and artfulness", reported 'The Examiner,' "but admit that she is a most fascinating woman."

The year 1809 had opened on a tragic note and the pursuit of the British forces through Spain culminated in the death of Sir John Moore on January 16th, killed by a French cannon ball on the battlefield of Corunna. As Charles Wolfe so impressively depicted, he was buried where he fell whilst his troops embarked once more for England.

We buried him darkly at dead of night,
  The sods with our bayonets turning,
By the struggling moonbeam's misty light
  And the lanthorn dimly burning.

No useless coffin enclosed his breast,
  Not in sheet or in shroud we wound him;
But he lay like a warrior taking his rest
  With his martial cloak around him.

Slowly and sadly we laid him down,
  From the field of his fame, fresh and gory;
We carved not a line, and we raised not a stone,
  But we left him alone with his glory.

Eight thousand soldiers also died, and of the army that set out to liberate Spain, twenty-six thousand ragged, filthy and exhausted men struggled back to England.

"It is impossible to imagine anything at all like the streets of Portsmouth," wrote General Dyott, deeply affected, "from the crowds of officers, soldiers, dragoons, and dragoon horses; as the greater part of the troops from Corunna were disembarking; such miserable, tattered beings I never saw, so wan and worn out . . . . I remained no longer in Portsmouth than was necessary to land my baggage."

In the House of Commons on January 25th, Lord Castlereagh proposed the erection of a monument to Sir John Moore in St. Paul's Cathedral, but two days later the death of one of England's most popular and successful soldiers was over-shadowed by Colonel Wardle's motion calling for an inquiry to investigate the conduct of the Duke of York as Commander-in-Chief of the British Army.

On Tuesday, January 31st, a messenger hurried from the House to summon the attendance the following day of witnesses to substantiate the Colonel's allegations of corruption and abuse.

Dr. Andrew Thynne arrived reluctantly, protesting that he had done no more than convey a message to Mrs. Clarke, and Mr. Robert Knight, thunderstruck, so he claimed, "to hear my name being mentioned in the way it has." But it was Mrs. Clarke that everyone wanted to see, and all over the country people waited impatiently to hear what she would have to say about the military junketing that went on in the privacy of Gloucester Place.

"The Honourable House is extremely full to-day, and very impatient to behold Mrs. Clarke," wrote John William Ward, 1st Earl of Dudley, ". . . . the whole story of his (the Duke of York) living with these ladies, which is now for the first time made public, will do him a great deal of harm. It was of course well enough known in London before; but the good people of the provinces, I really believe, fancied that he and his Duchess were the true models of conjugal fidelity and happiness. Her Royal Highness is at least even with him."

"The room for writing letters is emptied," he added in a hastily penned postscript, "so I presume Mrs. Clarke is arrived."

She came, blithely and buoyantly, a small, well-made woman, with a fair complexion and lively blue eyes, and an appearance of great vitality. "Her attire resembled a vestal's," commented one spectator caustically. "It was a light blue mantle with a veil, which she threw back that her face might by chance captivate some of her judges," he remarked, not knowing perhaps that the previous Sunday Mrs. Clarke had boasted that half the Members would fall in love with her!

One of the first Government witnesses was John Few, a London shopkeeper, whose evidence disclosing Mrs. Clarke's financial stratagems revealed also her powers of captivating Dukes and tradesmen alike. At the time of the transaction Mrs. Clarke was living with her mother and children at 14 Tavistock Place, and her life with the Duke had not yet begun.

"Did she order any furniture from you?" Sir Vicary Gibbs, the Attorney-General, asked John Few.

"No," he replied. "At that time I lived in Bernard Street, Russell

Square, and I had a share in a glass concern in Holborn. She called, and by direction of my partner, I waited upon her; it was to consult me about fitting up a Grecian lamp in her back room. After she had talked a little while, I sat down and drank some wine with her. In the matter of conversation, from one thing leading to another, she seemed to be acquainted with almost every person that I knew. I sat there perhaps about half-an-hour. A person whom I understood to be her sister was present".

"Did she represent herself as being a married woman, or a person who had been married?"

"She talked of her late husband, and of her children, who were then at school."

"What further passed?"

"Nothing more than general conversation. I conceived that she knew almost everybody that I knew. I can hardly describe her to you, for I never met with any person who, on the first interview, behaved so extremely polite and genteel to a stranger. I saw her two or three times, and drank wine with her, and she consulted me about the placing of some glasses, and the size and shape of some figures, whether they were too large for the room."

"Did she give any orders to you?"

"Yes, she desired I would have a Grecian lamp made, to fit up in the back room, which I believe came to about £20."

"When was the order given for this lamp?"

"About the middle of May, about the 18th or 20th May. The first delivery to her was the 24th May, 1803."

If John Few had fallen momentarily under the spell of Mrs. Clarke's beguiling ways he soon came to his senses as week after week went by and still the bill remained unpaid. As a widow, Mrs. Clarke's debts were her own concern, but as a married woman the responsibility for her financial foibles devolved upon her husband – and it was anybody's guess where the vagrant, impecunious Joseph Clarke might be found.

John Few now recalled with growing suspicion Mrs. Clarke's smooth talk about her husband and children, and either on the pretext of seeing that the lamp was properly hung, or because an unholsterer asked him to get "a sight of the house" – he forgot which – he called at Gloucester Place one morning and saw a cocked hat. Martha Favery readily explained that her mistress was a gay young widow who had been at a masquerade the night before, and John Few's misgivings were temporarily allayed. He continued to press his bill, Mrs. Clarke sat tight making no effort to pay, and at last in desperation he took her to court.

Mrs. Clarke now sprang her trap, and, pleading her coverture as a married woman under her husband's protection, John Few was non-suited.* Adding insult to injury he was not only prevented from collecting the money owing to him, but Mrs. Clarke's lawyer sent him a bill for her legal costs.

John Few seethed with indignation, and when he discovered her to be living in Gloucester Place under the protection of the Duke of York he presented her with an ultimatum.

Madam,

As I have not heard from you in reply to my last letter, I think myself justified in informing you that in the course of a week the inclosed hand-bill will be published, which no doubt will prevent any other tradesman from subjecting himself to similar treatment. As the wording of the bill has received the legal sanction of very able men in the profession, I am perfectly at ease in regard to any additional threats that may be held out to me.

I remain,

Your obedient servant,
John Few, jun.
22 June 1804

Mrs. Clarke,
No. 18 Gloucester Place,
Portman Square.

Hitting where it would hurt her most, John Few also sent a copy of the hand-bill to the Duke of York.

CAUTION TO TRADESMEN

"This is to give notice to the tradesmen in the neighbourhood of Portman Square, that they cannot recover, by law, any debt from Mrs. Mary Ann Clarke, formerly of Tavistock Place, Russell Square, but now of Gloucester Place, she being a married woman,

---

* Non-suited was where the plaintiff in an action abandoned his case at the trial before the jury had given their verdict, whereon judgment of non-suit was given against him. Before 1875 the advantage of this practice – which was peculiar to the common law courts – was that the plaintiff could bring another action against the defendant for the same cause or action.

and her husband now living, though his place of residence was unknown even to herself or her mother. These facts were proved on the trial of an action lately brought by a tradesman in Holborn, against this Mrs. Mary Ann Clarke, for goods actually sold and delivered to her; but she availing herself of her coverture (which, to the great surprise of the plaintiff she contrived to prove), he could not by law obtain any part of his demand; and, being consequently non-suited, an execution for her costs was, by her attorney, actually put into his, the tradesman's House!!!"

Mrs. Clarke capitulated. Although the Duke of York himself was harassed by debt on every side, and was unlikely to be as mortified by her behaviour as a man of greater rectitude, the risk of public exposure was intolerable. Through her lawyer, James Comrie, Mrs. Clarke paid the debt and costs.

Mrs. Clarke's attitude to money was that of the compulsive gambler; what she had, she spent, without any thought of what tomorrow might bring.

"What allowance did you receive from the Duke of York?" Lord Folkestone enquired of her.

"His Royal Highness promised me £1,000 a year to be paid monthly," she replied coolly, on being called to the bar, "but sometimes he could not make the payments good, which was the occasion of many distressing circumstances happening."

"Was it on the bare promise of £1,000 a year that you mounted such an establishment as you have mentioned, and with the expectation of no other means of defraying it?"

"His Royal Highness did not tell me what he would give me till I was in it."

"How long did he continue to pay it regularly?"

"Till almost the whole time that we were together in it. For three months before His Royal Highness left me he never gave me a guinea, though he was with me every day."

"How were the monthly payments made? By His Royal Highness' own hand, or by what other means?"

"His Royal Highness wished me to receive it from Greenwood but I would not subject myself to that, although it would have been more punctually paid."

"How did you receive it?"

"From His Royal Highness."

"Did you ever receive more than at the rate of £1,000 a year from His Royal Highness?"

"His Royal Highness, if anything unpleasant had happened, which was always happening, would sometimes contrive to get a little more and bring me."

"Do you know what is the total amount of the sums you received from His Royal Highness during the time you lived in Gloucester Place?"

"Certainly not."

"Were the sums you received from His Royal Highness adequate to the payment of the expenses of the establishment you kept up?"

"I convinced His Royal Highness that it did not more than pay the servants' wages and their liveries."

"Did you state that to His Royal Highness?"

"Many times."

It was an essential part of Mrs. Clarke's case to prove that the money she received from the Duke was a mere drop in the ocean towards the cost of maintaining her town and country establishments at the opulent level to which he was accustomed and that she expected, and that she was compelled by necessity to enter upon the profitable project of selling commissions and appointments. Far from concealing her reckless extravagance, she flaunted it as openly as her success in wheedling large sums of money from aspiring officers and ambitious placemen.

"Do you mean to say that none of the bills for the constant expenses were paid for by His Royal Highness?" asked Sir Vicary Gibbs.

"Yes, I do," Mrs. Clarke asserted.

"Did not His Royal Highness pay for the furniture of the house?"

"I did not mean to that, I understood constant expenses. I do not put the furniture as constant expenses," retorted Mrs. Clarke, pouncing upon the Attorney-General's non-sequitur.

"Did not the Duke pay for the furniture?" Sir Vicary Gibbs persisted.

"Yes, all of it except the glass," Mrs. Clarke agreed, not forgetting to enumerate the items for which she had paid. "I believe that cost me £400 or £500. The chandeliers, those I paid for myself."

"Did not His Royal Highness pay for the wine?"

"He sent in a great deal of wine, but I bought wine myself. I kept a great deal of company, and a great deal was drunk."

"Do you mean to say that a chief part of the expenses for wine was not defrayed by His Royal Highness?"

"His Royal Highness sent in wine, but it was never enough. I purchased wine myself, both Claret and Madeira; and even that he did send in, he used to scold very much that it went too fast."

Sir George Warrender was anxious to know who paid for the horses and carriages.

"Did the Duke of York defray the charge of no part of your expenditure such as horses and carriages, independent of the allowance?"

"He bought one carriage, which I stated before."

"Did he purchase any horses?"

"For about six months I had job (hired) horses, the others I always purchased myself. I lost about £900 in one year in the purchase of horses."

"Were those horses kept at the expense of the Duke of York, exclusive of the allowance?"

"No, they were not."

Colonel Wardle now had some questions to put to Mrs. Clarke, and both of them were well aware that by showing that she had paid out large sums of money, which could have come only from trafficking in commissions, it gave weight and substance to the charges brought against the Duke.

"You spoke of having a house at Weybridge. Was that house ever repaired at your expense?"

"Yes, it was thoroughly repaired, and I built a two-stall stable there. I laid out between £200 and £300 upon it, if not more – I believe more. There was £40 to £50 alone for oil cloth to screen His Royal Highness: to screen his visits when he was going backwards and forwards, from the neighbours."

" Do you know what your diamonds cost the Duke of York?"

"No, I do not. I never asked."

Sir Arthur Wellesley, later Duke of Wellington, was an attentive member of the House of Commons Committee, and writing to the Duke of Richmond on February 12th, 1809, he enumerated "the points on which any impression has been made against the Duke of York". He mentioned "principally the allowance of £1,000 per annum, which she stated he gave her, compared with the extravagant expenses of her house and establishment", but included also "the purchase of a service of plate from Ricketts (Birketts) for £1,850."

At a time when so many were subsisting on so little, feeling ran high against the Duke of York for such excessive prodigality, but even more significant to the Members of Parliament adjudicating on the fate of the Comander-in-Chief was the fact that the Duke paid only £1,321 towards the total cost of the service, and that Mrs. Clarke contributed £500. "Which sum," wrote Sir Arthur Wellesley, "it is pretended the Duke must have known she could produce only from impure sources."

Before the details of this purchase assumed sinister importance in the House of Commons inquiry nearly five years later, Birkett was dead. When Thomas Parker, his executor, was called he brought with him a ledger containing an account for the purchase of the plate, and although a detailed inventory of the service itself was lacking, the exorbitant cost of the additional items was proof enough of the sumptuous standard of life at Gloucester Place. The statement revealed also two other important points.

It confirmed Mrs. Clarke's assertion of having paid £500 in cash on account, and the fact that the Duke had paid almost all the balance with post-dated bills for £200 payable at two-monthly intervals exposed the precarious financial plight of a man with an income of £40,000 a year and as little money sense as his mistress.

The account was read, published in the Minutes of Evidence and newspapers, and people pored over it with indignant curiosity.

MRS. CLARKE, Dr.				PER CONTRA Cr.			
May 16, 1804	£	s.	d.	1804	£	s.	d.
The whole of the above - mentioned Articles for . .	1,363	14	10	May 18			
				By Cash on Account .	500	0	0
An elegant rich chased Silver Epergne, with four Branches, and rich cut Glasses to Do.	139	13	0	July 12			
				By a Bill at 2 Months	200	0	0
				Nov. 14			
Very large Oval Silver Tea Tray . . .	84	0	0	By a Bill at 4 Months	200	0	0
				By a Bill at 6 Months	200	0	0
An elegant Oval Silver Tea Pot, square Ivory Handle . .	16	16	0	By a Bill at 8 Months	200	0	0
				By a Bill at 10 Months	200	0	0
12 Gadroond Silver Soup Plates, to correspond with the others	105	0	0	By a Bill at 12 Months	200	0	0
				By Cash, a Draft on Coutts and Co.	121	0	0
June 15				23 July			
2 large Silver Gadroond Waiters . .	58	3	0	Abated		11	4
Putting on Silver Plates for Arms, and polishing the above	16	5	6				
Engraving Arms and Crest on the above	21	6	0				
Silver Tankard . .	15	15	0				
Pair Sugar Tongs .		18	0				
	£1,821	11	4		£1,821	11	4

Note:

Epergne – Centre ornament, especially in branched form, for dinner-table.

Gadroon – Convex curve or curves in series forming ornamental edge like inverted fluting.

Waiter – Tray or Salver.

Timothy Dockery, one of Birkett's employees at the time of the transaction was asked to explain to the Committee of Inquiry the way in which the account was paid.

"Do you know to whom that specific service of plate belonged before it was sent to Gloucester Place?"

"Yes."

"To whom did it belong?"

"The Duc de Berri."

"State what you recollect with regard to the payment for it."

"£500 was paid at the time the plate was delivered, and the remainder was settled by bills at different dates."

"State by whom the £500 was paid in the first instance."

"The £500 was not paid to myself, but it was paid, I believe, to Mr. Birkett, as well as I can recollect."

"Do you know how it was paid, whether in cash, in bank notes, or how?"

"In two notes, one of three, and the other of two hundred pounds."

"Do you recollect by whom those bills were drawn, by which the remainder was paid?"

"To the best of my recollection they were drawn by Mrs. Clarke."

"Upon whom were they drawn?"

"The Duke of York."

"Did you offer those bills to the Duke of York for payment?"

"I did."

"How did the Duke of York settle those bills?"

"By his own drafts upon Coutts."

To Mrs. Clarke living in debt was an accepted way of life long before her egregious elevation as mistress of the Duke of York presented her with unprecedented scope and opportunity. "Live now, pay later" was a philosophy that she embraced without qualm or scruple, confident of her ability to survive the maelstrom of bailiffs and court cases that eventually brought to an end her fairy-tale rise from rags to riches.

Mr. Simeon wanted to know more about the origin and extent of Mrs. Clarke's debts.

"Were you accurate in stating that what you had from His Royal Highness would only pay the liveries and wages?"

"Very soon afterwards I found it," she admitted.

"Had your distress begun before the end of six months? If not, how soon afterwards?"

"I was going on in credit at the beginning."

"Then you were indebted at the end of the first six months?"

"Very much so."

"Then your distress must have begun, and your pressure by bills must have begun, very shortly after that time?"

"Yes."

"Did they not continue during the whole of the three years?"

"Yes, they did."

"Can you say nearly to what number of persons you might be indebted on account of your establishment; what number of creditors you had?"

"That is quite impossible. I have a list of a great many at home, of all that I owe money to."

"Do you think you had fewer than fifty?"

"I should think not fewer than fifty. But it might be fifty, or perhaps more."

"They were all very pressing?"

"Most of them, as soon as I got into debt, pressed for places."

"Did they not press for money?"

"When they found I did not take them up in the other way."

"How long were they before they found that?"

"I always felt it was impossible to recommend a tradesman to any place, and one that was about me especially."

"Then they soon found they could get no places?"

"Yes, I suppose they did."

"Then they immediately proceeded to demand their monies, did they not?"

"Yes, they did, but they were always very willing to serve me because they were very handsomely paid in the end. They charged me quite as high as ever they charged the Duke himself, if not higher."

"Did not numbers of them proceed, at the expiration of six months or thereabouts, to bring actions against you?"

"Yes, they did."

"Did not many of those actions proceed so as to incur great costs, besides the debts?"

"Yes, very great indeed."

"What do you say you were indebted when the establishment in Gloucester Place broke up?"

"Under £3,000."

Mrs. Clarke's housekeeper, Martha Favery, bore the main assault of the tradesmen pressing for payment of their bills, and of the procession of witnesses called before the Committee her story was the most improbable of them all. She saw Mrs. Clarke imposing her personality, cleverly side-stepping the incriminating question, evoking laughter in the House and cheers in the streets, and what Mrs. Clarke could do, Martha Favery seems to have decided, she could do, too.

Colonel Wardle asked her whether she remembered a note being changed just before the Duke went to Weymouth, and Mrs. Clarke to Worthing.

"I know that the Duke's servant came in the morning, and I gave him this note," Martha Favery replied, "but I do not know the number of it, nor what note it was, and he returned about eleven o'clock, and gave me the money. I took it upstairs, and then the Duke was in the bed-room, and Mrs. Clarke. In short", she added impudently, "they were in bed."

Martha Favery was uneducated and illiterate. Launching into an absurd pack of lies about a previous employer, she declared him to have been a carpenter, that the family was dead, and spoke of incongruous journeys with them to Margate, Ramsgate, and Brighton, asserting one minute that they were for health reasons, and the next that "they were like a great many people, in debt, and went about in consequence, if I must tell the truth."

When the Rev. John Ellis was called to the bar it was discovered that he was not the carpenter that Martha Favery had represented him to be but a reputable clergyman, and a master of the Merchant Taylors School. His family, he said, was very much alive, and they had had only one seaside holiday during the two years that Martha Favery was with them.

Although exposed and her veracity discredited, Martha Favery's account of Mrs. Clarke's imbroglio of debt was nonetheless a rough and ready approximation of the truth.

"Was not the house in Gloucester Place to your knowledge kept at a great expense?" asked Colonel Wardle.

"It certainly was," came the emphatic reply. "There were sometimes two men cooks, sometimes three men cooks."

"Have you often known Mrs. Clarke distressed for money during that period?"

"She never could pay her debts properly after the first quarter.

People were tearing me to pieces for money, and saying that I kept it."

William Wilberforce took up the questioning.

"Did the tradesmen seem willing to send in articles merely on Mrs. Clarke's authority?"

"They sent what she ordered, as far as I know. Sometimes they would not."

"Did you use any arguments to them to induce them to send in articles, if they appeared unwilling to do so?"

"No, I did not. I said when she had money she would certainly pay them. Nothing further than that."

"Did they tell you they looked to a better paymaster than Mrs. Clarke, or anything of that kind?"

"They have asked me whether His Royal Highness had settled with her, and given her money; and I said no, as soon as she had it, she would give it to them."

Mr. Herbert wanted to know whether the Duke of York provided any money to pay these importunate tradesmen.

"You have mentioned that there were very considerable embarrassments happened, and that you have been applied to for money, and have been supposed to keep it instead of paying the different creditors. Did you tell her of those distresses, and apply to her for money? And if so, what answer did you get?"

"I did inform her. She said that His Royal Highness had been very backward in his payments to her, and I must put the people off, and accordingly I did as she said."

"Did Mrs. Clarke ever mention to you that His Royal Highness said that he would give or had given her sums of money to pay those debts?"

"No, I never heard that."

"Did you never mention to Mrs. Clarke that you wished her to ask (for) money from the Duke of York to pay those debts?"

"Yes, I did."

"What was the answer Mrs. Clarke made?"

"She said all would be paid as soon as she had it from His Royal Highness."

"You have stated that you applied to Mrs. Clarke telling her that she owed certain sums of money, to get it from the Duke of York. Do you know from your own knowledge that many of those debts were afterwards paid?"

"Some of the debts were paid while he was still there. I have paid the baker, and I have paid the butcher twice."

In an effort to prove that the general household expenses were frequently paid by the Duke, Mr. Herbert pursued the topic when Mrs. Clarke was again called to the bar.

"Did you, when you lived in Gloucester Place, always pay your bills yourself, or did you sometimes pay them through the medium of your housekeeper?"

"Sometimes myself, sometimes my housekeeper; but the common tradesmen, such as butchers and bakers, I never paid myself."

"Did Mrs. Favery ever represent to you that the creditors were so clamorous that she was accused of having most likely secreted the money by not paying it?"

"Yes, but then I never minded what she said."

"Did Mrs. Favery represent the absolute necessity of the Duke of York's supplying you with money to pacify the creditors?"

"Yes, of course. If she was teazed by people she teazed me."

"Did this often happen?"

"She is the best judge."

"Were not the creditors often paid in consequence?"

"Yes, if they were very clamorous."

"Were not those sums to a very considerable amount?"

"I do not know what is called considerable."

"Were they to the amount of £1,000?"

"She would speak of different tradesmen teazing for their bills. I do not know to what amount."

"Do you not know that bills were often paid, and to a large amount, in consequence of your application to the Duke upon the representations of Mrs. Favery?'

Mrs. Clarke knew no such thing, and categorically said so. "No, he never paid a bill for me on its being so represented, and I never had any credit with any of his people, nor never got money on his account."

Colonel Wardle asked whether her diamonds were ever in pawn during the two-and-a-half years that she lived with the Duke of York.

"Very frequently," Mrs. Clarke informed him. "And I recollect that when Mr. Dowler paid me £800 I took them out, so that Parker's book would convince about the time that he got his appointment . . ."

"Once or twice His Royal Highness gave me small bills* for £300 or £400, but they were his own signing and drawing," she told Mr. Lyttleton. "It was to get my necklace, or something in that way, from Parker's in Fleet Street."

Mrs. Clarke had discovered that drawing bills was a most useful device for raising ready cash when hard pressed by her creditors, and on three occasions during the summer of 1805 she drew bills in favour of her mother, although undoubtedly she kept the money obtained from the pawnbroker.

True to form, she was unable to pay the bills as they became due, and when the crisis broke it was the Duke of York who stepped in to avert the consequences. Financially embarrassed himself, he in turn played for time with post-dated promissory notes.

A bill for raising credit is endorsed both by the person drawing it and the person who would pay the money, and the ambivalent role of Mrs. Clarke's mother in this incorrigible practice did not escape the eye of one lampoonist:

Your Mother, too, of scrivening fame,
Draft-drawing, bill-endorsing Dame;
Tho' now her hand's convenient,
Full surely if your Interest clashes
To trample on her very Ashes,
You'll fancy most expedient.

Bailiffs, law officers, and court cases were all a familiar part of life to Mrs. Clarke, and the experience she gained in handling the brusque, impervious agents of officialdom served her well as she stood facing a barrage of questions from Members on both sides of the House. As Lord Folkestone discovered, she had no inhibitions about scoring points off friends as well as adversaries.

"Do you know a person of the name of W. Withers?" he asked.

"Yes, I do."

"What is he?"

"He is a Sheriff's officer."

---

*The term "bill' 'is used not as an invoice for goods delivered or services rendered, but as a written order for raising money on credit. The person to whom the bill was made out could obtain the money immediately, less an appropriate discount, while the person drawing the bill agreed to pay the amount due, plus the agreed interest, on the date specified.

"How came you acquainted with him?"

"He had some business with me in his own way."

"Was it in consequence of your pecuniary distresses that you became acquainted with W. Withers?"

"No one would ever know a man of that description but through that very thing," Mrs. Clarke retorted sharply.

It is a significant indication of Mrs. Clarke's incredible nerve and self-confidence that for almost three years she had been able to pick her way so close to the abyss of financial disaster and survive so long. At last, on May 10th, 1806, her luck had run out, and in that cold, brief interview in the drawing-room of Gloucester Place, William Adam had brought to an end her life of royal patronage. He explained to the House of Commons the background of events leading to this conclusion.

He had reason to believe, he said, that Mrs. Clarke's conduct "had not been so correct as it ought to have been, and that it had a tendency to prejudice His Royal Highness's interests, not his character in a military point of view or in a public capacity, but his interests and his name with regard to money. This led to further enquiry, and I conceived it my duty to intimate the results of these things to the Duke of York. I found the Duke not inclined to believe that there could be anything wrong in that quarter, and that he continued of that opinion almost to the last, till very near the close of the connection . . ."

Fifty-eight-year-old Scottish-born William Adam is said to have been a man of urbanity and probity. In spite of the Duke's reluctance, he was determined that the infamous Mrs. Clarke must go, and she was probably telling the truth when she reported the Duke as saying that "he was entirely in the clutches of Mr. Adam."

"The investigations were completed," William Adam continued, "and when they were, I think, either upon the 6th, 7th or 8th May, 1806, submitted in detail and in writing to His Royal Highness, accompanied with the proofs. It was," he added unctuously, "an unpleasant task . . ."

"It had been represented to me," he revealed, "that this person had defended an action as a married woman, having obtained the property for which the action was brought in the character of a widow."

Mrs. Clarke disputed on principle Mr. Adam's version of the separation, but shed little new light on the matter.

"Do you know why the Duke of York withdrew his protection from you?" Mr. Herbert asked.

"Mr. Adam states that it was in consequence of my pleading my marriage to a bill of £130, but I can prove the contrary to that, as I had done it once before, and he knew it. And the man sent threatening letters to him, and to the whole of His Royal Highness's family. His name is Charman, a silversmith in St. James's Street. I have my own opinion of the separation."

"Did His Royal Highness assign any reason for it?"

"No, he did not, but I guess the reason."

"Was it on account of your interference in military promotions?"

"No, it was what Mr. Adam stated, upon money matters. But not that one of the bill."

It was left to James Comrie, Mrs. Clarke's lawyer, to give the most explicit and dispassionate account of the circumstances leading to the dismissal of Mrs. Clarke.

"Do you recollect that he (the Duke of York) ever assigned any reason that was prejudicial to her character when he parted with her?" Colonel Wardle enquired.

"The Duke of York stated to me that he had been served with a subpoena to appear in the court of King's Bench. I think it was on a trial which was then pending in which Mrs. Clarke was the defendant, which subpoena had been accompanied by a very severe letter, describing her very improper conduct in having pleaded her coverture to an action brought for goods sold and delivered, and, I think, upon a bill of exchange, one or either, I do not immediately recollect which. His Royal Highness stated that that was the reason which occasioned the separation."

"Do you mean to state, that you understood from the Duke of York, that she had done so without his knowledge?"

"He did not state that, but he said, after such a thing as that, it was impossible but that they must separate, or words to that effect."

"Did he complain of any other bad conduct in Mrs. Clarke?"

"I do not recollect that he did . . ."

For Mrs. Clarke it had been a short step from reckless expenditure to accumulating debts, from the Duke's parsimony to dependence upon her accommodating admirer William Dowler, from borrowing money from Parker the pawnbroker in Fleet Street to visits from the bailiffs, until, finally, financial chaos had brought her ostentatious world tumbling about her ears.

Chapter Nine

THE FIRST charge of corruption brought forward by Colonel Wardle against the Duke of York concerned the purchase in 1805 of an exchange between Lieut.-Colonel Brooke of the 56th Foot Regiment and Lieut.-Colonel Knight of the 5th Dragoon Guards.

Until 1870 army commissions were legally bought and sold, and a system enabling the sons of wealthy aristocrats to obtain positions of command over more experienced and efficient officers was accepted as a legitimate prerogative. Lord Brudenell, Cecil Woodham-Smith discloses in "The Reason Why", paid between £35,000 and £40,000 for a lieutenant-colonelcy placing him in command of the 15th Hussars.

The system had one incomparable advantage. With the ruling class dependent for their position and privileges upon the energies and exertions of "The lower orders", their command of the army was the best safeguard of all against revolution or military dictatorship.

By going on half-pay or purchasing an exchange, it was possible for the wealthy officer to avoid uncongenial duties at home or unpleasant and inconvenient service abroad, and Cecil Woodham-Smith explains that "when a fashionable regiment had to do a turn of duty in India, it was notorious that a different set of officers went out from those who had been on duty at St. James's Palace or the Brighton Pavilion."

By 1805, Lieut.-Colonel Knight had served in the army for twenty-three years, and had fought in most of the continental campaigns. Owing to his poor state of health he was extremely anxious to exchange his lieutenant-colonelcy in the Guards with Colonel Brooke so that by taking an appointment in the infantry he might go on half-pay. There was, however, a serious obstacle to be overcome.

It was an army rule that no officer could be promoted to the rank of a field officer in the Guards with less than six years' service.

Although Colonel Brooke had been in the army for twelve years, he had served only five on full pay, and his cavalry experience was limited to a paltry four months.

On his original application papers was a pencilled note, "Cannot be acceded to; His Royal Highness does not approve the exchange proposed."

Dr. Thynne explained his part in expediting the exchange which the Duke had originally rejected.

"Did you attend Mrs. Clarke in your professional line in July, 1805?" Colonel Wardle asked.

"I have attended Mrs. Clarke for the last 7 years; I do not recollect that it was in July, 1805, more than any other time. I have attended when she was ill."

"Did you ever, by the desire of any person, apply to Mrs. Clarke respecting an exchange between Lieut.-Colonel Knight and Lieut.-Colonel Brooke?"

"I have applied to Mrs. Clarke respecting the exchange of Lieut.-Colonel Knight and Lieut.-Colonel Brooke. The application I made was in consequence of an application made to me by an old and valuable friend, Mr. Robert Knight, the brother of the Lieut.-Colonel. He understood that I was acquainted with Mrs. Clarke; he begged I would speak to her to expedite the exchange: and I did speak to Mrs. Clarke upon the subject, and delivered her the message I got from Mr. Knight and his brother, the Lieut.-Colonel, to whom I was then introduced."

"What passed upon that subject between Mrs. Clarke and yourself?"

"I was authorised to tell Mrs. Clarke that she would receive a certain sum of money. I specified the sum of £200."

"For what was the sum specified; upon what event was that sum offered?"

"It was offered for the purpose of inducing Mrs. Clarke to expedite the exchange . . ."

"Was it not under the consideration and conviction of her, at that time being under the protection of the Commander-in-Chief, that such application was made to her?"

"Of course, if Mrs. Clarke was not thought likely to expedite the thing, no application would have been made to her."

"Did Mrs. Clarke indicate to you the circumstances of the exchange being gazetted?"

"Mrs. Clarke sent 'The Gazette'* to my house . . . no money ever passed through my hands. If Mrs. Clarke received money, she received it from some other quarter. I solemnly declare that no money passed through my hands whatever. I sent 'The Gazette' to the parties, and what they did with 'The Gazette' I do not care."

"Did Mr. Robert Knight alone authorize you to offer the £200, or was Lieut.-Colonel Knight a party to that offer?"

"I was entirely influenced by Mr. Robert Knight. His lady was an old patient of mine; he was always a great friend of mine. I did nothing to refuse Mr. Robert Knight . . ."

Robert Knight was the next witness to take up the story.

"Did you know of any positive promise of the Commander-in-Chief, prior to the application to Mrs. Clarke, that the exchange should take place?" Colonel Wardle wanted to know.

"No."

"Where was the application made to Mrs. Clarke?"

"There was some delay in the business, from what cause I do not know, and I stated the circumstances to Dr. Thynne, who happened to be attending my family at that time. He replied that he thought he could be of service by applying to a friend of his, Mrs. Clarke. I told him I should be much obliged to him if he would apply to her, and that I should be happy to give £200 if the business could be carried into effect . . ."

"How did you send the £200 to Mrs. Clarke?"

"Under blank cover, as far as my recollection serves me, by my servant."

As the House had resolved itself into a Committee of Inquiry, every Member had the right to put questions to the witnesses brought forward, and Mr. Leach now rose to elicit further details about the transaction.

"Did you see Mrs. Clarke soon after the notice in 'The Gazette' that the exchange was effected, and for what purpose did you see her?"

"I saw her, I think, in the month of September, for the purpose of thanking her."

"Upon that occasion did Mrs. Clarke desire you to be secret with

---

* "The London Gazette" first appeared in November, 1665 as "The Oxford Gazette", and became "The London Gazette" in February, 1666. It was published bi-weekly on Tuesdays and Fridays, and was the official Government journal in which details of military appointments were published.

respect to this transaction, and did she assign any, and for what reason for that secrecy?"

"She did entreat me to keep it a secret, lest it should come to the Duke of York's ears."

"Have you seen Mrs. Clarke within the last month, and how did it happen that you saw her?"

"She wrote to beg that I would come to her, about a month ago . . . and she asked me the name of the officer who had exchanged with my brother. She made a number of complaints of her having been ill-treated by the Duke of York; that he had deserted her and left her in debt, I think to the amount of £2,000; and that she was determined, unless she could bring him to terms, to expose him in the manner in which she is now endeavouring to do. I said that that was her affair, but that I trusted she would not introduce either me or my brother. She said, "O Good God! no, by no means, it is not my intention, you can have nothing at all to do with it'. That passed in the drawing-room, and I took my leave . . ."

The call for Mrs. Clarke to be examined was a moment of high excitement and curiosity, and many Members stood to obtain a a better look at the woman with whom the Duke had chosen to share his Bacchanalian revelries and his bed.

Mrs. Clarke had been called as a witness by Colonel Wardle and he opened his examination by asking whether Dr. Thynne promised to pay her if she effected the exchange between Lieut.-Colonel Knight and Lieut.-Colonel Brooke.

"Certainly he did", replied Mrs. Clarke spiritedly, making it clear from the beginning that she was going to make a clean breast of her financial chicanery.

"Do you recollect his mentioning any particular sum?"

"Yes, I think he did say something about a couple of hundred pounds."

"Do you recollect afterwards receiving any pecuniary consideration?"

"Yes, I do."

"How much."

"A £200 bank note was sent to me."

"Did the Commander-in-Chief know from you the amount of the money you had received?"

"He knew the amount, because I showed him the note, and I think I got one of his servants to get it exchanged for me through His Royal Highness."

Mrs. Clarke and Dr. Thynne had been together in the witnesses' room and Mr. Windham was obviously suspicious that whilst Robert Knight was being examined that they had taken the opportunity to discuss the evidence Dr. Thynne had given.

"Has any conversation passed between you and Dr. Thynne since he has been examined in this House?"

"Yes, he has been sitting with me nearly ever since."

"To what purpose was that conversation between you?"

"Not at all relative to this business, it has not been addressed to me, it has been addressed to the two ladies with me entirely."

"Repeat as much of that conversation as you can recollect."

"I could not repeat after Dr. Thynne if his character is known at all to the gentlemen here, it would be very indelicate. He has merely been laughing at the gentlemen here."

Sir Thomas Turton now had a few questions to put to Mrs. Clarke.

"Did you upon that occasion desire Mr. Robert Knight to keep secret this transaction?"

"Yes, I should think I did; certainly I should say that. I do not recollect saying it, but it is very likely that I did."

"Do you recollect expressing a wish that it might be kept secret lest it should come to the ears of the Duke of York?"

"Oh no, never."

"Or anything to that effect?"

"Nothing like it."

"Are you quite positive of that?"

"Positive."

The small, sharp-featured Attorney-General, Sir Vicary Gibbs, now rose to question Mrs. Clarke, and although reported to have been "absolutely persuaded of his universal capacity and the universal unfitness of others", he soon discovered that Mrs. Clarke was not to be intimidated by either rank or reputation.

"Had you ever mentioned the transaction voluntarily to Colonel Wardle, till he attacked you upon it?"

"He asked me if it was true, and I told him yes."

"Had you stated this voluntarily of your own consent to Colonel Wardle, or only in answer to his enquiries?"

"When Mr. Wardle told me he had heard, and mentioned the circumstances to me, I said yes, it was true; that was all I said. I did not think I should be brought here upon it, or I might have been very apt to deny it."

"Would you willingly have concealed it?"

"I concealed it from the beginning, it was not a public thing. Certainly anything which ought to be priavte, I have sense enough to keep as such. I believe Mr. Knight spoke of it himself – it had got round."

"Who were the other persons that you spoke to of it, besides Mr. Wardle?"

"A few of my friends, I don't recollect who. I am not without friends."

"Can you recollect the day on which Dr. Thynne applied to you?"

"The day of the month or the day of the week?" enquired Mrs. Clarke, coolly baiting the Attorney-General.

"Either."

"I do not, it was such a trivial affair."

"Can you tax your recollection upon either one or the other?"

"Not upon such a trivial occasion."

One of the Duke's most tenacious defenders was the twenty-eight year old Irish-born Member for Downpatrick, John Wilson Croker and, despite a stutter which he never completely conquered, he was a talented and persuasive speaker. He was also one of Mrs. Clarke's most caustic adversaries, but their first encounter gave little indication of the bitter infighting that was to follow.

"Do you recollect particulars of the last conversation which you had with Mr. Robert Knight?"

"Yes, he asked me who had taken the house I was in, and if the Duke and I were upon intimate terms now; it was a sort of general conversation. Then the subject of the letters came up, and he asked me whether His Royal Highness had paid my annuity. I told him no; that His Royal Highness had not taken any further notice of me nor of the debts; that he had forgotten the annuity and indeed that he had sent me word that he had never made any. That the trades people were daily harassing me for the debts I had run into when I was under his protection, and it was impossible for me to plead my marriage to them all, the people not being contented, and that I would publish his letters, and give the money among the trades people. Mr. Robert Knight then desired me, if I was going to publish any sort of memoir, that I would be sure to spare his brother. That was the heads of the conversation that passed between us."

"Did you make any enquiries of Mr. Robert Knight concerning

the business now under discussion?"

"Mr. Knight told me, I believe, as well as I can recollect: 'Ah, by the bye, you got very well over the difficulty that my brother could not'; and then I asked him the name of the other man, but I knew it before, and what sort of looking man he was. He was an Irishman", Mrs. Clarke concluded, almost certainly tilting at Croker's nationality.

The burden of defending the Duke fell principally upon the shoulders of Spencer Perceval, the Chancellor of the Exchequer and Leader of the House. The Prime Minister, the old and ailing Duke of Portland, was a mute figurehead sustained by draughts of laudanum and opiates, and never spoke in Parliament during his two-and-a-half years in office.

Spencer Perceval laboured tirelessly to extricate the Duke of York from the web that Mrs. Clarke was spinning to enmesh her turncoat lover in her backstairs jobbery.

"At the time when you received the £200, was the Duke of York present in the room?" he enquired.

"No, he was not."

"How soon afterwards did you state to the Duke of York that Mr. Knight had fulfilled his promise?"

"The same day."

"Was it on the same day that you desired His Royal Highness to get the note changed for you?"

"I did not desire His Royal Highness to get it changed for me. He wished it himself as I could not do it."

"What was the name of the servant by whom that note was changed?"

"I do not know, I am sure. It is a very unusual thing to ask servants their names", Mrs. Clarke retorted, giving the Chancellor of the Exchequer a sharp lesson in the finer points of etiquette.

If it was true that one of the Duke's servants had, on his instructions, changed a bank note which the Duke knew Mrs. Clarke had received from Robert Knight it was an obvious inference that she dabbled in military matters with his connivance. Two days later the Duke's supporters produced Ludowick Orramin, his footman for eighteen years, to repudiate her assertion.

A German by birth, Orramin explained in broken English that he had an order to take the Duke's clothes to Gloucester Place at eight o'clock each morning, "and no other servant, and no other servant dared to do it."

"Are you sure that no other of His Royal Highness's servants but yourself went to him there?" asked Sir Vicary Gibbs.

"Yes."

"Were you ever directed, either by Mrs. Clarke or by His Royal Highness, to carry out from Gloucester Place a bank note to be changed?"

"No."

"Did you ever carry out a bank note from Gloucester Place to be changed?"

"No."

"Are you quite certain of that fact?"

"Yes."

For a moment it seemed as if Orramin's emphatic contradiction had successfully scotched Mrs. Clarke's attempt to embroil the Duke in her money-making activities, but Sir Francis Burdett was not so easily convinced of his impartiality.

"Have you had any intercourse with any one, previous to your coming to this bar, respecting the evidence you have given this night?"

"His Royal Highness asked me if I ever did receive a note from him or Mrs. Clarke."

"Have you had any intercourse with any other person besides His Royal Highness previous to your giving your testimony this night?"

"I was asked the same question by Mr. Adam."

"Had you any intercourse of the same kind with any other person?"

"A Mr. Wilkinson, and Mr. Lowten."*

Taking his cue from the Government supporters who had brought Orramin forward to give evidence in the Duke's favour, Wardle called upon David Peirson, Mrs. Clarke's butler for fifteen months, to tell the Committee what he remembered about the bank note alleged to have been changed by the Duke's footman.

"Do you recollect any servant being ordered by the Duke to get a bank note changed?"

"I recollect the housekeeper, Mrs. Favery, bringing down a bill in a morning, and Ludowick going out and getting it changed and coming back and giving it to Mrs. Favery again, and she took it upstairs."

---

* Thomas Lowten was the Duke's attorney-at-law and solicitor, and he employed John Wilkinson as a private inquiry agent.

"Do you recollect any servant being ordered by the Duke to get a bank note changed?"

"No."

"Do you recollect Ludowick taking out a bank note to be changed?"

"Yes, I do, on a morning."

"Did you hear him ordered to do so by anybody?"

"The housekeeper gave him the note. I saw her give him the note, and he took it out."

"Do you know the amount of the note?"

"No, I do not."

"Was the Duke of York in Mrs. Clarke's house at the time this note was delivered to Ludowick to get it changed?" asked Mr. Brand.

"Yes, he was upstairs," Peirson replied.

"At what time in the morning was this?" Colonel Wardle interjected.

"Near eight o'clock."

"Do you know that the Duke was up?"

"I am not certain of that."

Even this evidence was suspect as when re-examined three days later, Peirson admitted that he had spoken to Mrs. Clarke before being called to the House of Commons.

"The day before she sent for me into Baker Street, where she was in her carriage, to ask me whether ever I had changed any bill, or knew any bill changed. I said I recollected Mrs. Favery giving a bill to Ludowick and his going and getting the bill changed, and bringing it back again . . ."

Mrs. Clarke refused to commit herself as to the date when Dr. Thynne had asked her to expedite the exchange, but by a series of somewhat apocryphal calculations the Duke's supporters deduced that Dr. Thynne had approached her on July 25th, and Colonel Gordon produced documentary evidence that the exchange had been agreed to by the Duke of York on July 23rd, and that it had been sent to the King for approval on the 24th.

Sir Arthur Wellesley, who, as the Duke of Wellington, was to become Commander-in-Chief thirty-three years later, wasted no time in dismissing the accusation.

"It was also proved," he wrote to the Duke of Richmond, "that the Duke of York had consented to this exchange two days, and the King one day, before Mrs. Clarke had been applied to, to exert her influence to expedite it; so that there is an end to this charge."

"Tomorrow", he concluded, "we go upon another."

Chapter Ten

"THERE HAS appeared in the last two days a general system of swindling applicable to all the offices of the state," Sir Arthur Wellesley wrote on February 12th in his report to the Duke of Richmond of the proceedings in the House of Commons, "in which Mrs. Clarke has been most active, and a great gainer."

He enumerated the points on which any impression had been made against the Duke of York, and high on his list of damaging disclosures was "the purchase of a service of plate at Rickett's (sic) for £1,850, for which the Duke paid only £1,350, and Mrs. Clarke £500, as she says, from the money she received, with the Duke's knowledge, on account of her interference in French's levy."

Colonel French and Captain Huxley Sandon had officially applied to the Assistant Military Secretary early in 1804 for a letter of service authorizing them to undertake a recruiting levy, at a time when the army was preparing to meet the threat of a Napoleonic invasion.

After an uneasy peace lasting less than fourteen months, war between England and France had broken out once more on May 16th, 1803, and travellers returning from abroad reported a vast invasion fleet being built with feverish speed in every port and navigable river in France, of gigantic engineering operations at Boulogne to widen and deepen the harbour to accommodate the immense flotilla, and of the construction of great camps along the channel coast.

In September that year Lady Bessborough was excitedly communicating a conversation with a merchant from Amsterdam who had escaped with an American passport on board a Prussian vessel. "His account is tremendous. . . . The boats draw only two feet and a half water, have a sail, and a thing call'd a bridge to let down to fasten to the shore . . . the number of men to sail at the same time are 250 thousand!!!"

In the midst of this danger and consternation, the levy entrusted to Colonel French and Captain Huxley Sandon was a disastrous fiasco. At the end of nine months only one hundred and fifty-four men had been enlisted instead of four thousand as stipulated in the contract, each recruit was said to have cost the country £150, and French and Sandon were deep in disgrace.

But Mrs. Clarke was riding on the crest of the wave – with a profit of £1,700.

It was Dominigo Corri, her music master and sycophant, who set in motion the events that were to bring both Sandon and himself to the bar of the House of Commons.

"Captain Sandon", Dominigo Corri explained to Colonel Wardle, "was introduced to me by Mr. Cockayne (an attorney), and he told me that he knew that I was acquainted with the lady who had a great influence in the War Office; and he told me that if I would speak to this lady, she would have £200 for what, I recollect, was for the levy of troops. I told him I would speak to Mrs. Clarke and so I did, and gave him the answer that she would try what she could, but she said at the same time, it was a very difficult matter, that she was obliged to break through it gradually, and could recommend nobody but people of character, and qualified for the place, and to go through the War Office, as everybody else was. And this I told Captain Sandon."

"Do you of your own knowledge know any thing more of the bargain between Mrs. Clarke and Colonel French and Captain Sandon?"

"Yes, Captain Sandon came to me and said that the Duke had screwed them down very hard, and that he could only give £700. 'Well', I said, 'it is all the same to me what you will give, and I will tell her what you say', and I told Mrs. Clarke of this new proposal. In the meantime, Captain Sandon introduced himself to Mrs. Clarke, and I never heard any more of the business; they settled it by themselves. Except in the month of June 1804, Mr. Cockayne sent to me at the coffee house, the Cannon coffee house, and he brought a bill, I believe – which I never looked at – for £200 payable to my order, he said, upon Mr. Grant. I did not look at the bill. I put my name, and gave it to Mr. Cockayne, and said, you had better keep it yourself, I am under an obligation to you, you had better keep it. And that was the end of my business."

"Do you of your own knowledge know nothing further of the bargain that was made?"

"Nothing more. Several people came to me applying to me for places, and I told Mrs. Clarke, but I never heard any more. She was very anxious to get 'The Gazette' every night, expecting places, but I know nothing more of the parties, for I introduced them to her, and I had nothing more to do with it, and no more business of any sort passed between Mrs. Clarke and me, except the music."

Huxley Sandon was more emphatic about the part played by Dominigo Corri, and the fee he paid him for an introduction to Mrs. Clarke.

"Who gave you the information that took you to Mrs. Clarke?" Wardle enquired.

"Mr. Cockayne, who was my attorney, informed me that if I had anything particular to ask for in the War Office, or at the Commander-in-Chief's office, in all probability he could recommend me to a person who could do anything in that way for me that I chose to request."

"Did he recommend you to Mrs. Clarke?"

"He recommended me to her agent."

"Who was her agent?"

"I understood a music master of the name of Corri."

"Do you recollect giving a check (sic) upon Mr. Grant for £200 in favour of Mr. Corri, on account of the levy?"

"Perfectly well, but it was not a check, it was a draft at two months; but it was not for Mrs. Clarke, it was entirely for Mr. Corri, who had acted as the agent from her to Mr. Cockayne, the attorney."

Mrs. Clarke was equally explicit.

"How long have you known Mr. Sandon?" asked Sir Vicary Gibbs, the Attorney-General.

"Ever since Colonel French's levy."

"Was that the first knowledge you had of him?"

"If he did not come about Colonel French's levy, he came about some other appointments. I should rather think he brought me a list of officers for appointments, instead of the levy first."

"Did he come to you voluntarily, or did you send for him?"

"I could not send for him, for he gave Mr. Corri £200 for an introduction, him and Colonel French."

Captain Sandon was an invaluable con-man for Mrs. Clarke in her lucrative sale of army patronage, and perhaps alarmed at having wrecked his military career, or ashamed of his own depravity, he feigned forgetfulness, dissembled and lied as he faced a critical House of Commons.

Closely questioned by Wardle, Sandon at length conceded how

he and Colonel French obtained authority to undertake the levy.

"What means did you take to get the letter of service?"

"I understood from Colonel French that he was to give a certain sum of money for it."

"What passed between you and Colonel French upon the subject?"

"When I saw him, he told me that he had settled everything with Mrs. Clarke."

"Do you know what were the terms concluded by that settlement?"

"Yes, he informed me that he was to give her five hundred guineas."

A letter of service authorizing the levy was granted on April 30th, 1804.* Colonel French set off to enlist recruits in Ireland and Scotland, leaving England to Captain Sandon, but their efforts to induce men into the army were a dismal failure and there followed "a variety of alterations in the letter of service".

The bounty payable was raised from thirteen to nineteen guineas per man, ten boys were allowed in every one hundred recruits at the full capitation rate, and the maximum age was raised to thirty-five.

Captain Sandon was not prepared to say what influence Mrs. Clarke had exerted in having these alterations agreed to, but admitted that he had seen her some fifty times during the course of the levy and had paid her a considerable sum of money.

"You have stated that 500 guineas was to be paid to Mrs. Clarke at first, and then that you have paid her from £800 to £900 since?"

"I think £850. I have the exact sum in my pocket book; it appears by that that it is £850."

"Can you state whether that £850 arose out of any particular agreement, at so much a man raised, or in what proportion Mrs. Clarke was paid?"

"It was to be general. If our levy had succeeded we were to have made her a present of perhaps a couple of thousand pounds. It appeared to me that there was no explicit agreement that a certain sum should be given. But our levy failed, and we were much out of pocket. She was the only gainer, I believe, upon the business."

On February 9th, several minutes elapsed before Mrs. Clarke appeared when called to give evidence, and when she arrived she

* See Appendix for the text of this letter.

was sobbing violently. "A cry of 'Chair, a chair' resounded from different parts of the house," the Parliamentary Debates reporter recorded drily, and Mr. Wharton, the Chairman, told her that she had the permission of the Committee to be seated.

"Did you know Colonel French?" asked Colonel Wardle.

Still crying and dabbing her eyes, Mrs. Clarke made no reply, and the Chairman intervened to say that if she had any complaint of ill usage the Committee would hear it.

"I have been very much insulted," Mrs. Clarke blurted out. "I knew I should be protected when I sent for the proper person. I sent for the Serjeant-at-Arms to conduct me in." When the challenge to chivalry came, she insinuated, the Serjeant-at-Arms was the only Sir Galahad among them.

The Deputy Serjeant-at-Arms was called, and the questions put to him by Samuel Whitbread exposed Mrs. Clarke's display of distress as no more than feminine artifice.

"She sent me a message stating that she had been insulted, and she would not get out of her carriage until I came for her. When I got there I saw seven or eight people or a dozen people, I do not think more. Her carriage door was opened and she was handed out, and not a word passed . . . There was not a word said to her all the way I came with her here."

"Was there not a considerable crowd in the passage leading to the House?"

"Yes, there were several people, a great many servants, they were standing on one side . . ."

"Did any of those persons insult her?"

"Not a word passed to my knowledge."

Mrs. Clarke quickly recovered both her composure and her vocality, and as the linchpin in the case alleging the Duke's complicity, she seized every opportunity of implicating him in her chicanery.

"Did you state to the Commander-in-Chief that you were to have any pecuniary advantages if Colonel French was allowed to have a levy?" Wardle wanted to know.

"Yes, certainly," Mrs. Clarke replied without a moment's hesitation.

"Did the Commander-in-Chief promise you, after such an application, that Colonel French should have a levy?"

"Yes, he did."

"Did you in consequence of Colonel French having such a levy receive any sums of money from him or any other person on that account?"

"Yes."

"Can you state any particular sums that were paid to you on that account, and by whom?"

"I recollect having one sum, but I cannot tell whether it was Colonel French or Captain Sandon, of 500 guineas – bank notes, making up the sum of guineas. And I paid £500 of it on account to Birkett for a service of plate, and His Royal Highness paid the remainder by his own bills. I fancy His Royal Highness told me so."

"Do you recollect that either Colonel French or Captain Sandon applied to you to prevail upon the Commander-in-Chief to make any alterations from the original terms of the levy?"

"They teased me every day, and I always told His Royal Highness, or gave him Colonel French's notes, but I cannot tell what it was about for I never gave myself the trouble to read them. I was not aware of what they always asked me or wanted, but His Royal Highness always understood it I believe."

During her reign as mistress of the Commander-in-Chief and patron of army promotion, Mrs. Clarke was fully alive to the precarious way of life to which she was committed. Once her financial skulduggery became known at the Horse Guards, she would lose, she knew, not only an essential source of income but also her lover.

That Mrs. Clarke was well aware of the risks she was running was confirmed by Dominigo Corri, who informed the Committee that he had called upon her one afternoon just as she was leaving for Kensington Gardens. Her carriage was at the door and greatly perturbed she urged him to "For God's sake go home and burn the letters."

The letters were "just common things . . . a desire for Captain Sandon to go such a day to the War Office, or something of that kind," and his wife, so he said, went home and burned them.

When Mrs. Alice Corri appeared before the House of Commons she reluctantly admitted to having deceived her husband by preserving the letters in a box, but said that she had destroyed them shortly before the inquiry began. The cause of the commotion, she recalled, had been a satirical reference in one of the newspapers "relative to a female Clerk".

Captain Sandon had been less circumspect. A cache of letters from Mrs. Clarke was discovered at his lodgings, brought to the

House of Commons, sorted and sifted by a Select Committee, and those letters considered "relevant to the matters in question" were numbered, read in evidence, and reprinted in the newspapers.

Here, declared the Wardle coalition gleefully, was conclusive proof not only of Mrs. Clarke's nefarious association with Captain Sandon, but also of the culpability of the Commander-in-Chief.

"I gave the papers to His Royal Highness," Mrs. Clarke had written. "He read them while with me; said he still thought men high, but that an answer would be left at his office as the way of business. I told him if any was appointed to give the Colonel the preference. Burn this soon as read."

"I hope you will attend the Duke to-day, as Clinton (his Military Secretary at the time) leaves him on Thursday, and he has all the writings for you in hand. He will not leave his office till six. How comes on French?"

"The Duke told me this morning that you must get on faster with your men, he has written to town for that purpose. You had better send me the exact number of all you have sent, and I will shew it to him. *He complains of the slowness of recruiting the Levy.*"

"Do you think it at all possible for you and French to let me draw a bill on you for £200? I am so dreadfully distressed I know not which way to turn myself, and before that will be due you are aware of what is to be done for me in that negociation (sic)."

"Mrs. Clarke's compliments await Colonel Sandon,* thinks it best for him not to come to her box this evening, as Greenwood goes with both the Dukes this evening, and of course will watch where your eyes direct *now* and *then*; and should he see and know Colonel Sandon, may make some remark by saying or talking of the *Levy* business, and it may be hurtful to his and Mrs. C's future interest."

---

* Although Mrs. Clarke addresses Sandon as "Colonel", the records held by the National Army Museum show that he remained a Captain from 1794 until he was cashiered in 1809. People were often imprecise in their allocation of rank in personal correspondence at this time, and it is clear that Mrs. Clarke made a slip of this sort.

"Can you give me a call to-day, about one or two, or about five? I wish to see you much. Tell Spedding to write in for what he wants, as the Duke says that is much the best."

"I am thoroughly convinced of the money being too trifling, and I have mentioned it to a person who knows the full value of those things, so you may tell Bacon and Spedding they must give each of them *two hundred* more, and the captains must give me fifty more. I am now offered eleven hundred for an old officer."

"I am vexed to death. You well know the state of my finances, and I hit upon Spedding for Tuesday, when, behold, the regiment he is in, did their exercise so bad that the Duke swore at them very much, and has stopped the promotion of every one in it! . . . I must beg very hard for him. The Duke is very angry with you, for when he last saw you, you promised him 300 foreigners and you have not produced one. O, yes, master Sandon is a pretty fellow to *depend on*. I wish I had hit upon Eustace first. I told you, I believe, that they must be done gradually, his clerks are so cunning."

Everything it seemed was grist to Mrs. Clarke's mill, and one of her letters produced a gale of hilarity.

"I am extremely sorry to inform you (for the poor boy's sake) but it is impossible to admit him, as he has that misfortune you mentioned of being one-eyed."

Private letters brought out and read as evidence in public always create a powerful impact, and the hastily-scribbled notes that Mrs. Clarke dashed off to her confederate in 1804 made a profound impression on the whole House. They were unexpected, conclusive proof that she had been immersed up to her eyes in military racketeering.

But were the letters proof of the Duke's complicity? Was it true that he grumbled at her about the slowness of the recruiting levy? Had he instructed her to tell Spedding to write officially for the promotion that he was seeking? Did he really read Sandon's papers with Mrs. Clarke at his elbow, complaining to her of the high price of enlisting men?

Government supporters dismissed the letters as the guile of a licentious woman inducing the sinister Sandon to supply her with

A Gillray cartoon burlesquing Mrs. Clarke negotiating army promotions with the Duke of York, with Miss Taylor an alert and interested spectator.

A riotously imaginative engraving by Rowlandson of drunken debauchery at Gloucester Place. The Duke of York is on the far side of the table with his arm round Mrs. Clarke, and their glasses are raised for a toast.

A satire by Rowlandson mocking Mrs. Clarke's promiscuity. "The Original Cock and Breeches" sign-board above her head indicates a brothel.

A caricature by Williams depicting the end of Mrs. Clarke's reign as the mistress of the Duke of York when she was peremptorily dismissed by William Adam, the Duke's legal adviser, in an interview at Gloucester Place.

place-seeking customers and cash, but for the Radical faction leading the case against the Duke, the chance discovery of the letters was an exhilarating bonus. Here, it was claimed, was indisputable proof of the guilt of the Commander-in-Chief.

Any decision on the letters can only be reached by taking into consideration the personalities of the people involved and the tenor of their lives. In 1804 the Duke's passion for the witty, vivacious Mrs. Clarke was at its height, and, with more brains than he, she possessed also ample charm and subtlety to persuade him to grant favours to her military friends about whom he knew little.

As a contemporary journalist, Leigh Hunt had a better opportunity than most for assessing the situation, and he did not consider the Duke entirely blameless. "My own impression at this distance of time," he wrote forty years later, "and after a better knowledge of the Duke's private history and prevailing character, is, that there was some connivance on his part, but not of a systematic nature, or beyond what he may have considered as warrantable towards a few special friends of his mistress, on the assumption that she would carry her influence no farther."

Miss Taylor had dined frequently with the Duke and Mrs. Clarke, and Wardle asked her to tell the Committee what she could remember of the conversation around the dinner-table at Gloucester Place.

"Did you ever hear the Duke of York speak to Mrs. Clarke respecting Colonel French and his levy?"

"Once only," replied Miss Taylor, demurely dressed in a black velvet pelisse, black bonnet with a net veil, and with a cross-barred handkerchief tied round her neck.

"Relate what passed at that time."

"The Duke's words were, as nearly as I can recollect, 'I am continually worried by Colonel French; he worries me continually about the levy business, and is always wanting something more in his own favour.' Turning to Mrs. Clarke I think he said, 'How does he behave to you, darling?' or some such kind words as he used to use. That was all that was said."

"Do you recollect anything further passing than what you have stated?"

"Mrs. Clarke replied, 'Middling, not very well.' That was all that she said."

"Was that the whole of the conversation?"

"No."

"Relate the rest."

"The Duke said, 'Master French must mind what he is about or I shall cut him up and his levy too.' That was the expression he used."

Miss Taylor – there are no other words to describe her – was a riot.

From the more waggish Members, and from those already convinced that the Duke had participated in Mrs. Clarke's duplicity, chuckles, sniggers, and a buzz of conversation were sparked off by Miss Taylor's homely, off-duty cameo of the Commander-in-Chief and his mistress, whilst Perceval and his colleagues sat grim and stony-faced.

Through the newspapers and by word of mouth the conversation spread like wildfire, and ridicule fanned the flames of rancour and indignation.

The versifiers were among the first to exploit the absurdity of the situation.

How did they all behave
To you, my darling dandy?
I hope some plums they gave,
Sweetmeat and sugar candy.

Londoners, with irrepressible Cockney humour, had their own variation of an old pastime.

"The joke in the streets among the people", wrote Charles Abbot in his diary, "is not to cry 'Heads and Tails' when they toss up halfpence; but 'Duke and Darling' " – the regal figure of Britannia no doubt serving somewhat incongruously for the saucy Mrs. Clarke.

From the Government benches, Sir Vicary Gibbs, an unpopular man for his vanity and self-conceit, was the first to attempt to depreciate Miss Taylor's evidence, and quickly exposed her anxiety to stifle any enquiries about her parents.

"What are your parents?"

"My father was a gentleman."

"Do you live with your father now?"

"No."

"Is your father living?"

"Yes."

"Is your mother living?"
"Yes."
"Do you live with your mother?"
"No."
"Are you married?"
"No."
"With whom do you live?"
"My sister."
"Where do you live?"
"Chelsea."
"Are you of any profession?"
"If a boarding-school be a profession."
"What is your father's name?"
"The same name as mine."
"Taylor?"
"Yes."
"What is his Christian name?"
"Thomas."
"Where does he live now?"

"I had rather be excused answering", Miss Taylor replied, caught at last into imparting information that she knew could end only in exposure.

The Chairman instructed her to withdraw and Lord Folkestone protested that for her to answer this question might prove injurious to her father, and that he could not conceive that the information would materially benefit the inquiry.

Sir Vicary Gibbs disagreed emphatically, and declared that much of the credit of Miss Taylor's evidence depended upon the degree of respectability which both the witness and her connections held in society. "Would the noble lord or any Member in the House deny that the evidence of a prostitute, who might be picked up in a street, was to be equally relied upon with that of a person who supported a decent and respectable character?" he asked scornfully.

After some discussion it was agreed that the question should be answered. Miss Taylor was recalled, and again asked where her father lived.

"I don't know," she replied unconvincingly.

"Do you mean that your credit should rest upon the veracity of that answer, that you do not know where your father lives?" Spencer Perceval fumed.

"I don't exactly understand the question," Miss Taylor retorted.

Once more she withdrew, and once more Members argued the propriety of the question put to her.

One Member hoped that Perceval would not pursue the point, but the Chancellor of the Exchequer was adamant. "I cannot help suspecting," he declared, "that something will be disclosed by a direct answer to that question, that will greatly, if not wholly, discredit the testimony of the witness."

Wilberforce saw no good arising from compelling her to answer in a direct form, and tactfully suggested that the question should be put in another way.

Charles Yorke was determined that Miss Taylor should not elude them. "If such vigilance is not exercised, street walkers from off the Strand would probably be introduced at the bar of the House to criminate the character of the Duke of York," he objected hysterically.

"Do you mean seriously upon reflection to abide by your answer that you do not know where your father lives?" Perceval asked when Miss Taylor was again recalled.

"Yes."

"How long is it since you have seen him?"

"About a fortnight."

"Do you know where he was living when you saw him last?"

"At Chelsea."

"In what street at Chelsea?"

"I beg leave to decline answering that question."

"What reason have you for declining answering that question?"

"I do not like to tell so large an assembly where I live."

"What objection have you, who keep a boarding-school, to tell this House where you live?"

"I have answered that just now."

"Will you repeat it."

"I did not wish to inform so large an assembly of my residence."

In the general mud-slinging there were suggestions that Miss Taylor's boarding-school was, in fact, an establishment of a far more salacious sort, and that she was fortunate to derive such excellent publicity in an all-male assembly. There were rumours, too, that she was the illegitimate daughter of a disreputable stockbroker, and that her mother was in prison for debt.

"What reason have you for wishing to conceal where you live from so large an assembly?" Perceval continued.

"They will find I am poor, and doubt my veracity."

"You may be assured your veracity will not be doubted on account of your poverty. State the house where you live, and what street in Chelsea."

"China Row."

"What number?"

"No. 8."

"How long have you kept a boarding-school?"

"Two years."

"Did you keep that boarding-school under the name of Taylor?"

"Yes."

"Where did your father live at that time?"

"I beg to be excused answering any questions about my father."

The hunt was up, and before recalling Miss Taylor eleven days later the Duke's defenders were busily occupied in ferreting out the skeletons in the family closet.

With his long legal experience behind him, Perceval vigorously cross-examined her in an attempt to debase the character of her parents, and thereby to belittle the credibility of her own evidence.*

"Do you know whether your mother has been in custody for debt, within a short time?" Perceval asked.

"I cannot answer that."

"Do you know that your mother has been in execution for debt?"

Cornered at last, Miss Taylor burst into tears. "My mother has nothing to do with the present subject," she sobbed.

"Do you know that your mother has been in execution for debt?" Perceval repeated.

"I must appeal to the indulgence of the Chairman. I cannot answer it", Miss Taylor pleaded.

Mr. Wharton declined to interfere, and Perceval pursued his point relentlessly.

"Do you know that your mother has been in custody for debt?"

"Yes."

"How long?"

* This was, of course, an inquiry in the House of Commons and not a criminal case heard in a court of law, but looking back at the rigorous questioning to which many of the witnesses were subjected, it is perhaps particularly pertinent to recall that it was not until the Criminal Evidence Act of 1898 that it became legally inadmissible for the character of a prisoner to be made an issue unless the defence had previously made imputations upon the character of a Crown witness.

"Nearly two years," Miss Taylor replied almost inaudibly, dissolving into tears again.

Miss Taylor's distress provoked a wave of sympathy. For hounding her down Perceval faced a barrage of angry criticism, and in the debate that followed he replied to his adversaries with forthright asperity.

"Is not the evidence of Miss Taylor under such circumstances, rather in want of support and confirmation itself, than capable of giving support and confirmation to Mrs. Clarke?" remonstrated the man who in six months' time was to be Prime Minister of England. "She has, for years, lived, and is still living, in habits of strictest intimacy with Mrs. Clarke, a person of notoriously vicious principles, of depraved character, and loose habits of life; but what is most deeply to be lamented and condemned is, that so connected and so associating with one of the worst of her sex, she has set up a boarding-school; professing to educate young ladies in virtue; the guardian, the pattern, the instructress of their morals!"

"It was necessary to know who Miss Taylor was; what were her connections, what her habits of life. In tracing these particulars, it turned out that her parents were not married, that they had for some time been going from place to place, changing their habitations; and though undoubtedly nobody would contend that a witness was not to be believed because she was not legitimate, or because her parents were in distressed circumstances, yet I would ask any man, if the examination had turned out otherwise, and if she had appeared to be, as she would have done but for this cross-examination, the daughter of respectable parents, in circumstances of credit, we should not have heard her credit enchanced, from being so respectably connected. But this cross-examination has ruined her school, and involved her with her creditors! I am sorry, and I feel as much as any man for the distress of any fellow-creature, Miss Taylor as well as anyone else; but I cannot believe that her cross-examination ruined her school. It was enough to ruin her school that she appeared as the friend and companion of Mrs. Clarke, and I confess I cannot bring my mind to lament that Miss Taylor's business as a school-mistress to young ladies is put an end to. I have some feeling for the parents, I have some feeling for the children; my feelings are not wholly absorbed by Miss Taylor."

In spite of Perceval's dissection, public sympathy and sentiment remained firmly on the side of Miss Taylor. Even Charles Yorke was won round, and sixteen-year-old Fanny Perceval complained bitterly about him in a letter to her brother.

"Do you know I am quite in a passion with Redhead Yorke," she wrote with filial solidarity. "He has behaved very ill about this, he too talks up Miss Taylor, and in his last paper he calls her 'a martyr to truth & sensibility'."

In spite of Miss Taylor, Mrs. Clarke remained the star performer whom everyone wanted to see and hear, and Colonel French was the ruffian whom the Duke had threatened to cut up to protect his darling. "Mrs. Clarke," wrote one reporter laconically, "ushers in the first mouthful at meals and waits upon the last. The weather is no longer the presiding genius of English sympathies."

Colonel French's levy had begun on a note of nepotism and bribery, and ended as a total flop on April 23rd, 1805, when the letter of service was officially withdrawn.

Mrs. Clarke, as Captain Sandon had said, was the only gainer.

Chapter Eleven

Among the Windham papers in the Department of Manuscripts of the British Museum is a long, defamatory poem dedicated to Mrs. Clarke, which for some undisclosed reason Charles Abbot, the Speaker, copied into his diary with a few minor alterations on March 17th, 1809, as the protracted debate on the conduct of the Duke of York was coming to an end.

> Old Dowler wails his thousand pounds,
> While crowds of Mothers wish thee drown'd,
> All trembling for their calves;
> And brides in disappointed gloom,
> Complain their Dearys, when at home,
> Are husbands but by halves.

In fact, far from bemoaning the loss of the thousand pounds that he had paid for his appointment as an assistant commissary of stores and provisions, thirty-six-year-old William Dowler was only too ready to admit the favours bestowed upon him by Mrs. Clarke.

"How long have you been in the commissariat?" asked Lord Folkestone.

"Since 1805."

"How did you obtain your situation in that department?"

"I purchased it of Mrs. Clarke."

"Did you apply directly to Mrs. Clarke for the appointment?"

"Certainly not; she suggested it to me."

"Did you pay any money to Mrs. Clarke for the benefit you received from it?"

"I first of all gave her £1,000, and at other times other sums to a very considerable amount."

"Did you ever make any other direct and regular application to obtain that situation?"

"To no one."

"You are positive as to that fact?"

"Positive."

Dowler explained that the question of his appointment only arose because Mrs. Clarke was hard pressed for money, and she had asked him to help her as the Duke had not been punctual in his payments.

"I applied to my father in consequence; he hesitated, and I told her I could not furnish her with more money than I had then given her. She then promised not the situation I now hold but another . . ."

The Commissariat Department was responsible for supplying the army with provisions, carrying out behind the lines the clerical work of book-keeping, requisitioning and accounts. Although commissariat officers received a commission from the War Office they were responsible to the Treasury, and were regarded as beings of very inferior status by other army officers.

Mrs. Clarke happily acknowledged her dexterity in obtaining Dowler's appointment, and added a few corroborative details of her own.

"Do you recollect in what sums you received the £1,000 that Mr. Dowler gave you for his place?"

"Perfectly well."

"State them."

"£200 first, and £800 afterwards, in one sum, which his father came up to town to sell out of the funds."

"You have mentioned having received various sums of money from Mr. Dowler, and in particular two sums of £200 and £800. State upon what consideration those sums were received."

"It was for Mr. Dowler's appointment, but previous to that he was not to have paid me money."

"To what appointment do you allude?"

"In the commissariat; assistant commissary."

"Whom did you apply to for that appointment for Mr. Dowler?"

"His Royal Highness."

"From whom was it notified to you that that appointment had been made?"

"His Royal Highness. He told me that he had spoken to Mr. Charles Long upon it, and it was settled at last . . ."

"How long have you been acquainted with Mr. Dowler?" Croker asked.

"As I have seen the papers it is almost useless to ask me because I might agree with him."

"How long have you been acquainted with Mr. Dowler?" Croker repeated.

"Eight, nine or ten years," Mrs. Clarke replied, corroborating Dowler's evidence. "I cannot say which."

"Have you not at various times received sums of money from Mr. Dowler?"

"Some few sums."

"Do you owe Mr. Dowler any money?"

"I never recollect my debts to gentlemen," Mrs. Clarke answered contemptuously, as the crowded benches rocked with laughter.

"Have you not frequently recognized debts to Mr. Dowler and promised to have them paid?"

"I only recollect one, where I had two or three carriages seized in execution or something. I had nothing to go out of town in to Weybridge. I sent a note to Mr. Dowler's lodgings, and begged he would buy or procure me a carriage immediately. He did so in a few hours, and I told him His Royal Highness would pay him for it. His Royal Highness told me that he would do so for it, or he would recollect him in some way."

Mrs. Clarke maintained that during the time she lived with the Duke she was constantly harassed for money, and that Dowler had "relieved several things as well as His Royal Highness, and I think oftener. I do not recollect His Royal Highness doing anything above twice."

"Once or twice (Dowler) paid something for me to my housekeeper. When she has told him something that was distressing he has given her money to pay for things when His Royal Highness was not in the way."

To trace the original recommendation for Dowler's appointment was the responsibility of the Secretary of the Treasury, the "tall, slouching, and ignoble-looking" William Huskisson.* Huskisson produced documents confirming Dowler's appointment with effect from July 10th, 1805, at the rate of fifteen shillings a day, but admitted that although he had enquired "of every gentleman in the treasury at that time as to any knowledge they might have respecting the manner in which Mr. Dowler had been recommended,

---

* William Huskisson is probably best remembered as the first man to be run over by a train, when, in September, 1830, against medical advice, he insisted on being present at the opening of the Manchester and Liverpool Railway. He tripped crossing the line and died from the injuries he received when an engine ran over his leg.

none of those whom I have seen profess to have any knowledge of the quarter from which he was recommended."

At the time of Dowler's appointment, Sir Brook Watson, the commissary general, and Dowler's father, were both common councilmen for the same ward of the City of London, and Dowler was vigorously pressed to acknowledge that he obtained his commission through Sir Brook Watson and not Mrs. Clarke.

This Dowler denied, and maintained that he did not know Sir Brook Watson sufficiently well "to bow to him even passing in the street".

Sir Brook Watson had died two years earlier, and although William Huskisson instructed the present commissary general and Sir Brook Watson's executor "to examine such papers as were in their possession they have not been able to find, either in the public records of the commissariat department, or among his private papers, any trace of a recommendation by him, either official or private, of Mr. Dowler, to the situation he now holds . . ."

It proved, as Sir Arthur Wellesley reluctantly conceded, "that Mrs. Clarke had influence to obtain such an appointment."

Dowler's evidence seriously threatened the Government hopes of exculpating the Duke, and every effort was made to dismiss him as an infatuated dupe caught in the toils of an outrageous adventuress.

"Indeed, this gentleman appears to have been one of the most faithful gallants which our *élégante* encountered in the course of her Cyprian career. We find him pouring forth his cash as if his purse were an inexhaustible cornucopia; nor was he less in her good graces, even when her charms had attracted a noble lover."

Dowler had admonished Mrs. Clarke for her shady profiteering in army patronage, prophesying that it could only end in disaster. Mrs. Clarke was highly indignant at such effrontery, and a chill wind had blighted their relationship for several months. When at last her activities had enveloped them both in a blaze of publicity it is to Dowler's credit that in the crisis he did not desert her.

Dowler returned from Lisbon with despatches the day after the inquiry began and, pouncing upon his evidence in support of Mrs. Clarke, Croker was convinced that behind it lay collusion and complicity. He decided that it might be extremely profitable to know what opportunities they had had to discuss the details of the purchase four years earlier of Dowler's appointment as an assistant commissary.

"You have stated when you were last here that you had seen Mr. Dowler but twice since his arrival in England; once on a Sunday when he called relative to the business now under inquiry, and once in the Witness's room in this House. Do you abide by that assertion?"

Mrs. Clarke bristled as she faced the cold, unsympathetic Member for Downpatrick. "I will not be caught in a story about that, and therefore I shall say I did see him once besides."

"Do you mean to say that you were caught in a story before when you represented that you had seen him but twice?"

"No; it is now perhaps your wish to catch me in one."

"Did you not say that you had seen Mr. Dowler only twice?"

"It is very likely that I might have said so."

"Is that true or false?"

"It is true that I have seen him twice, and it is also true that I have seen him three times."

"Where did you see Mr. Dowler the third time which you now allude to?"

"In this House," Mrs. Clarke retorted blithely.

"How often have you seen Mr. Dowler besides those three times since his return from Portugal?"

"Once since – yesterday."

"That is the whole number of times that you have seen Mr. Dowler since his arrival in England?"

Mrs. Clarke's patience was exhausted. "I believe that the honourable gentleman can tell pretty well, for his garret window is very convenient for his prying disposition as it overlooks my house," she snapped as the House roared with laughter at her impudence.

"That is the whole number of times that you have seen Mr. Dowler since his arrival in England?" Croker persisted doggedly.

"Yes."

"You are sure of that?"

"Yes."

"You are not now afraid of being caught in a story? You answer with perfect recollection?"

"If the honourable gentleman wishes it I will say I have seen him oftener, if it will at all tend to anything. I do not wish to conceal that Mr. Dowler is a very particular friend of mine."

The Chairman intervened to rebuke Mrs. Clarke, and told her that she had not been called to make observations on the gentlemen who examined her, but to give correct and proper answers to the questions put.

"I have as well as I can recollect," Mrs. Clarke replied, afraid of no one.

"At what other places than those you have already mentioned, and at what other times, have you seen Mr. Dowler since his arrival in England?" Croker continued.

"I have seen him at his own hotel."

"When?"

"The first night he came home, I believe, but which was to have been a perfect secret, as I did not wish my own family, or any one, to know I saw him that night."

The inquiry was repeatedly held up by the intervention of Members objecting to the irrelevant interrogation to which some of the witnesses were subjected, who then withdrew whilst the whole House solemnly debated the probity and pertinence of the questions proposed.

Wilberforce, obsessed with the profanity of sexual promiscuity and now alarmed at the prospect of the salacious details which the incorrigible Mrs. Clarke might divulge, protested that Croker's questioning served no useful purpose as they were all well aware of the character of the witness, and that this was no occasion for elucidating it further.

William Fitzgerald – perhaps afraid that his own association with Mrs. Clarke might be disclosed – and Sir George Warrender agreed, but Perceval, Croker, William Adam and Charles Bragge Bathurst were determined that she should not be let off so easily, and insisted that she should publicly admit to having spent the night with Dowler on his return from Portugal.

"You have stated that you saw Mr. Dowler at his hotel. How often did you see Mr. Dowler at his hotel?" Croker asked, resuming his interrogration.

"I have told you, once," Mrs. Clarke replied tetchily.

"On Thursday?"

"Yes, on Thursday."

"What time of the day did you see him at his hotel on the Thursday?"

"At night."

"Did you pass under your own name of Clarke on that occasion?"

"I passed under no name."

"At what hotel did you see him?"

"At Reid's in St. Martin's Lane."

"Were you in company with Mr. Dowler for a considerable time upon that occasion?"

"I have stated that I was in company with Mr. Dowler, and I beg leave to ask the Chair whether this is a proper question, whether it is not unbecoming to the dignity of the House?"

Again Mrs. Clarke withdrew, and again the House argued the propriety of the question. When recalled she outmanoeuvred Croker with dignified decorum.

"My visit," she informed him with cool assurance, "continued till the Friday morning."

Even Wilberforce was perplexed, and confided to his diary that "Mrs. Clarke by fascinating the House has prevented its degradation by appearing to stifle the inquiry, and take too strong a part with the Duke of York – curious to see how strongly she has won upon people."

Mrs. Clarke had been talking her way out of tight corners all her life, and was cock-a-hoop at having routed such a formidable adversary as the brilliant young Irishman, John Wilson Croker.

"When he set at me," she boasted afterwards, "it must be in the recollection of every one who was in the House at the time, that I turned him round my finger to the continued mirth and pity of the House."

The fact that Mrs. Clarke had spent the night with Dowler immediately he arrived in London was hailed as a discovery of far-reaching significance, and Perceval and his friends were resolved to make the most of it.

It was conclusive proof, they claimed, of Mrs. Clarke's shameless promiscuity, and John Fuller, M.P. for Sussex, was so incensed at the thought of the money lavished "on such a baggage" by the Duke of York that he regretted that the House had ever proceeded with such a silly and foolish inquiry.*

It was a safe assumption that Mrs. Clarke had posed as Mrs. Dowler when spending the night with him at his hotel, a positive

* The following year Mr. Fuller was himself in disgrace when he entered the House in a highly inebriated condition, "and too audibly mistook the Speaker for an owl in an ivy-bush". He was immediately named and handled over to the Serjeant-at-Arms, and the following day "the speaker administered a severe but dignified rebuke". (Horace Maybray King, M.P. in "Before Hansard". J. M. Dent and Sons Ltd., 1968.)

indication, said the Duke's henchman, that she could lie with impunity to suit her purpose or the convenience of the moment.

But most significant of all, why had she rushed to Dowler the moment he set foot in London? A woman with as many talents as Mrs. Clarke, it was inferred, was as capable of seducing her lover with her brains as with her body, and that she had deluded Dowler into testifying that he had obtained his appointment through her influence.

The night she spent with him at the hotel in St. Martin's Lane was not the first time that she was alleged to have masqueraded as Mrs. Dowler, and much was made of the evidence of Nicholls, the baker from Hampstead, that Dowler was a frequent visitor whilst she lodged with him in 1807/8. Mrs. Clarke agreed that Dowler slept at the house on several occasions – "but not with me" she was quick to add.

Nicholls also asserted that Mrs. Clarke told him that she was married to Dowler, but that she did not take his name because "if the Duke of York knew that she was married he would send Mr. Dowler abroad". As the Duke had parted from Mrs. Clarke nearly eighteen months earlier it seemed as dubious a tale to tell as it must have been for Nicholls to believe.

But if Nicholls gave little tangible help in bolstering the attack upon Mrs. Clarke, the hotel proprietor and his staff were a far sounder proposition.

Samuel Wells, a waiter, agreed that he knew a lady by the name of Mrs. Dowler, that he had heard her called by that name, and confirmed that she had stayed one night at the hotel on Dowler's return from Lisbon.

George Robinson, the porter, told the Committee that he saw the lady he now knew "by the public talk" as Mrs. Clarke with Dowler at the hotel, living with him as his wife, and that he had delivered wine addressed to Mrs. Dowler to 14 Bedford Place, and "at the end of the King's Road. I believe it is called Westcott Buildings, or something of that sort, leading to Sloane Square."

John Reid, the proprietor, was even more explicit.

"How long has Mr. Dowler frequented your house?" Perceval wanted to know.

"About two years."

"Do you recollect his coming there at any time with a person whom he represented to be his wife?"

"I do."

"Do you know who the lady was whom he so represented as his wife?"

"I do not," Reid replied, making it essential that he should identify Mrs. Clarke to substantiate his evidence.

"When was that person last at your house, that you knew her to be there?"

"I think last Friday sennight,* the day that Mr. Dowler came to town."

"Did the lady who came with Mr. Dowler go by the name of Mrs. Dowler?"

"Certainly she did, or she would not have been in my house," John Reid replied indignantly.

"Did you ever address her yourself by the name of Mrs. Dowler?"

"I did."

"Did she answer to that name?"

"Most certainly."

"Have you ever heard Mr. Dowler call her by the name of Mrs. Dowler?"

"Yes, I have."

"And she answered to that name?"

"Yes."

As a bizarre climax, whilst Mrs. Clarke was giving evidence two days later, John Reid was called to the bar to identify her as the woman he believed to be Mrs. Dowler. It was a situation that Mrs. Clarke did not appreciate and, although surprised to be confronted with the proprietor of the hotel in St. Martin's Lane, she had faced too many awkward situations to lose either her composure or her tongue.

"Is there any precedent, may I ask," she appealed to the Chairman amidst loud laughter, "for having two witnesses at the bar of this House at one time?"

She was told that the Committee would call what witnesses they liked, so standing aside she awaited her opportunity.

"Do you know the witness at the bar?" Perceval asked John Reid.

"Yes."

---

* A period of a week. Sennight was a very popular expression with the Georgians, but, unlike fortnight, has now been dropped from our vocabulary.

"Is the witness at the bar the person whom you represented as having been frequently at your house with Mr. Dowler?"

"Yes."

"Before Mr. Reid leaves the place," Mrs. Clarke spoke out, "I beg leave to say that I never said I was Mrs. Dowler; he might put what construction he thought proper upon it. It was very proper he did perhaps."

Perceval ignored the interruption.

"Did she ever answer to the name of Mrs. Dowler in your presence?"

"To my servants I have no doubt that was her answer. Upon all occasions whenever I spoke to her I suppose I always said 'Ma'am', but if I mentioned any name it was Mrs. Dowler."

"Have you ever heard Mrs. Clarke say that her name was Dowler?" enquired Charles Adams.

"I never heard her mention her name at all," John Reid conceded.

"Would you not have been afraid of the credit of your house if you had called her by any other name?"

"Good God!" exclaimed the outraged Mr. Reid, "I should not have thought of any thing of the kind."

"Did Mr. Dowler lodge (at the hotel) at any time?" Wardle asked.

"Yes."

"And the lady came occasionally?"

"That was when the bailiffs were after me," Mrs. Clarke gaily informed the crowded House, adding another diverting detail from her chaotic life.

John Reid withdrew, and perhaps convinced that the last word was a female prerogative, Mrs. Clarke again seized the initiative.

"May I speak a word?" she addressed the Chairman. "I merely wish to ask a question of some of the Crown lawyers."

Whilst the Members roared with laughter at her irrepressible presumption, Mr. Wharton told her brusquely that it could not be permitted.

With the general public, Mrs. Clarke's panache effectively turned the tables on the attempts to denigrate and discredit her. Croker's encounter with her produced endless hilarity, and the caricaturists gave full reign to their imagination.

One of the most popular satires was Rowlandson's coloured engraving of "Chelsea Parade, or A Croaking Member Surveying the

Inside, Outside and Backside of Mrs. Clarke's premises." Whilst Croker prys upon the scene with a periscope from his attic window, Wardle, in officer's uniform and cloak, slips a purse into the hand of a young woman at the door wearing a belt inscribed "Favorit". "Engaged five deep at present," she reports, "but despatch quick so pray enter and your business shall be done in a crack." Mrs. Clarke leans from an upstairs window with her breasts exposed and above the door is a lantern announcing "Now exhibiting wonder upon wonders, or Mrs. Clarke's Puppet Show which has given satisfaction to Po(pulace) and Princes."

Below, a board proclaims "All the world's a stage and men and women merely players – some play the under part . . ." Wearing a mitre and carrying a crozier, the Duke of York walks disconsolately away from the house with William Adam, and across his bishop's robe is printed "Men have their Entrances and their Exits." "To part with my Dear, and not allow four hundred a year," he grumbles.

If Croker and the Duke of York were the butts of public jocularity, the unfortunate Dowler was the cuckold, the weak-willed plaything of an unscrupulous woman. He had returned to England on official business and without warning found himself projected into the House of Commons as one of the principal witnesses supporting the charges of corruption levelled against the Commander-in-Chief.

"Long and severe cross-examination took place of Dowler," commented 'The Courier' reporter, 'but never did we read of witnesses going through them with more steadiness, consistency, modesty, and firmness, than Mr. Dowler." He successfully repulsed all the efforts of government supporters to contradict his assertion that he had purchased his commission as assistant commissary through Mrs. Clarke, and one versifier dipped his pen in gall to vilify this aristocratic turncoat:

> It seems – it is – the noted Mrs. Clarke,
> In dalliance late, with Dowler in a ditch –
> 'Tis she – and my next Almanack shall mark,
> Conjunction of the dog-star with the Bitch.

Chapter Twelve

On the fourth day of the inquiry, like a conjurer producing a rabbit from a hat, Mrs. Clarke sprang another of her sensational surprises.

When she was called before the Committee for a second time late in the evening of February 9th, Richard Brinsley Sheridan, the playwright turned politician, rose to question her. His attendance after nearly thirty years in Parliament was by now erratic and John Ward describes him disparagingly as "drunk, lazy, discontented, and declining rapidly in his faculties".

Skilled dramatist though he was, the fifty-eight-year-old author of "The School for Scandal" can scarcely have anticipated the aspersions that Mrs. Clarke was waiting to cast upon one of the ecclesiastical sycophants who came within her orbit.

"Do you recollect to have had any negotiation respecting other promotions, entirely disconnected with the Military department?" Sheridan probed.

"If you will point out what those things were, I will answer to it," Mrs. Clarke informed him peremptorily.

"Had you any negotiation or money transactions respecting promotions in the Church?"

"I never received any, but a Dr. O'Meara applied to me. He wanted to be a Bishop. He is very well known in Ireland."

"Did you ever communicate Dr. O'Meara's offer for a bishopric to the Commander-in-Chief?" Perceval asked, taking over the questioning.

"Yes, I did, and all his documents."

"Did Dr. O'Meara specify any particular sum, and what was that sum?"

"I think the gentleman must be a friend of his," replied Mrs. Clarke brashly, "and he must know better than I do, and he may recollect perhaps."

"Did Dr. O'Meara specify any particular sum?" Perceval demanded.

"I forget, and I have burnt almost all my papers. I might recollect but not at the moment."

Charles Yorke wanted to know when this enigmatic Irishman made his application for a bishopric, and Mrs. Clarke obliged with a colourful anecdote of her life as the mistress of the Duke of York.

"In 1805, the very night that the Duke was going to Weymouth, he called upon me the moment the Duke had left the house, between twelve and one o'clock. I think he watched His Royal Highness out, as he had seen that his horses were waiting in Portman Square, and then he came in just as I was upon the stairs, and said it was a very good opportunity for he was going to Weymouth immediately, and asked me to come down stairs again, and write him a letter of introduction to His Royal Highness, and I did so."

The idea of Mrs. Clarke dispensing ecclesiastical patronage was too much for Wilberforce. It was bad enough listening to the sordid story of the Duke's immorality, but Dr. O'Meara, he concluded, was "only a creature of her imagination".

Stung perhaps by the scepticism of the incredulous, Mrs. Clarke decided to confound their cynicism with indisputable proof, and when she stepped to the bar of the House four days later she held in her hand a dozen letters.

"To show I did not tell a story about Dr. O'Meara," she informed Lord Folkstone, "I have a Letter of Recommendation from the Archbishop of Tuam – not to me, but to the doctor himself."

'How did you come by the letter of the Archbishop of Tuam?" John Beresford asked.

"It was left amongst Dr. O'Meara's papers, among his documents, by accident, and I did not destroy it because I thought it might be of some future service to him. When I gave him his papers this was left by accident."

The Archbishop's testimonial was a dull document, confirming that he "had assurances from persons in whom I place the most implicit confidence, that you are a gentleman of most unexceptionable character in every respect, of a respectable family, and independent fortune."

No one was particularly interested in either Dr. O'Meara's respectability or his money, but the Archbishop's recommendation was tangible evidence that he had solicited Mrs. Clarke's help to promote his ecclesiastical ambitions.

Among the letters she had with her, she informed Lord Folkestone, "There is another from the Duke, in which he acknowledges about Dr. O'Meara, that he would serve him as he could. It does not speak of the Archbishopric, it merely acknowledges that he knows such a man."

The Duke's love-letter to Mrs. Clarke was read to a crowded House of Commons, printed in the papers, and mocked and mimicked all over the country.

My beloved

August 4th, 1805.

How can I sufficiently express to My Sweetest, My Darling Love, the delight which her dear, her pretty letter gave me, or how much I feel all the kind things she says to me in it? Millions and millions of thanks for it, My Angel, and be assured that my heart is fully sensible of your affection, and that upon it alone its whole happiness depends.

I am, however, quite hurt that My Love did not go to the Lewes Races. How kind of her to think of me upon the occasion, but I trust that she knows me too well not to be convinced that I cannot bear the idea of adding to those sacrifices which I am but too sensible that she has made to me.

News, My Angel cannot expect from me from hence. Though the life led here, at least in the family I am in, is very hurrying, there is a sameness in it which affords little subject for a letter. Except Lord Chesterfield's family, there is not a single person except ourselves that I know. Last night we were at the Play, which went off better than the first night.

Dr. O'Meara called upon me yesterday morning and delivered me your letter. He wishes much to preach before Royalty, and if I can put him in the way of it I will.

What a time it appears to me already, My Darling, since we parted. How impatiently I look forward to next Wednesday sennight!

God bless you, my own Dear, Dear Love! I shall miss the Post if I add more. Oh believe me ever, to my last hour, Your's and Your's alone.

Addressed: Mrs. Clarke, to be left at
the Post Office, Worthing.

When an affair has ended, the love-letters that survive are a derisory reminder of human frailty and folly and, as Mrs. Clarke had shrewdly anticipated, the Duke's letter was a sensation, producing reactions as diverse as they were critical.

It had, wrote Sir Arthur Wellesley despondently, "created a terrible impression."

An anonymous pamphleteer scathingly denounced it as "of the sort of style that can only be compared to those of his uncle, the late Duke of Cumberland, when he corresponded with Lady Grosvenor; fond and familiar in the extreme, but in no degree to be said *Sensible*."

Writing forty years after the event, Leigh Hunt was more tolerantly disposed towards the Duke. "He even let her recommend him a clergyman," he wrote in his autobiography, "who – as he phrased it – had an ambition to "preach before royalty". He said he would do what he could to bring it about; probably thinking nothing whatsoever – I mean, never having the thought enter his head – of the secret scandal of the thing, or not regarding his consent as anything but a piece of good-natured patronizing acquiescence, after the ordinary fashion of the 'ways of the world'."

For the lampoonists the episode was a heaven-sent opportunity for displaying their talents:

Dr. O'Meara, pious liver!
To me your letter did deliver:
He says, he something good could reach
If he before the King could preach:
This for him I'll try to do,
And all, my love, for sake of you.

Dr. O'Meara had duly delivered Mrs. Clarke's letter to the Duke in Weymouth, where he was spending a few days with his father, George III. Weymouth was the King's favourite seaside resort, and during the summer the life of the town revolved around the royal family.

Three frigates and two royal yachts were anchored in the bay, a camp of sharpshooters kept a permanent look-out for the Napoleonic invasion that never came, and Hanoverian cavalry careered on the sands singing martial choruses. From half-past seven until nine the King took his morning constitutional up and down the esplanade, twice a week a party of the local nobility were entertained at the royal lodge, and on the remaining four evenings the royal entourage attended the play.

It was the sober, stereotyped routine that spelled stability and security to the unimaginative monarch and his wife, but which drove many of their staff to the brink of frustration. "On the whole," complained General Dyott, the King's Aide-de-Camp, "it's but a tiresome kind of life we lead . . . The same sameness is more tiresome than anything ever was."

On Sundays the royal household assembled for divine service, and two months after the Duke's visit to Weymouth in 1805, Dr. O'Meara's worldly aspirations were finally consummated when he preached, as Cobbett commented caustically, "from under the wing of Mrs. Clarke." O'Meara declared that he preached before the King the previous year, but he is conclusively refuted by a report of his sermon in 'The Morning Post' under the dateline Weymouth, October 3rd, 1805."

Taking his text from St. Paul's Epistle to the Romans – "So we, *being* many are one body in Christ, and every one members one of another" – he preached, 'The Morning Post' reported, an excellent sermon on Universal Benevolence.

"He expatiated with great eloquence on the relations which the public and private affections bear to each other, and their use in the moral system. . . . The King was very attentive, and stood for nearly the whole of the sermon (which we never observed before) and expressed his high approbation to the Earl of Uxbridge and others, whilst the Queen and Princesses, and the whole audience were melted into tears."

If publicly Mrs. Clarke's protégé appeared to have achieved considerable episocopal progress, in private the Duke informed his mistress that the King – obsessed with the nightmare of Catholic emancipation, and convinced perhaps that an embryonic Catholic lurked in every Irish breast – did not like the big 'O' in the Doctor's name.

Once again the lampoonists gibed at the idiosyncrasies of the royal family:

> For we're told that the King has aversions to 'O',
> As strong as if asked to salute the Pope's toe.

The saga of Dr. O'Meara ended as capriciously as it had begun. "The sackful of letters" that Nicholls had recued from the fire in in Hampstead included several written to Mrs. Clarke by Dr. O'Meara, who, defending himself against the charge of "an indecent production", declared disingenuously that "In the Microcosm of London, it is difficult to distinguish ladies under protection from ladies of fashion."

He had received, he said, a letter from Mrs. Clarke, declaring herself weary of the pomp and vanities of a wicked world, and that Mary Magdalene was not more penitent. Entreating him to comfort the weak-hearted, she begged that he would find her a cheap and safe asylum in Ireland.

The Rt. Hon. Charles Williams Wynn was on the Select Committee entrusted with the task of deciding which of Mrs. Clarke's letters should be put before the House as relevant to the inquiry into the conduct of the Duke of York, and he reported to his brother that "Some were highly ridiculous, particularly one from O'Meara, the Candidate for a Bishopric, who invited her to a Tour in Ireland, and assures her that he 'Will guard her from Pikes and threshing machines'."

Constantly searching for new activities and new excitement, it was probably an intriguing experience for Mrs. Clarke, after the steady stream of military men seeking appointments, promotion and exchanges, to have this ludicrous ecclesiastical humbug fawning upon her for favours. It flattered her vanity; it was the light relief that added to life a dash of whimsical absurdity.

No one seriously imagined that Dr. O'Meara had paid Mrs. Clarke for her services, and although she herself was almost over-eager to give details of the profit she made in her military sphere of operations, she denied receiving any money for her efforts to further the Doctor's preferment.

Ironically for the Duke, the two cases in which Mrs. Clarke reaped no financial gain swung public opinion violently against him, and there could have been no greater contrast than the Irish imposter in search of a Bishopric, and the eighteen-year-old footman to whom she presented a commission.

At the beginning of the enquiry on February 1st no one supposed that the examination of witnesses would continue almost without interruption for the next three weeks. "In the meantime all other business is at a stand" complained Sir Arthur Wellesley, "and nobody talks or thinks or anything but Mrs. Clarke."

Curiosity attracted large crowds to the precincts of St. Stephen's, anxiously hoping to catch a glimpse of her on her way to Westminster, and "some of the persons present", 'The Sun' primly observed, "very indecorously huzzaed her as she passed."

She arrived one evening to a less cordial reception and before she could alight, her brother, Captain Thompson, as improvident and unscrupulous as she herself, was arrested at the door of her carriage for a large unpaid tailor's bill.

* * *

To further her money-making intrigues, Mrs. Clarke had depended principally upon two crypto-agents conveniently in contact with cash-paying customers in search of appointments, promotion or exchanges – Captain Huxley Sandon, serving with the Royal Waggon Train, who had disembarked at Plymouth a week before the inquiry began, and Jeremiah Donovan, an ex-army lieutenant and surgeon, who informed the Committee that he had been so badly wounded in the War of American Independence that he had been unable to take off his clothes or lie down for five years.

To encourage her agents and their prospective clients, it was alleged, Mrs. Clarke had circulated a "List of Prices of Commissions", contrasting her own charges with the official rates.

	Mrs. Clarke's Prices	*Regulated Prices*
A Majority	£900	£2,600
A Company	£700	£1,500
A Lieutenancy	£400	£550
An Ensigncy	£200	£400

Mrs. Clarke firmly repudiated all responsibility. "No, I never did; that did not belong to me," she informed Mr. Lockhart. "I have seen such a thing. I saw it in Cobbett, but it is not true."

Such a blatant overture was certainly not Mrs. Clarke's method of conducting her affairs, and it is far more likely, as "The Annual Register" suggests, that it was Jeremiah Donovan's contrivance to attract customers and increase his commission.

Mrs. Clarke denied also having received a long list of names for promotion. "I never received more than two or three names. This I had for two or three days. It was pinned up at the head of my bed, and His Royal Highness took it down."

The Committee of Inquiry was obviously sceptical and a few days later she elaborated the point. "The second morning His Royal Highness took it down, drew the curtain and read it. I saw it when he was pulling out his pocket-book sometime afterwards, when one or two promotions had taken place, with his pen scratched through those names – when he took out his pocket book to look at some other papers. I only make this remark as I have heard a gentleman on my right hand say that I had picked his pocket."

"You are quite sure His Royal Highness read it?" Charles Adams insisted.

"I am quite sure," replied Mrs. Clarke confidently. "He read it in my presence, drew up the curtain, and afterwards came to me and made the remark that he would do everyone by degrees, or make them, or to that effect."

The lampoonists embellished her reminiscences with ribald glee.

When we retire to bed
Enchained in love's embraces,
A list is at the head,
Of numsculls wanting places.

In the middle of her examination by Mr. Lockhart about the list of officers that she had pinned above her bed, Mrs. Clarke made a startling digression. "I have received a letter this instant which has exceedingly interested me, begging me that I would not go on, or to that effect," she announced.

The Chairman intervened, asking her to hand the letter to the Committee, but Mrs. Clarke was a firm believer in giving her gentlemen a good run for their money.

"I will perhaps in a few days," she teased him, "but not tonight. I have hardly read it over."

Mrs. Clarke's delaying tactics won her little respite. She was instructed to produce the letter, and it was read in silence to a Committee grimly perplexed by this unexpected diversion.

Westminster Hall,
Thursday night,
8 o'clock.

Madam,

I am most anxiously desirous to see you tonight. The lateness of the hour will be no difficulty with me. It is, I trust, quite unnecessary to observe that business alone is my reason for expressing by this solicitude in so earnest a way. If you think a more unreserved communication might take place at Westbourne Place, I would be there at your own hour tonight. To what this particularly refers you may have some guess, but it would be highly improper to glance at it upon paper. . . .

Most sincerely your friend,
William Williams

William Williams, Mrs. Clarke informed the Committee, had called upon her the previous day. "When he came into the drawing-room yesterday he asked me whether there was anyone in the back room. I said upon my word and honour not, but I told him as my character now seemed so much hacked about with everyone I would open the door and convince him, which I did. He then began to question me how I felt towards the Duke of York, if I had any revenge, or if I had any wishes that His Royal Highness had not satisfied, and if anything would induce me now to abandon the country with my children, and take all the blame on my own shoulders. That no sum whatever would be backward if I would say I would . . . he had no authority from the Duke of York, but it was the Duke's friends."

The letter had been handed to Mrs. Clarke by one of the messengers at the door of the chamber, and greatly alarmed at this alleged attempt to suborn their principal witness, Thomas Brand, one of the Members for Hertfordshire, urged the necessity of bringing the writer before the Committee immediately. "The doors of the House were instantly ordered to be secured", and the Serjeant-at-Arms was instructed to take William Williams into custody "wherever he could be found".

In the meantime a dozen Members proffered their opinions, suggestions, proposals. "The prodigious tumult prevented us from collecting the tenor of their observations," complained the Parliamentary Debates reporter querulously.

When William Williams was brought to the bar the episode ended on a note of farcical absurdity. Aged about forty, corpulent, with prominent features, ruddy complexion and bald, he was, he said, a clergyman from Somers Town, but in the precincts of Westminster he was well known as a preposterous eccentric labouring under a mental derangement.

"My reason was to attempt, if I could," he murmured lamely, endeavouring to explain his indignation at the spectacle of Mrs.

Clarke inculpating the Duke of York in her shady practices, "to persuade her from that ironical, sarcastic, witty animadversion that sometimes has fallen from her with reference to the person before alluded to."

How Mrs. Clarke must have laughed at her success in despatching the whole House of Commons on a wild goose chase after the mad parson from Somers Town!

Chapter Thirteen

THE CRACKPOT CLERGYMAN was not the only curious character the committee brought forward to support its most persuasive, scintillating and unaffectedly articulate witness. Another soon followed in the unexpected and unsolicited appearance of Brigadier-General Clavering.

The association between Mrs. Clarke and the General had been neither compatible nor successful; it ended in mutual antipathy, and both of them smouldered with old scores to settle.

On the morning the inquiry had begun, Mrs. Clarke had written to Jeremiah Donovan about the cases of corruption Wardle proposed to lay before the House.

"I wish from my soul," the words tumbled out, "Mr. Wardle had taken it up less passionately; he might have done more good. Why do you not send me a line? I dare say Clavering is hugging himself as he did not send the recommendation."

It was only too true that General Clavering was highly agitated at the thought of being dragged through the mud in the wake of Mrs. Clarke, but the inquiry had been in progress a week before he wrote to her, *"particularly to beg* that you will take every care that *my name* be, in no shape whatever, or *on any account,* brought before the House of Commons. As being a family man, the world would be inclined to attribute motives to our acquaintance which, though not existing, all the arguments in the universe would not persuade them to the contrary."

Mrs. Clarke was not the woman to allow even a Brigadier-General to escape the penalty for such an impertinent and blatant slur on her virtue.

The following day Clavering suddenly changed his tactics. He discussed the position with Thomas Lowten, the Duke of York's solicitor, and perhaps afraid to rely on Mrs. Clarke's discretion, or possibly persuaded that the best method of defence was attack, he wrote to the Attorney-General asking that he might give evidence "to impeach the veracity of Mrs. Clarke."

When called on February 10th, the best that General Clavering could do to incriminate Mrs. Clarke was to revive the allegation that she had represented herself as being under the protection of Mr. Mellish, the Member for Middlesex. As William Mellish had already testified that he had never seen Mrs. Clarke until her appearance in the House of Commons, and Mrs. Clarke herself had roundly denounced such a ridiculous rumour, it was a detail of trivial significance, and a tale that no one believed. General Clavering had no further proof to offer of Mrs. Clarke's mendacity, and there was a strong feeling that he was wasting the Committee's time. Before leaving the bar, however, he found himself neatly enmeshed by Colonel Wardle.

"Do you of your own knowledge know that Mrs. Clarke used her influence in favour of any person whatever in the Army with the Commander-in-Chief?"

"I do not."

"Do you of your own knowledge know of any person that asked her to use her influence with the Commander-in-Chief upon that subject?"

"I am not acquainted with any person that ever did. I have heard reports of that nature, but I cannot bring to my recollection any person positively."

"Then you state positively that you do not know of any transaction of that nature?"

"None, to my certain knowledge."

When Mrs. Clarke appeared three days later she promptly proceeded to nail the General's lies and ingratitude.

"General Clavering, I fancy," she told Lord Folkestone, "informed the honourable gentlemen here that he never had any thing to say to me upon military affairs. General Clavering being a distressed man, he was then a Colonel, I spoke to the Duke respecting him, and had a great deal of difficulty, more so than any other man that I ever applied for, in getting any sort of employment for him . . . At last I prevailed upon the Duke to give him a District, and with it he made him a Brigadier-General, entirely through my means. He afterwards asked me to get him a regiment, and fearing they might all be given away before His Royal Highness came to town I wrote to him when he was reviewing along the coast.

"Here is the letter which His Royal Highness wrote to me," she said like a gambler producing the ace of trumps, "in which he mentions General Clavering's name."

The Duke's second love-letter, so people said, was no more sensible than the first, and loud laughter and repeated calls to order by the Chairman punctuated the reading of the document which Mrs. Clarke had so maliciously produced to corroborate her testimony and confound the misguided General.

Sandgate,
August 24, 1804

How can I sufficiently express to My Darling Love my thanks for her dear, dear letter, or the delight which the assurances of her love give me? Oh, My Angel! do me justice and be convinced that there never was a woman adored as you are. Every day, every hour, convinces me more and more that my whole happiness depends upon you alone. What a time it appears to be since we parted, and with what impatience do I look forward to the day after tomorrow: there are still however two whole nights before I shall clasp My Darling in my arms! How happy I am to learn that you are better. I still however will not give up my hopes of the cause of your feeling uncomfortable.

Clavering is mistaken, My Angel, in thinking that any new regiments are to be raised. It is not intended, only second Battalions to the existing Corps. You had better, therefore, tell him so, and that you were sure that there would be no use in applying for him.

Ten thousand thanks, My Love, for the handkerchiefs, which are delightful, and I need not, I trust, assure you of the pleasure I feel in wearing them, and thinking of the dear hands who (sic) made them for me.

Nothing could be more satisfactory than the tour I have made, and the state in which I have found everything. The whole of the day before yesterday was employed in visiting the Works at Dover; reviewing the Troops there, and examining the coast as far as this place. From Folkestone I had a very good view of those of the French Camp.

Yesterday I first reviewed the Camp here, and afterwards the 14th Light Dragoons, who are certainly in very fine order; and from thence proceeded to Brabourne Lees to see four regiments of Militia, which altogether took me up near thirteen hours. I am now setting off immediately to ride along the coast to Hastings, reviewing the different Corps as I pass, which will take me at least as long. Adieu, therefore, My Sweetest, Dearest Love, till the day after tomorrow, and be assured that to my last hour I shall ever remain,

Yours and Yours alone.

Addressed: George Farquhar, Esq.,*
18 Gloucester Place, Portman Square.

When General Clavering was recalled he reluctantly conceded that he had written to Mrs. Clarke promising her £1,000 if she could obtain permission for him to raise a regiment, and he made matters worse with the extenuating plea that although it was his "decided opinion that she did not possess any influence over His Royal Highness in the distribution of military promotions . . . I conceived it would be a fair speculation to try whether that influence did exist or not."

The application was not successful, and the Duke, Mrs. Clarke informed the General, "scouted the idea" and would not hear of him raising a regiment.

Less than a fortnight later General Clavering tried again.

"My proposal then," he wrote to Mrs. Clarke from Bishop's Waltham on September 5th, 1804, "was to raise a battalion for *general and unlimited service,* by the voluntary offers of a stipulated number of men from each regiment of militia . . ."

"Should an opportunity occur, to submit the plan to His Royal Highness without arguing too strongly upon it, as he must be tired to death with proposals, and as I would not appear, even through so circuitous a channel, to trespass on his patience, when so recently under an obligation for my present appointment."

For Brigadier-General Clavering the consequences were calamitous. Many Members seethed with indignation at his hypocrisy, his lies, and his attempts to whitewash his nefarious conduct, and he was committed to Newgate Prison for contempt.

---

*"George Farquhar", Mrs. Clarke explained to the Committee, was a fictitious device the Duke frequently used when writing to her to allay suspicion and to deceive the inquisitive. "There is no such person in existence, I believe," she said. "It was one of my brothers. I lost two in the navy and that was one of them."

It was Mrs. Clarke's turn to hug herself now for having so strategically manoeuvred the General's downfall, whilst the lampoonists inevitably found him a place in their execrable doggerel:

For thee, along each crowded street,
Hot Pulses, every moment beat,
New Slaves your Empire court,
Nor threatening oft, and sore annoy'd,
Can Dukes or Claverings well avoid,
Their old and loved resort.

Mrs. Clarke introduced the Duke's love-letters into the inquiry for two distinct purposes. They were first of all indisputable, corroborative proof that he allowed her to meddle in military matters, as well as to further the ambitions of a pretentious cleric and, from a purely personal point of view, they were the best possible publicity for the book of biographical reminiscences that she was threatening to publish. In both spheres she attained her objective with unerring accuracy.

"The love-letters,"said Sir Arthur Wellesley, "have created a terrible impression," but by one of the unpredictable quirks of fate it was not the love-letters but a note of seventeen words about which Mrs. Clarke said she knew nothing that created the maximum disarray and damage to the Duke's defences.

A fierce controversy raged around this note produced by Captain Huxley Sandon who, like William Dowler, returned to England from overseas service to find himself immediately projected into the House of Commons inquiry as one of the principal witnesses.

Sandon landed at Plymouth a week before the inquiry began, and, desperately perturbed at the thought of being exposed as one of Mrs. Clarke's most active agents, he consulted his superior officer, Colonel Hamilton, and confessed his culpability. He told him, too, that he had in his possession an incriminating note from the Duke of York to Mrs. Clarke about the promotion of Captain Tonyn of the 48th Regiment to a Major in the 31st.

The story of Tonyn's promotion began in March, 1804, when Sandon called upon Jeremiah Donovan and told him that he had an opportunity of promoting a gentleman to a majority. He asked Donovan if he knew of an officer willing to pay £500.

Donovan mentioned the offer to Captain Tonyn, who had served in the army for twenty-three years, and perhaps because he had waited nine months with dwindling hope for a favourable response to his father's application for him to be appointed to the rank of major, Tonyn was persuaded to purchase his promotion through Mrs. Clarke.

He became restive and suspicious, however, as the weeks passed with still no sign of his promised majority and, in May or June, he informed Sandon that he was withdrawing his deposit and would take his chance in the regular line of promotion.

With some difficulty Sandon persuaded him to curb his impatience, and immediately hurried round to tell Mrs. Clarke of the Captain's indignation at the delay. Mrs. Clarke, so Sandon said, dismissed Tonyn as "a shabby fellow", complained bitterly of her desperate financial straits, and gave Sandon a note she had received from the Duke to inveigle the precipitate Tonyn to wait a little longer.

"You are quite sure you received a note from her?" Perceval asked.

"Yes, I am quite sure I received a note from her."

"Do you recollect what you did with the note? Did you give it to Major Tonyn?"

"That I do not recollect," Sandon lied, "whether I gave it to Major Tonyn or what became of the note."

From Plymouth, Sandon had proceeded on leave to London, and during a further conversation with Colonel Hamilton he showed him the note that he had received from Mrs. Clarke. Colonel Hamilton took a copy, and when Sandon said that he was going to destroy it with the rest of his papers, the Colonel strongly impressed upon him to do no such thing.

As he stood to testify in the House of Commons, Sandon was totally oblivious that Spencer Perceval had been fully informed of his conversations with Colonel Hamilton; like the ignoramus in a fool's paradise he was blissfully unaware that immediately before he was called for examination, Perceval had exposed him to the whole Committee, and that every Member knew the context of the note that he was recklessly attempting to suppress.

"Did you not state to Colonel Hamilton," Perceval asked, "that the note which you showed to Major Tonyn was in the handwriting of the Duke of York?"

"I do not recollect that I did."

"Are you sure that you did not show him the note?"

"If I had, I certainly should not have forgotten it."

"That is not an answer to the question."

"I had not the note to show him."

"Did you not either give or permit Colonel Hamilton to take a copy of this very note that we are talking of?"

"Not that I know of."

"If you had the note in your possession surely you would be able to bring to your recollection whether you gave him an opportunity of copying it."

"I rather think there was something of a note", Sandon conceded.

"You now recollect that there was a note and that you showed it to Colonel Hamilton?"

"Yes, perfectly."

"What is become of that note?"

"I believe the note is mislaid."

"When did you see it last?"

"I saw it about six days ago I think."

"A note that you did not recollect to have been in existence when you began your examination you now recollect to have been in existence six days ago?" Perceval fumed.

"Yes," Sandon admitted.

"You have done all you could within these few days to find it?"

"I certainly have," Sandon lied again.

"Are you quite sure you have not actually destroyed it?"

"I am very confident that I have not."

Unless it was possible to obtain the note alleged to have been written by the Duke, the Tonyn case would remain an inconsequential, infuriating frustration, and the Committee was determined to coerce Sandon into producing the evidence that he was wildly trying to conceal.

As he prevaricated and perjured himself, Member after Member rose in an effort to compel him to disclose what had become of the note that he had shown to Colonel Hamilton.

"I have searched everywhere and I cannot find it . . . I am pretty clear that it is not destroyed," he assured Samuel Whitbread.

"I have mislaid it somewhere," he informed Perceval, "among some other papers which I had in my bureau."

"In what room in your house is this bureau in which you say you put it?" Sir Vicary Gibbs wanted to know.

"It is in my sitting-room. I have but one sitting-room."

"Do you think that if a messenger was sent with you now to your rooms you could find the papers?" Sir Samuel Romilly suggested.

"I really cannot tell. I looked two or three times for it, and I could not find it two days ago. It is mislaid in some place or other."

"If I could find it," he promised Charles Bragge Bathurst smugly, "I should produce it with the greatest of pleasure."

The Committee grew increasingly restive at Sandon's contortions to extricate himself from the predicament into which his lies had led him, and a shout of "Withdraw, Withdraw" that was taken up on both sides of the house was the signal for his ignominious eviction.

The Speaker's resolution that Captain Huxley Sandon was guilty of gross prevarication was carried unanimously, and he suggested that Sandon be either committed to the custody of the Serjeant-at-Arms, that all access to him should be denied, or that he be sent to Newgate. Before the Committee had decided which course to adopt, the Serjeant-at-Arms unexpectedly appeared to say that Captain Sandon respectfully asked to be permitted to say a few words.

"I beg pardon of the house for my prevarication, and I beg that the House will do me the honour to excuse my extraordinary behaviour," Sandon said as Members listened in critical silence.

"With regard to the note in question, it is not destroyed. I have it in my possession at my chambers. If it is required I can go and fetch it; I think I can put my hands upon it. The note that you were speaking of was given me to show Major Tonyn, and to say that his promotion would not go on unless he paid the money. I took the note, and produced it to Major Tonyn with that message. I showed him the note, desiring him to wait three or four days . . . I brought back the note, and I have it now in my possession. He was gazetted, and the £500 was paid to Mrs. Clarke and the £25 to Mr. Donovan. If the honourable house would wish to see the note I will go and fetch it. As to who wrote the note, I cannot take it upon me to say: Mrs. Clarke told me it was written by the Duke of York."

Sandon was despatched to his lodgings under escort to produce his papers, and it was decided that this was an excellent opportunity to see what Mrs. Clarke had to say about the matter.

She had been waiting in the witness's room and, as she knew nothing of Perceval's statement or of Sandon's evidence, she could not tailor her testimony to the facts already disclosed. Her relies to Perceval's carefully phrased questions are an admirable example of the cool, intelligent way in which she faced her interrogators, punctuating her answers with shrewd observations or counter-questioning.

"Do you recollect what passed between you and Captain Sandon in consequence of any application from Major Tonyn, expressing his impatience at the length of time that elapsed before he procured his appointment?"

"No, I really do not . . ."

"You do not remember any representation having been made to you by Captain Sandon that Major Tonyn intended to withdraw the deposit he had made, in consequence of the delay?"

"No, I do not recollect it, though he might perhaps have mentioned it."

"Do you recollect having sent any paper to Major Tonyn by Captain Sandon?"

"What sort of paper?"

"Any paper."

"I could speak more positively if it was mentioned what sort of paper."

"Any written paper."

"Of my own writing, or any other person's?"

"Any written paper."

"I do not recollect. I was always very cautious of giving any written paper out of my hands."

"As you were so cautious in putting any written paper out of your hands would you not have recollected the circumstances if it had occurred?"

"If he meant to insinuate that there was any writing of the Duke of York's," Mrs. Clarke replied categorically, "I never did in my life to anyone."

"Did you or did you not send any note to Captain Sandon?"

"I never recollect sending him any note, but more especially any note of the Duke of York's, because I should have been afraid of entrusting it to him."

"If Captain Sandon has presented any note to Major Tonyn purporting to be a note written by the Duke of York, and given to him by you, is it true?"

"I do not think it is, and I am almost sure that it is not. Perhaps he has written one himself."

When Sandon returned to the bar of the House, he brought with him not only the note given to him by Mrs. Clarke, but the forty-one letters mentioned previously that she had written to him in her heyday as mistress of military promotions, proving more effectively than all her evidence the scope and extent of her lucrative traffic in the sale of army commissions. The note itself was unsigned, ambivalent, and very dirty.

I have just received your Note, and Tonyn's business shall remain as it is. God Bless you.
Addressed: George Farquhar, Esq.

Mrs. Clarke was inevitably the first witness to be confronted with the note wrested with so much difficulty from the recalcitrant Sandon, and although it was obvious that she genuinely remembered nothing at all about it, she was characteristically only too willing to lend Perceval a hand in solving the riddle.

"Do you recollect ever seeing that paper before?"

"I suppose I must have seen it before, for it is His Royal Highness's handwriting."

"What reason have you to suppose you have seen it before?"

"I do not know how it could have got into that man's possession unless I gave it to him, and it was a direction I used very often to get from His Royal Highness, 'George Farquhar, Esq.'."

Having obtained a copy of the note from Huxley Sandon during his conversation with him in London, Colonel Hamilton had immediately contacted William Adam. William Adam informed the Duke about the note in Sandon's possession, and together the two men hurried round to consult Colonel Gordon.

"I think last Saturday week," the Duke's military secretary testified, "about half-past ten at night, the Duke of York and Mr. Adam called at my house. I had been extremely fatigued and was going to bed; I was undressed. I went in my undress into the room where were the Duke of York and Mr. Adam. The first word that was said to me was by the Duke of York, and I think the words were these, 'Here is a very extraordinary business. Here is a forgery'."

No one knew exactly what the note was intended to convey, but if it could be proved that the Duke had written it at Mrs. Clarke's behest to restrain Tonyn's impatience, the Commander-in-Chief's prospects of remaining in office were bleak indeed. Totally unable to believe that he had written this note, the Duke conceived himself the victim of an infamous forgery, and Mrs. Clarke, Perceval was convinced, was the evil genius whose skulduggery knew no bounds.

"Have you ever imitated other hand-writing?" he asked.

"No, not to make any use of it. I might, with two or three women, laughing, or anything in that way, imitate a hand," she replied, gaily pulling a red herring across Perceval's path, "but not to make any use of it whatever. Not to send it out ever."

"You have done it to see whether you could do it?"

"I do not know that I have done it, but it is very often when women are writing that they might say, 'Come, you write a hand, and see whether it is like anyone's hand.' I have done it lately. Several of us were sitting together and we were playing at some kind of game. Perhaps there may be some bad construction put upon that," she gibed.

"What have you done?"

"I have said, 'Is not this like such a sort of hand, and that like such a sort of hand?' "

"What sort of hand were you imitating at the time . . .?"

"I do not know. It is very ridiculous to mention here I think. There is a game you play at, you put down a man's name and then a woman's, and where they are, and what they are doing, and then make a long roll of it."

Perhaps "Consequences" was a party game that the Percevals never played, and the Chancellor of the Exchequer wanted to know whether it was "any part of the skill in that game to write the name as nearly resembling the handwriting of the person whose name it is as possible?"

"No, I should think not. I wrote without knowing it something in the office here, that I was told was very like the writing of a person here."

"Whose writing did they say it was like?" Perceval innocently inquired.

"They said it was like the Speaker's hand," Mrs. Clarke blithely informed him.

"Have you never told anybody that you could imitate the handwriting of any one?"

"No, I do not recollect that I have. There was a story went about that I had forged for £2,000 with the Duke of York's signature 'Frederick', but I never did. I never signed his name in my life except when he has been there, and we have been trying together how near I could write to him, and he to me."

"You have tried sometimes to see how near you could write to the Duke of York?" Perceval pounced triumphantly.

"Yes, but I never did it but when he was by."

"Could you write very near when you tried?"

"I do not know. He is the best judge of that. I believe if he was asked he would not say I had ever made use of his name in any writing."

"You know his handwriting?"

"Yes, he fancied it was a great deal like his signed 'Frederick'. That was all I ever attempted about it."

"Do you know a person of the name of Town?"

"Yes, I do, a velvet painter."

"Do you not recollect having told him that you thought you probably might make considerable proficiency in that art as you made great proficiency in writing, and copying handwritings?"

"No, I never told him any such thing. You will recollect he is a Jew. It is ridiculous."

"You are quite sure you never said any such thing?"

"No, I should never have said such a thing to such a man."

"Did you ever, in a playing way, attempt to imitate the handwriting of the Duke of York?"

"I do not think I did to him."

"Not to Mr. Town?"

"No."

"Have you to anyone else?"

"I do not think I have, but he has seen a great many ladies when he has been with me in a morning, and if he listened to any of our conversations and made remarks upon them three or four years afterwards, I cannot say anything to such a thing. The only question is to ascertain whether I ever did make use of the Duke of York's name. If I had I am sure it would have been against me long before this. Perhaps he might have stolen something that might have been lying about the house."

What was the truth about the note which raised such a storm of controversy in 1809? Unfortunately it is no longer in existence, presumably lost in the fire that almost entirely destroyed the Palace of Westminster in October, 1834, and it is only possible to reach an objective conclusion from a careful appraisal of contemporary opinion.

A whole host of witnesses were called, and after a careful scrutiny of the Duke's two love-letters they were asked to say whether or not they believed that he had also written the enigmatic note.

The Inspector of Franks at the General Post Office thought that the Tonyn note had been written by the Duke. "It resembles it (the Duke's handwriting) so nearly I should think it was," he said, an opinion with which his deputy concurred.

Thomas Nesbitt, in charge of the Letter of Attorney Office, flatly disagreed. "After a great deal of attention and care in looking at almost every letter in the note, I am of the opinion that it was not written by the same hand."

Thomas Bliss, an expert in detecting forged bank notes, had complete confidence in his professional ability. "From an examination of the three letters," he said, "which I looked at as carefully as possible, I thought they were all of one handwriting."

Thomas Bateman, who had been engaged in examining powers of attorney for twenty years, was less categorical. "I can only say that there is a very marked similarity," he informed the Attorney-General.

Public opinion had no doubt at all that the note had been written by the Duke, and the experts, with less unanimity, agreed. It is highly probable that in the midst of a busy life, responsible for a large amount of official and private correspondence, he had forgotten a brief message of three lines written five years earlier.

George Canning spoke of "any man who knows what it is to be in a situation to receive twenty, and write perhaps a dozen letters in a day," told the House of finding the copy of a recent letter to a lady, and of being utterly unconscious to what it related, and to whom.

"Madam," the Secretary of State for Foreign Affairs had written, "I have received your valuable present, and have only to assure you that you may depend on my discretion." It was not a bribe, a crime or a confederacy, Canning related, but a promise to a poetess to keep secret her "Ode to Vaccination".

The Duke, the majority of people decided, found himself in a similar plight, and had genuinely forgotten a hasty note dashed off to his mistress as he sat at his desk at the Horse Guards embroiled in a mass of correspondence, detail and discussion.

The note bore the Duke's private seal, a highly embarrassing hall-mark, so it seemed, of its authenticity. Some of the Duke's defenders suggested that Mrs. Clarke had surreptitiously appropriated one of his two signet rings as he relaxed at Gloucester Place, others that she had used the unbroken seal from an old letter, but they were sophisms that no one believed, and which Mrs. Clarke dismissed with appropriate contempt.

The implication of forgery was scarcely credible, and no one seriously imagined that a woman as perspicacious as Mrs. Clarke was likely to have run the risk of detection, and an ignominious end to her life of high society as the Duke's mistress. It seemed also impossible that she had either the time or patience to acquire the skilful proficiency that baffled even the experts.

Mrs. Clarke had many talents but that of forgery seems totally out of character. During the inquiry, William Jerdan, "The Morning Post" reporter, received an invitation from Mrs. Clarke to call at Westbourne Place after having been introduced to her whilst visiting her sister, and he has left a vivid picture of her subtlety and guile.

"Her object, as may be surmised," he wrote in his autobiography, "was to neutralise my pen, and the wiles to which she resorted would make a delicious chapter in the history of woman's ingenuity. I found myself as a bird, I suppose may do when caught in a net; but the meshes were of many shapes and kinds, and reticulated with infinite skill and cunning. Wheedling confidential secrets, allurements, prospects of advantage, piquant familiarities, *recherché* treats and lies. Never was a greater variety of artillery brought to bear upon a newspaper scribbler; and at least, *Madame* so far accomplished her wishes, that I did moderate my tone about her personal performances."

Perhaps Sir Arthur Wellesley may be permitted the last word about the note that for days was the controversial talking point in drawing-rooms, kitchens and public houses throughout the country, and which played a decisive part in the resignation of the Duke as Commander-in-Chief. Sir Arthur was one of the most regular Members of the inquiry, and in apologising to a correspondent for the delay in answering his letters he pleaded that he had been much pressed by the business in Parliament in the last week, which generally lasted until four, five and six o'clock every morning.

The future hero of Waterloo was reluctant to believe that the Duke was "a party to Mrs. Clarke's plunder of Tonyn," and "I doubt," he wrote on February 17th, "the handwriting being the Duke's, although it resembles it much. . . . But I acknowledge that from other circumstances attending the note, namely, its seal, the direction, the difficulty with which we got it from the holder, and Mrs. Clarke's real, unaffected ignorance of its existence both before and after it was produced, I am induced to fear that it is the

Duke's handwriting. The impression is strong against the Duke both in and out of the House."

The note created a major sensation, but there was also a whole crop of minor incidents to occupy the newspaper reporters and whet the public appetite for every possible scrap of information about the mercurial Mrs. Clarke.

Chapter Fourteen

Mrs. Clarke was recalled for a second interrogation late in the evening of February 13th: it was her seventh appearance before the house since the inquiry began a fortnight before. At first highly elated at such a unique outlet for her vanity, she was by now becoming tetchy at the endless barrage of questions.

"Had you a footboy of the name of Samuel Carter?" Wardle demanded.

"Yes, I had," Mrs. Clarke replied sharply. Turning to the other Members she added with genuine indignation, "Colonel Wardle told me he would not mention that."

It was the first intimation of a new case of corruption that Colonel Wardle was bringing against the Duke, and one, Mrs. Clarke alleged, that he had promised to disregard. Bad blood was beginning to flow between Wardle, the Duke's accuser, and Mrs. Clarke, his principal witness, but Wardle was totally absorbed in pursuing his brief and never dreamed the day of reckoning lay ahead when Mrs. Clarke would turn her talents against him.

Samuel Carter had been introduced to Mrs. Clarke by Captain Thomas Sutton, an ex-army officer who had lost a leg whilst on active service with the grenadiers. After his discharge from the army, Thomas Sutton had experienced considerable difficulty in finding employment, but was eventually appointed deputy fire-master at Woolwich. "He had been an esteemed friend of the Prince of Wales and of the Duke of York for twelve years," Mrs. Clarke informed Perceval maliciously, "but nearly died of want except through me."

Encouraged by his acquaintance with the Duke of York, Sutton had written to him on December 7th, 1801, requesting a special favour.

"The kindness that your highness has at all times most graciously bestowed on me, emboldens me to address you on behalf of an orphan lad, nearly sixteen years of age, of the name of Samuel Carter (whose father lost his life in the service, and whom I have brought up and educated), in hopes that your highness will be graciously pleased to appoint him to an Ensigncy."*

It was an inauspicious moment for Captain Sutton to choose for his application. Following the Peace of Amiens in March, 1802, the war between England and France was briefly at an end, the strength of the army was being reduced, and he received a reply stating that "from present circumstances it is not in the Commander-in-Chief's power to recommend any person for a commission, but His Royal Highness has directed Mr. Samuel Carter's name to be noted, to be provided for at a future opportunity."

No further applications were made on behalf of Samuel Carter, but in March, 1804, he was officially appointed to an Ensigncy in the 16th Foot Regiment.

The Duke's supporters endeavoured to show that it was customary for applicants to wait two or three years before being appointed, but Wardle pertinently pointed out that "however well disposed the office might have been towards his application, to have given effect to it, they must have known that he was alive, and the place of his residence, which could not be the case without a fresh Memorial."

With characteristic aplomb, Mrs. Clarke took upon herself the credit for Carter's commission.

"To whom did you apply for the commission for Samuel Carter in the 16th regiment?" Perceval asked.

"To His Royal Highness," Mrs. Clarke replied predictably.

"Did you apply to His Royal Highness for a commission for Samuel Carter in the name of Samuel Carter?"

"Yes, it was his real name."

"Was that the name he was usually called in your family, and even to His Royal Highness, the Commander-in-Chief?'

"Yes, it was."

'Was His Royal Highness aware that it was the some person who had occasionally waited upon him at your table, for whom you asked that Commission?"

"Yes, he was."

"What interval elapsed from the time Carter was in your service till he obtained the commission?"

"I should think he was living with me near a twelvemonth

* The lowest commissioned officer in a foot regiment, equivalent to 2/Lieutenant.

altogether, not entirely in Gloucester Place but in Tavistock Place likewise."

"Did he go immediately from your service into the army?"

"Yes, he did."

"Did His Royal Highness see Samuel Carter subsequent to his being gazetted?"

"Yes, he did."

"Did he speak to Samuel Carter on the subject of his having a commission, either before or after he obtained the commission?" Sir John Sebright interjected.

"I don't know what His Royal Highness said to him, but he saw him after he had been down to the Isle of Wight, and joined the depot. He came up to me for some money, and His Royal Highness saw him in Gloucester Place."

The odium heaped on the head of the Duke of York in the case of Samuel Carter sprang from feelings of outraged propriety, from the strict conventions of an age that contemplated class distinction as a way of life as sacrosanct as it was inviolate. Was it possible, people asked each other, that the Commander-in-Chief could stoop to the folly of promoting his mistress's footman to the position and privileges of a commissioned officer?

To circumvent the calamitous hostility that the case engendered, Perceval and his friends endeavoured to establish that Carter was not the orphan that Captain Sutton had purported, but his own natural son, and that far from being a menial lackey to Mrs. Clarke, he had lived with her as one of the family. Unfortunately, Captain Sutton had died two years earlier, and it remained a matter of conjecture whether Carter was an officer's son and a gentleman, or merely the servant to whom Mrs. Clarke had good-naturedly presented a commission.

"Did you not understand that Samuel Carter was a natural son of Captain Sutton?" Perceval asked Mrs. Clarke.

"No, I did not," she contradicted him. "People have said so, but he told me to the contrary himself."

"Did not Captain Sutton take care of his education?"

"Captain Sutton always had the boy about him. He had several and Sam was one. He had been strongly recommended by Mrs. Fitzherbert, I believe, but they denied that at one time."

"Did Captain Sutton educate the boy?"

"He was not well educated till he came to me. He used to go to school while he was in my service, every leisure hour."

"Don't you know that Captain Sutton took care of his education?"

"I know that he took some pains to instruct him in his leisure time. He was a very good boy."

"You have stated that Samuel Carter was a boy," Charles Yorke addressed Mrs. Clarke. "What age was he when he got his commission?"

"I called him a boy," Mrs. Clarke answered promptly, "because he was short. I believe he was eighteen or nineteen; of a proper age for the commission."

Mrs. Favery was equally obstructive about Carter's parentage, and told Perceval that she knew nothing about the suggestion that he was Captain Sutton's illegitimate son.

"Did you never suppose that ?"

"No. I cannot tell what other persons supposed", she answered.

Having made no headway in their attempts to establish Carter as an officer's son, fully entitled to follow in his father's footsteps, the Government now contended that Mrs. Clarke, with an only boy of six, had accepted him into her family as an older, adopted son, and that he was not the footman she represented him to be.

It might be profitable, the Duke's friends decided, to see what her servants had to say about Samuel Carter.

"He cleaned the knives, cleaned the plate, attended the carriage and waited at table on His Royal Highness," Mrs. Favery maintained. That seemed conclusive enough, but although Mrs. Favery was responsible for paying the servants their wages, she had conveniently forgotten whether Samuel Carter was among them. "I really cannot say what I gave him," she declared. "I have given him money a great many times when he has asked for money to buy himself shoes and things he wanted."

Thomas Walker, the coachman, confirmed that he remembered Carter at Gloucester Place five years earlier. He agreed also that he went behind Mrs. Clarke's carriage, and that although they both waited at table, neither of them wore livery.

William M'Dowall, a footman at Gloucester Place in 1804, was very muddled. "He did the work along with me, that is all I can say," he declared, but prodded by Lord Palmerston he recalled that Carter had his meals with the other servants, and "acted as a servant as far as I know."

M'Dowall's confused evidence and unsteady stance at the bar of the House suggested that he was drunk, and he was ordered to withdraw whilst Members solemnly debated what action to take.

Strongly prejudiced by the criterion of stern military discipline, Colonel Vereker urged the House to make an example of such a person, obviously hoping to see him speedily locked up in Newgate for contempt.

Charles Bragge Bathurst was more moderate, and thought that M'Dowall had given his evidence as clearly as could be expected "from a man in his situation of life", and that it was beneath the dignity of the House to take any notice of the state he was in.

Mr. Sumner was not prepared to see M'Dowall escape so lightly. He should be censured in some way, he proposed, and his evidence expunged.

William Smith, a Unitarian and the Member for Norwich, wanted to know when a man was to be judged as being drunk, and thought "every Member might often find himself puzzled."

For nearly an hour the charade went on as the House debated what they ought to do with a drunken footman. When at last it was decided to recall M'Dowall, his evidence was as incoherent and irrelevant as it had been before, and one is as mystified as amused that he was ever summoned at all.

Strangely enough it was Carter himself who provided the most eloquent testimony of his relationship with Mrs. Clarke. Among the letters preserved by William Nicholls were three written by Carter after obtaining his commission whilst waiting to sail to the West Indies on active service, a centre of bitter colonial rivalry with Napoleonic France.

The letters revealed not only the nineteen-year old soldier's affectionate dependence upon the woman who had befriended him, but also her impulsive generosity.

Isle of Wight,
September 20th, 1804,

Honourable Madam,

I wrote to the Inspector General (Gwynn) for leave of absence on the 14th, but received no answer . . . The Adjutant informs me, if I have not my regimentals ready when called upon, I shall be put under arrest. Permit me, madam, to hope that your goodness (which I have experienced so often in the greatest degree possible) will extricate me from so unpleasant a situation by obtaining me leave of absence speedily.

"Honourable Madam, the favour of a line would tend to disperse those fears which have been some time prevalent with me, which was occasioned by your silence, viz., that some part of my conduct has offended you. From gratitude, I say with energy, God Almighty forbid. Accept madam, the sincere thanks and acknowledgments of your grateful servant,

Sam Carter.

Note: Having wrote to His Royal Highness for leave, I received an answer directing me to apply to the Inspector General.

Carter obtained his leave, and immediately he returned to the Isle of Wight he wrote to Mrs. Clarke again.

2nd October, 1804.

I was extremely sorry at not having had it in my power to wait until you came in from the baron's, in order to thank you for the kind benevolence I have ever experienced from you, and which has made so deep an impression on my heart and mind as not to be erased by time. Honourable madam, I have still to beg the continuance of that benevolence; for, having placed me in a situation which requires a great number of expensive things at first, and notwithstanding having laid out my money with the greatest economy, I find it inadequate. I have now the offer of a barrack room (which will save the expense of lodgings), but I have no cot, or any money to buy one; neither have I any to subsist on till the 24th. If, madam, you will extend your kindness towards me once more, it will ever be gratefully remembered by, madam, your sincerely thankful servant,

Samuel Carter.

Honourable Madam, I have set the things down which I bought, by which you will see the state of my purse.

	£	s.	d.
Belt and Feather	1	8	–
To Sword and Sash	6	3	–
Gorget and Sword-knot	1	8	–
Paid Lewis	7	–	–
,, Laundry Maid	0	10	6
,, Taylor's Bill	2	3	–
Trunk	1	11	6
Gloves and Stockings	1	2	–
Silk Handkerchiefs	0	14	–
Round Hat Trimmed	1	14	–

Watch from pledge	2	3	–
Boots and Shoes	3	10	–
Expenses down	2	5	–
Borrowed at Depot	6	2	6
To Jacket and Trimmings	4	5	–
	£41	19	6

Presumably Mrs. Clarke complied with Carter's request for further financial help, but on January 4th, 1805, he was writing to her again from the Clarendon Transport at Portsmouth.

Honourable Madam,

Impelled by my dreadful situation, and my perfect knowledge of your goodness, I trust you will pardon the liberty of addressing you again . . .

"I have no stock for the voyage, neither have I any money to purchase those little things which are absolutely necessary. I have to keep watch four hours every night, and have nothing to eat but salt meat three times a week, and water to drink, the rum being so bad 'tis impossible to drink it.

Your goodness to me has ever been such as leaves not the smallest doubt that you will not suffer me to starve in the situation you have been pleased to place me, and which is such as will ever tend to make me the most grateful and happy of beings. Should, Madam, you be induced to take into consideration my wretched case, and by a little pecuniary aid save me from everything that is horrible, it will be an act worthy of yourself, and imprint that upon my heart which will never be erased.

I am, Madam,

Your grateful servant,
Samuel Carter.

In an age when nepotism flourished, it was at least comprehensible that Mrs. Clarke had made the most of her opportunities as mistress of the Commander-in-Chief to boost her precarious finances by turning her hand to a profitable excursion in army brokerage, but it revealed neither discrimination nor discretion when she extended her patronage to an impossible Irish preacher and the footman who waited on her at table. It indicated, Wardle declared indignantly, "to what extent Mrs. Clarke's influence went, and it made it difficult to say where it might stop."

Still convinced that Carter was an officer's son, Perceval appealed "to the feelings of the House and the country, whether an act like this is to be imputed to the Duke of York as a crime! If a man is to be punished for his vices it may be well; but let him not be punished for his virtues."

"If there is any praise due on account of Samuel Carter," Sir Francis Burdett trenchantly corrected him, "it belongs not to the Duke of York, but to Mrs. Clarke."

As usual, Croker was in the vanguard of those ready to denounce Mrs. Clarke at every turn. "Having falsely represented herself as having raised Mr. Carter from the situation of a footboy to that of a gentleman," he railed, she now turns round, as it serves her present purpose, to degrade a gentleman to the level of a footboy. She had, as his letters gratefully own, assisted him with money for his outfit. With accidental malice she had adorned the victim she meant to sacrifice. She had given him money, and she fancied in her mean calculation, that she had purchased a right over his character.

"Let us consider, too," Croker inveighed, "the actual situation of Carter when she makes this attempt. Where now is the object of her ruinous kindness? Under a burning sun, in a distant and fatal climate, fighting the battles of the country that at this moment rings from side to side with his dishonour! Perhaps she concluded he was dead . . ."

The scandal-mongers salaciously suggested that Carter's services were not entirely confined to the dining-room and the carriage.

"It were to be wished that no one shared her bed during her keeping with His Royal Highness," wrote one gossip, "but suspicions are entertained of a great many, and one in particular, Samuel Carter, her footman, for whom she procured a commission in the 16th regiment of foot, since gone to the West Indies."

Perhaps when the newspapers reached Samuel Carter nearly five thousand miles away, he decided it was preferable to be fighting for King and country under a burning sun than facing a barrage of questions into his relationship with Mrs. Clarke in the House of Commons.

* * *

On February 20th, Mrs. Clarke took to her bed, but was she really at the point of mental collapse after eleven searching examinations, or physically exhausted from the whirl of Westbourne Place, "the resort of dozens of M.P.'s, and curious strangers," where she could be found still holding court long after the lights of Westminster had been extinguished? Or had she at last turned her back in anger on the interminable bombardment of questions fired at her by Perceval and his colleagues?

Dr. Metcalf told the House that she was totally unfit to attend for two days, but the less credulous whispered that she had, in fact, been ordered to bed out of Perceval's reach by Colonel Wardle, who was alarmed that she might be tricked into betraying that behind the inquiry he had instigated, hovered the enigmatic figure of the Duke of Kent, maliciously endeavouring to oust his brother from his office at the Horse Guards.

Despite strenuous Government efforts, the tide of public feeling was running strongly against the Duke. Five days before the inquiry ended, Sir Arthur Wellesley reported to the Duke of Richmond that the Commander-in-Chief had been burnt in effigy in Suffolk and Yorkshire, and Charles Williams Wynn informed his brother that "it is admitted that he made her foot-boy an Ensign in the Army. These are facts, which though they are not crimes as a Court of Justice could take cognizance of, yet prove such flagrant misconduct that the House of Commons would neglect their duty, if in some way they do not recommend that the person who has been guilty of them, should be removed from the important and responsible situation of Commander-in-Chief."

Mrs. Clarke arrived at the House for the last time on February 22nd. Lord Folkestone, one of her staunchest supporters, rose to request that the Committee would examine her immediately so that she might be detained as short a time as possible.

A chair was ordered and she replied to Perceval's final questions with the same sangfroid and saucy repartee. Perhaps in deference to her indisposition, perhaps bleakly aware of the tide of opinion running swiftly against the Duke, Perceval's examination was less rigorous, no one mentioned the Duke of Kent, and Mrs. Clarke returned to Westbourne Place undaunted and undefeated.

The inquiry ended at 3.30 in the morning of February 23rd, and at a quarter to eleven the next night there was a spectacular distraction from the contrivances of Mrs. Clarke when Drury Lane theatre was destroyed by a fire which started, it was said, as a result of negligence by some plumbers who had been working in the passages leading to the water-closets.

The wooden interior exploded in a massive conflagration. The London sky was ablaze with light, and the flames were clearly visible at Twickenham twelve miles away. The Perceval children watched in tense excitement from the roof of their Downing Street home, whilst the light shining through the windows of the House of Commons sent Members rushing into Palace Yard to obtain a better view of the breath-taking blaze that lit up the London streets as bright as day, creating pandemonium in the middle of a speech by the Foreign Secretary on the progress of the war.

"I think even the dreadful calamity of the burning of Drury Lane will not be without its advantages", wrote Fanny Williams Wynn, sanctimoniously shocked by the outrageous Mrs. Clarke, "if it makes people think and talk of something else."

Chapter Fifteen

THERE WAS a fortnight's respite for the Members of Parliament after the inquiry ended before they were launched into a seven-day debate on the conduct of the Duke of York and the character of Mrs. Clarke, but, if there was a temporary lull at Westminster, the Duke and his mistress were still the hub of conversation from Carlton House to St. Giles, from the barrack rooms at Brighton to Inverness.

From his home in Northumberland, Lord Grey had found the scenes in the Commons disgusting, and deeply regretted that the opposition had not immediately and publicly disclaimed all association with Wardle's accusations.

"It is impossible to believe that anything more can be imputable to the Duke," he wrote with pompous condescension, "than might have happened to any man who has had the misfortune to keep a mistress."

Alarmed at the catastrophe into which the Duke's extra-marital excursion had led him, other men took a closer and more critical look at their own amours. It was customary at the beginning of the nineteenth century for a man to give his paramour a pledge of financial support, and one Royal Admiral "endeavoured to get the weather-gauge of his mistress" by requesting her to return the bond which he had executed in her favour. He was not, however, to be liberated so lightly, and received in reply the warning torn from the bottom of an old playbill. "No money is returned after the curtain is drawn up."

For the caricaturists and satirists the advent of Mrs. Clarke was a heaven-sent opportunity of illimitable scope, and in the incomplete national collection of prints she emerges an easy winner in the 1809 popularity poll with 130 appearances, followed by the Duke of York with 107, and Wardle with 51.*

---

* "English Political Caricature, 1793–1832". M. Dorothy George, Oxford, 1959.

The versifiers also commemorated Mrs. Clarke's activities with sledge-hammer humour:

Come all you brave Fellows who wish for promotion,
Whether Captain or Colonel or a General's your notion,
A Warehouse I keep for the sale of commissions,
You will be treated with Honour if you secrecy mark, Sir,
For my master is Noble and I am his Clarke, Sir.

As for bubbling and cheating you need have no fear,
No false hopes are held out to our customers here,
All is fair and above board, our House is known well,
And the sign you'll observe is the Grand York Hotel,
So hand over the ready and fear nothing my spark,
For my Master is honest and so is his Clarke.

As for Petticoat Angels, let them say what they will,
When once they engage I'll be bound they fulfil,
Then 'ere the firm breaks, to me take a trip,
You know the old proverb, 'twixt the cup and the lip,
But forget not the ready (Gold or notes), for pray mark,
My Master wants Money, and so does his Clarke.

One quatrain was suggestively risqué –

Who for the Tricks he has done in the dark,
Is content to be his Darling Clarke's Clerk,
And to cure her from being more love sick,
Has given her a Royal Duke's Bishopric.

Perceval had borne the brunt of the Duke's defence, and before the inquiry ended he decided that if the Government was to succeed in refuting Wardle's allegations it was imperative for the Commander-in-Chief to make a public declaration of his innocence. On February 18th, he secretly consulted the Speaker about an address from the Duke to the House of Commons, who agreed that he "had long thought such a communication would in substance become necessary."

Lord Melville had reached the same conclusion. He sent the Prime Minister a suggested letter which the government could submit to the Commons, but when it was circulated for comment Lord

Mulgrave roundly denounced it as no more than "a gratuitous and futile public censure of the royal family's morals".

There are contradictory accounts as to how the Duke's public apologia finally came to be written. One version contends that Perceval prepared a draft of inordinate length for cabinet approval, but from his letter to the King dated February 23rd, it seems evident that the draft was not written by Perceval but by the Duke himself.

"It was not till after a very full and deliberate examination for some hours in the Cabinet this morning, of every sentence in the letter, and approbation of its contents, that Mr. Perceval submitted to H.R.H. the few alterations which appeared in it from the draft as first proposed by H.R.H."

The Duke considered the revised letter too mortifiying, and further amendments were made by Colonel Gordon before he agreed to sign. At half-past four on February 23rd, the Speaker read the much disputed document to the whole House.

Horse Guards,
February 23rd, 1809.

Sir,

I have waited with the greatest anxiety until the Committee appointed by the House of Commons to enquire into my Conduct as Commander-in-Chief of His Majesty's Army had closed its examinations, and I now hope that it will not be deemed improper to address this Letter, through you, to the House of Commons.

I observe with the deepest concern, that in the course of this Enquiry my name has been coupled with transactions the most criminal and disgraceful; and I must ever regret and lament that a connection should ever have existed which has thus exposed my character and honour to public animadversion.

With respect to any alleged offences connected with the discharge of my official duties, I do in the most solemn manner, upon my honour, as a Prince, distinctly assert my innocence, not only by denying all corrupt participation in any of the infamous transactions which have appeared in evidence at the Bar of the House of Commons, or any connivance at their existence, but also the slightest knowledge or suspicion that they existed at all.

My consciousness of innocence leads me confidently to hope that the House of Commons will not, upon such evidence as they have heard, adopt any proceeding prejudicial to my honour and character; but if, upon such testimony as has been adduced against me, the House of Commons can think my innocence questionable, I claim of their justice that I shall not be condemned without trial, or be deprived of the benefit and protection which is afforded to every British subject by those sanctions under which alone evidence is received in the ordinary administration of the Law.

I am, Sir,

Yours,

Frederick

The Speaker of the House of Commons

The letter was received by Members on both sides of the House as an ill-advised and regrettable expedient, and Sir Samuel Romilly bitterly resented the Duke's attempt to prevail upon the Commons either to acquit him, or to commit him for trial by his peers, when their specific purpose was to decide the Duke's fitness to remain as Commander-in-Chief.

"I wish I had the power to expunge (the letter) from the Journals of the House," he declared vehemently, "and to blot (it) out from the memory of all its Members."

It was a view with which Wilberforce was in complete agreement. "The letter," he said, "ought never to have been received, and had better be forgotten."

When the debate opened on March 8th, Perceval was gloomily aware that he was fighting a rearguard action to save the Duke from an ignominious removal from office. To make matters more difficult, from Windsor the King was obstinately insisting that the interests of the crown were at stake, and that whatever the cost his favourite son must be vindicated.

Arthur Wellesley also had a melancholy presentiment of disaster and defeat.

"The Duke of York is certainly in a bad way," he reported to the Duke of Richmond two days before the debate began. "All that we can do will be to acquit him of corruption, and indeed I doubt whether we shall be able to carry him so far as to acquit him of suspecting Mrs. Clarke's practices, and allowing them to go on. If we should succeed in both these objects, the question will turn upon the point whether it is proper that a Prince of the blood, who has manifested so much weakness as he has, and has led such a life (for that is material in these days), is a fit and proper person to be entrusted with the execution of the duties of a responsible office. We shall be beat upon this question, I think. If we should carry it by a small majority, the Duke will equally be obliged to resign his office; and most probably the consequence of such a victory so hardly earned will be that the government will be broken up."

The debate was opened by Colonel Wardle before a packed House, and after thanking Samuel Whitbread, Francis Burdett and Lord Folkestone for their support, he spoke for three hours on "the evidence which has been taken at the Bar, as well as the documents upon the table." He recapitulated the details of the exchange between Lieutenant-Colonels Knight and Brooke, and of Colonel French's levy; he repeated the part played by Mrs. Clarke in Dowler's appointment, in the promotion of Samuel Carter from footboy to officer, and in Dr. O'Meara's attempt to nobble a Bishopric.

He concluded by moving that the "faithful Commons most humbly submit their opinion to His Majesty's gracious consideration, that His Royal Highness the Duke of York ought to be deprived of the Command of the Army."

Perceval had intended to speak first in the Duke's defence, but at the last minute stood aside to make way for Francis Burton, a distinguished judge, who, although totally blind for ten years, had attended every meeting of the Committee with dedicated fervour. His wife, the sixty-four-year-old judge informed the House, had read all the evidence to him, and had re-read the important passages two or three times.

The Duke's guilt or innocence depended largely on the evidence of Mrs. Clarke, and Francis Burton was the first to cast a stone at her credibility.

"Among the foremost of false witnesses stands also Mrs. Clarke, the accomplice," he declared. "In her testimony is to be found an absolute tissue of falsehood. I have reckoned up myself as many as twenty-eight positive assertions, in some of which she is contradicted by herself, in almost all by other unimpeachable witnesses . . ."

To justify his denunciation of Mrs. Clarke as an inveterate liar, Francis Burton reminded the House that on several occasions she had posed as a widow, and repeated the evidence that she had masqueraded as the wife of William Dowler. Her other lies he did not think it necessary to enumerate. "I have in my pocket a list of twenty-eight," he asserted blandly, "which any gentleman is welcome to inspect." If no one doubted the judge's integrity, many Members were abashed that he had not fully substantiated his accusation.

At midnight Perceval rose to speak, and he was still on his feet when the House adjourned three hours later. He continued his defence of the Duke the following day, and delivered, Arthur Wellesley generously remarked, "the best speech I ever heard in Parliament."

Even Wilberforce, deeply shocked by the disclosure of such "a shameless violation of decency" was impressed by Perceval's sincerity. "The Duke of York's business deciding," he wrote in his diary that night. "Perceval's capital speech, which greatly changed my opinion as to his guilt, softening though not quite turning me."

To Spencer Perceval, Mrs. Clarke was anathema. A puritanical evangelist, the father of twelve children, and a devout believer in the sanctity of family life, he had ten years earlier been one of the most active advocates for making extra-marital intercourse an offence punishable by law. Lord Auckland's Bill for the Better Prevention of Adultery had been rejected by an assembly of men unwilling to place a public restraint upon a private propensity, and now, for three weeks, they had been compelled to tolerate the intrusion of the profligate Mrs. Clarke. It was an experience that Perceval was not prepared to suffer in silence.

"Her sarcastic insolence, her playful pleasantry, as if there was nothing in her evidence that weighed heavy upon herself, her general cleverness and versatility, the art and wit she displayed in answering those questions which she thought proper to answer, the most unblushing effrontery with which she disclosed things which would have abashed the boldest witness, the mode in which she was continually evading the questions which she wished to avoid, presenting new topics to the examiner, misleading him, turning him beside his object, and at last, when pressed and driven to extremity, sheltering herself in a total forgetfulness," Perceval exploded.

"The House cannot forget it . . . Perhaps, sir, they might wish to forget but they cannot but remember how indulgently they tolerated her jokes, how they seemed to forget her vice in her wit, and be almost reconciled to her infamy by her manner of displaying it."

Finally, Perceval proposed a resolution expressing the opinion of the House that there was no ground to charge His Royal Highness with the crimes imputed to him, and confidence in the integrity of his conduct in the discharge of his duties as Commander of the Army.

Throughout the centuries it is the woman who has been expected to observe the protocol of rectitude and sexual morality, and the man who has been permitted a more tolerant measure of licence and liberty. As if to atone for this unfair advantage there have always been men ready to defend the woman who has overstepped the boundaries of decorum, and Samuel Whitbread suggested to Perceval that there were other aspects to consider before admonishing Mrs. Clarke for her unedifying behaviour.

"I think some indulgence may be extended to her," he urged. "Her sex, the novel situation in which she was placed, the extraordinary and interesting scene, herself the object of the eager curiosity of every eye in the House, are all to be taken into consideration. If some flippancy at the beginning produced a great deal of mirth, was it extraordinary that she should persevere in a course which had produced that effect? The House must take some share of the blame."

Perceval became increasingly aware as the debate continued that the real danger threatening the Duke and the downfall of the Government lay in the outraged consciences of Wilberforce and his friends. Sex was the basest of all sins to these earnest evangelists, and their energetic reforming efforts, which began in 1788 with a Proclamation against Vice and Immorality, did not exculpate the Duke for his affair with Mrs. Clarke.

On March 10th, Henry Bankes proposed an amendment, which, although acquitting the Duke of corruption, urged his dismissal for "a course of conduct of the worst example to public morals, and highly injurious to the cause of religion, which if not discountenanced by His Majesty and by this House cannot fail to have a pernicious effect upon those main springs of social order and well regulated society . . ."

The twenty-nine-year-old Lord Folkestone, descended from a Huguenot family which settled in Canterbury in the sixteenth century, had been partly educated in France, and his humanitarian sensibilities had been deeply stirred by the bitter struggle of the French revolutionaries. He returned to England a staunch advocate of popular rights, and defended Elizabeth Taylor with warmth and compassion.

"A virtuous young girl," he declared amidst loud laughter from the government benches, "I repeat, a virtuous young girl, and however the gentlemen on the other side of the house might laugh at the term, I will say there was nothing in the evidence, nothing in the deportment of Miss Taylor at the bar, which justified them in their merriment, or at all contradicted the justice of the term as applied to her – I will repeat, this virtuous young girl, when her family was in their distress, took a boarding-school for the support of herself and her younger sister. She had a dozen pupils before she was summoned to attend this house as a witness, and in consequence of the answers which had been extorted from her in the course of her examination, nine of them have been withdrawn. Her creditors soon found out her misfortunes, and no time was lost in laying an execution on her goods. Her furniture has been seized, the carpets torn off the floors, and she herself obliged to seek an asylum in a friend's house. And yet, although such distress and ruin had been occasioned in her little establishment, it appeared that all the debts she owed in the world amounted only to about £150."

Sir Francis Burdett, who had seconded Wardle's original motion, was a perpetual thorn in the side of the government, and he found Mrs. Clarke's guile an admirable pretext for tormenting the Crown lawyers. "She stood at the bar like a potent witch," he declaimed with graphic rhetoric, "and no sooner did the sable band encounter her, than their faculties seemed to be withered, as it were, by the wand of an enchantress. She routed the whole troop, horse and foot and chariots . . . Mr. Attorney-General verily believed he had got a witch at the bar, but still returned to the attack, and still retired, baffled, vexed and defeated."

Samuel Romilly had heard a great deal about the fascination of Mrs. Clarke, but was not impressed when she first appeared at the bar, although he modestly admitted that this might have been due to his want of sensibility. He deplored her unguarded manner, her levity, and the general impropriety of her conduct, but pointed out that this was not the way a witness would testify who had come to give false evidence, and contrasted Mrs. Clarke's behaviour with that of Sandon and Donovan, whose primary concern had been to protect themselves. He also reminded the House that on several occasions she had been threatened that if she prevaricated she would be sent to Newgate.

On March 14th, John Wilson Croker delivered a long speech, and although only a young back-bencher of twenty-eight, and afflicted with a stutter which he never completely lost, his cogency and vigour did much to bolster the Duke's tottering defences. It was an impressive performance for a man who had been in Parliament only eighteen months, and when Perceval became Prime Minister in October, he offered Croker the post of First Secretary of the Admiralty, an office he occupied for the next twenty-one years.

Wilberforce spoke late at night the next day, and although he had prepared his speech with customary thoroughness, he lacked enthusiasm, and felt ill at ease. To condemn immorality in the abstract was one thing, to be confronted with it in the persons of the Duke of York and Mrs. Clarke another.

It was necessary, he said, to make some reparation to public morals and decency, and public safety required that the command of the army should no longer be confided to the Duke of York. He objected also that "it was customary in the House to call things by very soft and gentle names. That which used to be called 'adultery' was now only 'living under protection'."

Perceval became increasingly apprehensive of the government prospects of defeating the improbable combination of Wilberforce and Wardle, and in the long, exhausting struggle to retain the Duke in office, it was undoubtedly the defection of Wilberforce that rankled most bitterly.

At last, at six in the morning on March 17th, more than six weeks after the inquiry had begun, Members trooped into the Division lobbies to give their verdict on the conduct of the Duke of York.

They defeated first by 294 votes to 199 the amendment proposed by Henry Bankes, and rejected Wardle's original address by 364 votes to 123.

That evening the debate continued, "made intricate by the form of the amendment," the Speaker noted in his diary, "and noisy by the arrival of the Irish Members from their anniversary dinner on St. Patrick's Day." At 4.30 the following morning, after another all-night sitting, Perceval's resolution was carried by 278 votes to 196.*

"It is no wonder that His Royal Highness has been acquitted," commented Mrs. Clarke with her usual witticism, "when a blind judge charged the jury."

It was an ominous portent that of 474 Members, 196 had voted against the Duke's complete acquittal, and Bragge Bathurst, who disapproved of all the resolutions upon which the House had voted, had tabled a further hostile motion for debate the following Monday, observing "with the deepest regret, that in consequence of a connection the most immoral and unbecoming, a communication on official subjects, and an interference in the distribution of military appointments and promotions, has been allowed to exist, which could not but lead to discredit the official administration of His Royal Highness, and to give colour and effect, as they have actually done, to transactions the most criminal and disgraceful."

Perceval and his colleagues had little confidence in their ability to defeat the motion proposed by Bathurst, but before the debate was resumed on Monday, March 20th, the Duke of York had resigned.

. . . on last Saturday morning," Perceval informed the House, ". . . His Royal Highness the Duke of York, of his own immediate and spontaneous motion, waited upon His Majesty and tendered to him his resignation of the Chief Command of His Majesty's Army, and that His Majesty had been graciously pleased to accept that resignation."

Referring to the case nearly twenty years later, the Duke said in his posthumous letter published in 1827:

"If it should be expected of me, that I refer to the charge and accusation of Mr. Wardle—I may be permitted to say, that it was completely in my power to have suppressed the whole of that most unfair proceeding. I might have been disposed thus to have acted, had I believed that any woman could have been so base, as to

---

*An interesting sidelight on the divisions on the conduct of the Duke of York is the disparity of the voting figures. It must be remembered, however, that in 1809 party discipline as we know it today scarcely existed, although there were at that time "place men" dependent upon the government of the day for the continuance of salaries and places not granted to them for life. There was also a certain amount of personal loyalty, for instance, many Members in 1809 still considered themselves "the friends of Mr. Pitt", although he had been dead for three years.

have treasured up a private correspondence, written in the moment of an infatuated and infatuating connection; as the future means of threat and annoyance to one, whose fault as towards such female was a careless and most unguarded confidence. The charges against me sprung out of the consequences of an unsuspecting and too artless a disposition; nor had I the least consciousness of the extent of surmise with which a cold-hearted and intriguing woman had surrounded me. I could not believe, and did not imagine, that in a character which appeared all frankness, and seemed never more pleased than in endeavouring to oblige, and render Services; evidences of good temper and kind disposition were but the cloak of a cold and calculating and venal mind, of which I became the dupe. —Men of much stronger and more resolute tempers might have been caught by a less skilful tempter, and consummate hypocrite. I am very ready and willing to admit; and I do trust—that every other period of my long and unremitting service to my King and country, as "Commander-in-Chief," justify me in asserting—that these momentary weaknesses were *exceptions* to the general tenor of my conduct and the principles which directed me in the bestowing of military preferment.

"Nor was it ever objected to me, that the very individuals which were benefited by the intrigue and recommendations of Mary Ann Clarke, were unfit objects, or unworthy to hold the King's Commission. I should have felt much more acutely on this matter, had such been the case; and that, in addition to the manner of attainment, the bad quality or the unfitness of the promoted had been urged against me. If such then was the case (*and I contend strongly that such was the case*), it would seem—that my general character and official habits had been such, as to deter the favourite from daring to propose to my consideration any unworthy object. Thus, the extreme point of accusation would extend to this:—that by means of an acquaintance with Mary Ann Clarke, some few were brought under my notice sooner than, without such means, they otherwise might have been."

A broadside by Gillray grimly predicting "Blood an' Thunder when Whore and Rogue are rentasunder."

In an acrimonious exchange in the House of Commons, Mrs. Clarke accused John Wilson Croker of spying upon her visitors from his garret window, which inspired a bawdy skit by Rowlandson on the activities at her fashionable Chelsea residence.

Mrs. Clarke was supplanted in the Duke's affections by the actress Mrs. Carey, which provided Williams with material for an amusing caricature on the amorous escapades of the Duke of York.

Cruikshank's satire on the re-instatement of the Duke of York as Commander-in-Chief. The Duke is mounted on the shoulders of the decrepit General Dundas, and the Prince Regent ushers him back into office with a pleased smile. Spencer Perceval, the Prime Minister, clears the way with a broom, pushing aside Wardle, who lies on his back whilst a perky little dog, with the head of Mrs. Clarke superimposed, stands over him urinating.

Chapter Sixteen

ON THE EVENING that Perceval informed the House of the Duke's resignation, Mrs. Clarke, with her impeccable sense of timing appeared in a box at the Opera House in the Haymarket for a benefit performance of "The Honeymoon".

"It will be rather awkward to be sure to resign at the end of a month," soliliquized the actor in the role of the Mock Duke, to an uproar of laughter and wild applause, "but like other great men in office, I must make the most of my time and retire with a good grace to avoid being turned out, as a well-bred dog always walks down stairs when he sees preparations on foot for kicking him into the street."

Mrs. Clarke had too much finesse to join in the ovation, but it was an exhilarating experience to savour the public recognition of a job well done.

The loss of an office that he had held for nearly fourteen years was not the only sacrifice the Duke was compelled to make, and bowing before the public clamour and private criticism of his sexual peregrinations, reluctantly he dismissed Mrs. Carey, the actress, who had replaced Mrs. Clarke in the royal four-poster.

"The establishment at Fulham has been entirely given up, and the lady has retired into the country," reported one gossip, whilst the versifiers celebrated the event with their usual irrepressible humour:

O pity, pity me,
In future I'll be wary,
I never, never will
Kiss either Clarke or Carey.

If the outcome of the inquiry appeared catastrophic for the Duke, he did not retire to Oatlands and cut his throat as Mrs. Clarke had grimly predicted. He knew that his withdrawal was a strategic manoeuvre, and that when the hubbub had died down he would be quietly reinstated at the Horse Guards.

In the meantime, Elizabeth Taylor, Colonel Wardle and Mrs. Clarke proceeded to reap their own particular rewards.

Miss Taylor, Wardle said, had begged him not to call her as a witness to support his charges of corruption, and pleaded that if he forced her forwards "it would be the ruin of herself and her dearest connections."

Lord Folkestone had defended her with chivalrous compunction. But Cobbett did not propose to leave Miss Taylor in the exclusive care of His Lordship, and beseeched the public to exercise their best feelings and efficient protection by paying her debts, "because upon that, perhaps, even her life may depend, and that, I think ought to be followed by the raising of money sufficient to secure her a small annuity."

It was an excellent opportunity to take a further swipe at the late but unlamented Commander-in-Chief, and as the money poured in, the names of the subscribers were published in "The Times", "The Courier", and "The Statesman."

An Enemy to Whoremongers and Adulterers	£1	–	–
S. Whitbread, Esq.	21	–	–
A private in the line	0	1	–
Found in my regimental small clothes	1	–	–
A Little Boy at Mr. and Mrs. Barker's School	0	5	–
How Does French Behave to you Darling?	2	2	–
His Grace the Duke of Somerset	10	–	–
V stands for Viper and Vicary	1	1	–
The profits arising from the sale of 6 pots of Dr. O'Meara's "Celestial Unction" and 3 sacks of his "Live Coal"	–	–	6
Mr. Groves, boot-maker, Walting Street, and may the Advocates of Corruption have long corns and wear tight boots	–	7	–

By April 24th, the total contributions had soared to £2,217, and Cobbett relaxed happily in the knowledge that he had rescued Miss Taylor from ruin and imprisonment.

For three months Wardle basked in a glow of idolatry and acclamation, "having boldly dared single-handed to attack the Hydra of corruption and assail her even in her very den."

The immaculate patriot, as Mrs. Clarke spitefully dubbed him, was a national hero, whilst at Westborne Place she dined alone, neglected, irascible – and unrewarded. It was entirely her efforts, she claimed, that had raised Wardle to this pinnacle of popularity, and as the days passed without either word or visit, her bitterness grew, and the seeds were sown of rancour and revenge.

From every part of the country adulation and gratitude were showered upon the chauvinistic Colonel. The Corporation of London voted him "the Freedom of the City, in a gold box, the value of one hundred guineas", and on April 1st, the Mayor, Aldermen and Liverymen of the several Companies of the City of London in Common Hall assembled –

"Resolved unanimously that it has long been a matter of notoriety and has lately been proved beyond the possibility of Doubt that Abuses of a most corrupt nature and ruinous Tendency have existed and still exist in various Branches of the Administration of Public Affairs . . ."

"That to detect such abuses and expose to detestation those men who have wickedly connived at or participated in them requires no small degree of Virtue, Independence and Patriotism, all of which have been eminently displayed by Gwllym Lloyd Wardle Esquire . . ."

The town of Liverpool presented him with a service of plate valued at a thousand guineas; the people of Rochester contributed two hundred guineas for a Silver Cup.

Colonel Wardle was the most popular man in the country, and votes of thanks poured in from Deal to Rutherglen, from Lewes to Londonderry, from Hereford, Hythe and Hull, from Kilmarnock, Nottingham, Plymouth, St. Ives and Berwick-upon-Tweed.

For "The Mushroom Patriot", to borrow another of Mrs. Clarke's endless epithets, it was his finest hour.

For the moment, Mrs. Clarke was busily preoccupied with her own affairs. She had threatened William Adam the previous summer that if the Duke did not pay her annuity she would publish "every circumstance ever communicated to me by His Royal Highness", and in the House of Commons she hinted that she was preparing to add a new dimension to her popularity and her purse.

"Have you not stated that you have several letters – which you call love-letters – from the Duke of York in your possession?" enquired Mr. Thompson.

"Yes, I have," Mrs. Clarke replied. "And some of my friends have," she added ominously.

From the alacrity with which she produced the Duke's two love-letters in the House of Commons it seems probable that she had already embarked upon her memoirs before the inquiry began, and that when it ended, with her name on every lip, she knew that it was the best opportunity that she would ever have of making a lucrative coup in the best-seller market.

Whilst living in Hampstead she had become acquainted with Sir Richard Phillips, the Radical book-seller and friend of Tom Paine, the English revolutionary, but after reading her manuscript he decided that her revelations were too hot to handle, and recommended her to another publisher. At the same time he alerted the Duke of York's friend, Lord Moira, of the potion that Mrs. Clarke was brewing.

Stringing together half-a-dozen adjectives, one of the Duke's contemporaries described him as "a big, burly, loud, jolly, cursing and courageous man"; he was also neither reticent nor circumspect. As he prattled on at Gloucester Place about the affairs of the Royal family, about their adultery, their avarice and their pretensions, Mrs. Clarke had listened and remembered.

The Prince of Wales, she told her friends, was an idle sensualist, with just enough brains to be guided by any laughing, well-bred individual who would listen to stale jokes and impudent ribaldry. The Duke of York she dismissed as a big baby, not out of his leading strings.

But for Queen Charlotte, the haughty, plain-faced wife of George III, she received her most splenetic comments. She was, she said, a dominating matriarch, who hated everyone who would not bow down to any idol that she chose to set up. The Queen, Mrs. Clarke maintained, bitterly resented Princess Caroline, the estranged wife of the Prince of Wales, and her daughter, Charlotte, and seethed with jealousy in case they acquired too much influence over the heir to the throne.

Pierre M'Callum, Wardle's go-between, never forgave Mrs. Clarke for deserting the cause of reform by permitting the suppression of her memoirs. An embittered psychotic, he viciously assailed her in a manuscript that he left unfinished when he died the following year, but the anecdote he ascribes to her is more probably the product of his own fevered imagination.

"One night the Doctor (Mrs. Clarke's pet name for the Duke) came home very much inebriated, and would have somewhat for a relish," M'Callum related. "Having nothing on hand, some cold beef and ham were procured for him, which increased the thirst of intoxication in the night to a violent degree. He rose to get somewhat to quench it, and the neglect of the maid occasioned a ludicrous mistake. As she had forgotten a certain utensil, I had substituted another in its place, and the Doctor, seizing the water bottle, took a long pull, and smacking his lips, swore it was the finest cooler he had ever tasted in his life. His unqualified praise of the cooler made me desirous to taste it, and I had taken two or three gulps, before my nose and palate informed me of having taken a saline draught of our own compounding. This discovery affected our stomachs so violently that our bed and furniture were covered with the effusions of our nausea."

With the Duke in disgrace, the image of the royal family bespattered and tarnished, and the government faltering, the threat of Mary Ann Clarke festering public opinion still further was an intolerable prospect. Lord Chichester, the Joint Postmaster-General, was entrusted to negotiate the purchase of the manuscript and the destruction of all the printed copies of her memoirs, and on April 1st, an agreement was prepared.

Mrs. Clarke was to receive £7,000, her annuity of £400 was to be restored and paid to her two daughters on her death, and Gillett, the printer, indemnified with a payment of £1,500.

"In consideration of the Terms proposed and agreed to I promise to deliver up every Letter, Paper, Memorandum and Writing in my power or custody respecting the Duke of York, or any of the Royal Family, and particularly all Letters, Memorandums or other Writings written or signed by the Duke. I also promise to procure all the Letters not in my custody, entrusted by me to others and to concur in any application for any such Letters or Memorandums and deliver them to the Duke's Friend. I also agree that I will (when required) make a solemn Declaration on oath that I have delivered up all the Letters and other Writings from the Duke to me as far as in my power or possession, and that I know of no other. I promise to procure from the Printer and the Persons employed to print a publication of my Life, every Document in their possession and all such parts of the Work as may have been printed. I further promise not to write Print or Publish, or cause or allow any other Person to write, print or publish any article respecting the connection between me and the Duke, or any Anecdote either written or verbal that may have come to my knowledge from the Duke.

"I also promise that the printer shall enter into an Engagement binding himself in a Penalty that he has delivered up every Manuscript which he may have been entrusted with respecting the intended Publication, and he shall make oath that he has done so. And that he shall on oath deliver all such parts of the said Work as may have been printed.

"I further consent that on failure of my complying with the several stipulations above stated that the Annuity agreed to be paid to myself for my life, and to my Daughters upon my Decease, shall become absolutely forfeited.

"I will deliver up all the Letters but the Manuscript and all that is printed thereof shall be burnt before any person appointed for that purpose.

"I also promise to keep no copy or copies of any of the Duke of York's Letters or of the Manuscript or any part thereof. Dated this first of April, 1809."

Before she signed the agreement, Mrs. Clarke had second thoughts. She had always known that life was tough, and for many years she had lived in a man's world of bluff and hard bargaining. Her jewels were still in pawn, rent and taxes were due on the house in Westbourne Place, she probably had little idea how much she owed the tradesmen, and £7,000 was scarcely a fortune to a woman of her spendthrift habits.

Two days later a codicil was added to the agreement.

MEMORANDUM THIS THIRD DAY OF APRIL, 1809

"The sum of Seven Thousand Pounds agreed to be paid by the above agreement has been increased to the sum of Ten Thousand Pounds which has been paid to me as per my receipt dated this day – The Annuityes hereinbefore mentioned to be granted, are to be granted agreeably to the above Stipulations."

MARY ANNE CLARKE

A receipt was drawn up, signed and sealed, and Mrs. Clarke was solvent once more.

It would have been an intriguing experience to have deluged the country with her life story, to have lived again the experience of being a sensation in an age of scandal, but the Earl of Chichester took possession of her love-letters, and as 18,000 copies of her book were slowly consumed by the flames in Salisbury Court it was like a funeral pyre marking the end of her dreams and aspirations.

Extracting the last ounce of merriment from the incorrigible Mrs. Clarke, the lampoonists depicted her on one knee before the Altar of Repentance contritely committing to the flames "all that gives my Darling pain."

The Newcastle Pottery produced a large earthenware mug satirizing "Burning the Books of Curious Arts", one of which may still be seen in the Henry Willett collection in Brighton Museum. The mug is decorated with caricatures of the Duke and Mrs. Clarke, who holds in her left hand a copy of the agreement consenting to the destruction of her memoirs. "Burn away – I would burn half the Universe for the money," she chortles as the books are piled on the fire. "You may preserve a copy or two for Doctor O'Meira (sic) and a few private friends – Now for my Brimstone Carriage."

The money and mockery mingled uneasily, notoriety merged with caricatured burlesque, and for Mrs. Clarke life was never quite the same again.

Chapter Seventeen

During the inquiry, and for a few days afterwards, Mrs. Clarke was almost a national heroine, having exposed, with unaffected candour, corruption and abuses in high places. Lady Williams Wynn choked with choleric indignation at the idea of a public appeal to recompense Mrs. Clarke for her services to the radical cause.

"Shocked I am to hear that there is actually a subscription opened in the city for purchasing an annuity of £1,000 per ann. for Mrs. Clarke!" she wrote to her daughter-in-law. "That some have already put down their names to £100 and that they give out that sixpences will be received in order that the majority of the people may have the satisfaction of contributing."

Before finally agreeing the terms for the destruction of her memoirs, Mrs. Clarke had approached Wardle urging him to promote a national appeal, but his reply on March 24th dashed all her hopes of any financial support from the politician whom, she claimed, she had raised "from insignificant obscurity to the apex of popular admiration."

"I had hoped that your arrangement about your book would have warded off all present difficulty . . .", Wardle churlishly informed her. "That you deserve well of your country, I believe to be a very general sentiment, but the idea prevails that you are living in splendour, militates forcibly against anything you suggest."

When it became known that she had accepted £10,000 from the government for the suppression of her memoirs, Mrs. Clarke lived in a no-man's land, exiled and execrated by both political parties, and the prospect of a public subscription disappeared in an onslaught of ridicule and gibes.

"Mrs. Clarke in sheets hot pressed," the satirists scoffed as her memoirs were incinerated in Salisbury Court, whilst the lampoonists mocked her with the hostility of Cobbett and his friends:

Mary, Mary,
Quite Contrary,
Who's your Guardian Now?
When injured Belles,
And Patriot-Swells,
Their Malice at you throw.

Amateur poets were fired with venomous anger, and one anonymous author bestowed upon her "a garland" of sixteen scurrilous sonnets:

With Vixien, forth, I walk'd into the Park;
And, as I pac'd along in Rotten Row,
She flew at people, and began to bark:
Angry at which, I bawl'd out "Here, Bitch, ho!"
Now, whether by mistake, I do not know,
But, at that instant, up came Mrs. Clarke.

William Jerdan reported that during the inquiry there had been envy, jealousy, backbiting and all uncharitableness between Wardle, Mrs. Clarke and their associates, and when it was over the disenchantment festered. The dirty linen was dragged out, and, no longer united by a common purpose, animosity ran wild.

The prospect of financial gain prompted Mrs. Clarke to lend her support to the campaign to rout the Duke of York from the Horse Guards, but her attack on Wardle sprang from revenge and taking up her pen she sent the mushroom patriot a furious blast to bring him back to reality again after the heady intoxication of public adulation.

May 14th, 1809.

Dear Sir,

When I sent for you the other day, and you were accompanied by Major Dodd, to enquire what were your intentions with respect to putting your promises into execution, you seemed unwilling to admit that they were made but conditionally; *this I deny.* The only construction I can put upon it is this, that you felt yourself under a heavy responsibility to me, and of which both yourself and Major Dodd thought to get rid of by future promises as futile and evasive;

neither of which ought or can succeed. I will here put you once more in mind of those promises, and of my expectations, which if you value yourselves as men of honour, you cannot but accede to, nor can you think I require anything but what I am fully entitled to; nothing less than five hundred a year, and as my children have been equal sufferers with myself in the public opinion, as being the daughters of so incorrect a mother, they demand from me everything I can or ought to command, and therefore, as five hundred a year for my life, which may be short, would be nothing to them, I think that by letting you off for ten thousand pounds is not half your promises to me. Yet as I feel aware of what you mentioned the other day of not having it in immediate power to accomplish, I expect that you and Major Dodd enter into a joint bond, as you did into joint promises, for ten thousand pounds to be paid me within two years, and till that be accomplished, to pay me the five hundred a year, commencing from March last, and to pay Wright the remainder of his bill.

This is all, and surely it is not half the value of the promises made me, which were these. As my son was then under the protection of the Duke of York, of course he would lose that protection as soon as I began upon the Duke's ruin. He was to have equal protection from the Duke of Kent. I withdrew my son, and I have him now on my hands. The next was a situation for Captain Thompson in some way enough to keep him, *or in the event of the Duke of Kent coming in as Commander-in-Chief to get him reinstated in the army*. He remains as he was!!! The next, the payment of the arrears of annuity, as promised me by the Duke of York, and the annuity to be continued to me during my life of four hundred per annum. My debts to be paid, those contracted while I lived with the Duke of York, and those since.

The debt of twelve hundred pounds, which is owing to Mr. Comrie, for which he stops my jewels and furniture.

My present house and furniture to be paid for, of which a part only is paid by you and Dodd.

Now let me ask you if the ten thousand pounds is equal to half these promises, and for the fulfilment of each you pledged yourself in the most solemn manner to see performed, and to which I paid the most implicit confidence and belief, or why did I resist and expose during the investigation, the overtures made me by Williams of whatever sum that I might ask for being ready for my acceptance, to make me affluent for life. Think upon this. I shall add but little more, but even were this sum to come out of your *own* pocket, the character you have acquired *through my means* would not be more than I am fully entitled to.

I remain, Dear Sir,
Yours, etc., etc.
M. A. Clarke.

Whilst living with the Duke, Mrs. Clarke had spent £2,600 on furniture with Francis Wright, the upholsterer of Rathbone Place, and still owed him £500. When she moved to Westbourne Place in November, 1808, she had decided that in return for her evidence in the House of Commons supporting Wardle's charges of corruption against the Duke of York, Wardle should have the privilege of paying the remainder of Wright's bill, as well as furnishing her new home in appropriate style and elegance. It was a simple matter to persuade Francis Wright that she had found a new and wealthy protector.

From time to time Wardle and Dodd had accompanied her to Wright's warehouse, and during December, January and February, an expensive selection of furniture and fittings arrived at Westbourne Place. A handsome sideboard was delivered, and two Grecian couches costing a hundred guineas each; curtains for the drawing-room at £100, and a set of dining chairs; a large mirror, three writing desks, and a lamp at eighteen guineas.

At the beginning of June, Wardle received a bill from Francis Wright for £1,919 14s. 2d.

Of an inherently mean disposition, and financially dependent upon his wife, Wardle was not the man to be intimidated by Mrs. Clarke's predatory designs. It still rankled that she had excluded him from the negotiations for the suppression of her memoirs, for which she had received £10,000, and she was quite capable, he decided, of paying for her own furniture.

When Wardle refused to pay Francis Wright for her furniture and fittings, Mrs. Clarke's fury knew no bounds. She had played her part in exposing the Duke of York in the House of Commons and, now that he no longer needed her, Wardle had repudiated his promises of financial support. She was determined that he should not escape so easily, and effectively deploying her powers of persuasion she prevailed upon Francis Wright to take Wardle to court for debt.

There was nothing that Mrs. Clarke enjoyed more than stirring up the dust, and the thought of bringing Wardle publicly to his knees was an exciting distraction. As the principal witness for Francis Wright, she would scintillate in a court of law as she had done in the House of Commons. Once again there would be the éclat and the ballyhoo, and if in the process she killed the radical hopes of reform by publicly admitting that she had been bribed to testify against the Commander-in-Chief, what was that to her?

The case of Wright v Gwyllym Lloyd Wardle, Esq., was heard before Lord Ellenborough and a special jury on Monday, July 3rd, 1809, at the Court of King's Bench in Westminster Hall, and Mrs. Clarke arrived with her usual gaiety, fashionably dressed in a spotted muslin cloak lined with pink silk, and a white muslin gown. She wore a white handkerchief tied loosely round her neck, the newspaper reporters busily noted, primrose-coloured gloves, and her silk hat was trimmed with ribbons and a veil.

The appearance of Sir Vicary Gibbs, the Attorney-General, as counsel for Francis Wright, provoked excited comment. "His performances," declared Henry Brougham, "were rated at the most exorbitant value," but it was common knowledge that it was Mrs. Clarke, and not the upholsterer Wright, who was to pay for his services.

There was a strong impression, too, that party politics had induced the Attorney-General to pit himself against Wardle, the man who four months earlier had brought the government to the brink of defeat. Vicary Gibbs never successfully adapted his legal talents to the rigours of the political arena, and in the House of Commons Wardle had emerged the victor.

In Westminster Hall, Vicary Gibbs was meeting on his own ground the adversary that he had failed to defeat upon his, and if he could prove that Mrs. Clarke had been bribed to testify against the Duke it would be an end to Wardle's brief hour as the champion of reform.

Serjeant Best appeared as Wardle's counsel, and he asked Mrs. Clarke to tell him how she and Wardle came together. "Was it in consequence of a correspondence with M'Callum that you became acquainted with Colonel Wardle?" he enquired.

"Yes, if you call one letter a correspondence," Mrs. Clarke snapped back.

"I was to give Colonel Wardle every assistance and information in my power respecting the inquiry he was about to institute," she maintained, "and in return he was to furnish my house . . . He was with me daily. He was ever coming without any invitation. He ran over the house from the kitchen to the garret."

On one occasion when Wardle went with her to Rathbone Place, she said, Francis Wright was in bed following an accident, but she introduced Wardle to Wright's brother, Daniel, as the man who was to pay for her furniture.

"Colonel Wardle made no reply when you said he was to furnish the house?" commented Vicary Gibbs.

"No, why should he?" Mrs. Clarke replied promptly. "He went on purpose to give his credit."

"Colonel Wardle accompanied me to Wright's several times," she continued, "and once or twice went in with me. Once, in particular, he and Major Dodd accompanied me. They did not approve of the pattern of a carpet which had been sent in for the drawing-room. I chose a blue and white; Colonel Wardle chose a scarlet and bronze. At last, as I could not bring him to my taste, I observed in the presence of Wright, 'Well, as you are to pay, I'll take what you please'."

One day a large mirror was delivered to Westbourne Place, but Wardle protested that as there was already a large lustre in the room the mirror was unnecessary. "He was in a great passion," remarked Mrs. Clarke, "so much so that the man nearly dropped it . . . Upon this occasion he observed that Wright would not be so ready to send things in if he did not know that he was to be his paymaster."

For the first time the public heard how Wardle, Dodd and Glennie had taken Mrs. Clarke with them on a four-day visit to the Martello Towers at the end of November, 1808. "At the time I had several friends about me," Mrs. Clarke maintained, "and Colonel Wardle was afraid they could persuade me not to give the evidence he wanted, and he therefore took me out of the way."

Two or three weeks later, it was alleged, Mrs. Clarke informed Wardle that Wright was insistently demanding money, and implored him to help her. Wardle discussed the matter with Major Dodd, who arranged for his wine merchant in Pall Mall to pay Wright £500, which Wardle and Dodd re-paid to the wine merchant in equal shares. This circuitous arrangement was agreed upon, it was said, so that there should be no trace of any direct payment to Francis Wright by either Colonel Wardle or Major Dodd which, if discovered, would reveal that Mrs. Clarke had been bribed to appear in the House of Commons as Wardle's principal witness.

Again and again the Attorney-General urged Wardle's counsel to call Major Dodd. "I repeat this challenge," Sir Vicary persisted, "because if they do call Major Dodd I shall make him confirm my witnesses, and if he does not come it will make my case still stronger."

Major Dodd never arrived, and in his summing-up Lord Ellenborough told the jury that Wardle would deny at his peril the circumstances of the money paid to Wright through the wine merchant in Pall Mall. He complained also that in his bill Wright had included the cost of insurance, carpenters, bricklayers, painters, plasterers, ironmongery and coal, which the Attorney-General agreed should be struck out.

The jury returned with their verdict at nine o'clock at night after deliberating for an hour and a half. Wardle, they decided, should pay Wright £1,095 8s. 6d. for the furniture supplied to Mrs. Clarke, and costs amounting to £1,194.

Success was a potent draught to Mrs. Clarke. In less than six months she had unseated the Duke of York as Commander-in-Chief of the army, and toppled the mountebank Wardle from "the apex of popular admiration".

There was little time, however, to savour her triumph – and still less to reflect that revenge is sweet only in the imagination – as two days later, with his integrity ridiculed and his popularity shattered, Wardle issued a frantic

"APPEAL TO THE PEOPLE OF THE UNITED KINGDOM"

Honoured as my Parliamentary conduct has been by the approbation of so many of my countrymen, I feel myself called upon, in consequence of an event that yesterday took place, immediately to address you . . .

The detail of the evidence the public prints will afford. It is with me to state that my Counsel, satisfied in their own minds that the jury would not, upon such testimony as had been given by the plaintiff's brother and Mrs. Clarke alone, find a verdict against me, did not comply with my *earnest entreaty, repeated to them in writing during the trial in the strongest terms,* that Major Dodd and Mr. Glennie and other respectable witnesses might be examined, as I knew their testiomony would be founded in truth, and in direct contradicition to what had been sworn against me . . .

There only remains for me, before God and my country, to

declare that it was obtained by *perjury alone,* and I do pledge myself to prove that fact at the earliest moment the forms of the law will allow me to do so . . ."

G. L. WARDLE

James Street,
July 4th, 1809.

His friends were dismayed, the public scoffed, and Mrs. Clarke awoke to the fact that going to law is a beginning and not always an end. For ten days she lay low, and then hit back with contemptuous condescension.

TO THE PEOPLE OF THE UNITED KINGDOM

Honoured as my testimony before the House of Commons has been with the confidence of the country at large, and sanctioned as my evidence has been in a recent instance by a jury of my Countrymen, I feel myself called upon – after affording time for the most deliberate reflection – to address you . . .

Colonel Wardle, inflated by a popularity the extent of which was as unexpected as it will be found to have been undeserved, has vainly flattered himself that this same popularity would protect him against the justice of his country. Disappointed at the verdict, he has lost his prudence with his temper, and without giving himself time for reflection, has made an unusual appeal to the People of the United Kingdom against the verdict of a jury.

If he had been content to throw the blame of his failure upon Counsel, it would have been no business of mine, they are able to defend themselves, but to be charged with a crime so disgraceful, so low, so contemptible, and by a person who of all men best knows how abhorrent to my nature is anything like falsehood – to be charged with perjury is really too bad.

It only remains for me to declare before God and my country that the evidence I gave was strictly true, and that my intimacy with Colonel Wardle merely related to my evidence and his promises.

Most anxiously, therefore, do I look forward to the period when the futility of Colonel Wardle's attempts to prove the contrary will recoil upon himself and others. I trust that till then the public will suspend their judgment upon Colonel Wardle's intemperate accusation . . .

I have the honour to be,
With the greatest respect,
M. A. Clarke

Like most people of a combative disposition, spoiling for a fight at every opportunity, Mrs. Clarke effervesced with animation and inexhaustible energy when she was herself the aggressor, but when attacked she fumed, protested, and blazed with indignation. A few days after Wardle publicly announced that he was charging her with perjury, she also found herself facing another attack from a totally unexpected quarter.

On March 27th, Huxley Sandon petitioned Parliament for his release from Newgate. He had served in the army for thirty-two years, and pleaded that in a fall over a precipice on horseback "he had received so severe a contusion on his head that his faculties had been materially impaired, and his recollection greatly weakened."

The Speaker discharged him with icy condemnation. "You have closed a long career of corrupt practices with disgrace and infamy," he said, and ten days later Sandon was cashiered on Cabinet advice.

Immediately after Wardle's overthrow by the upholsterer Wright, Sandon announced that he was commencing proceedings against Mrs. Clarke for obtaining money under false pretences by promising the Duke of York's support for Colonel French's levy.

"Such a trial must give rise to much curious discussion," commented one newspaper editor laconically.

The time had come, Mrs. Clarke decided, temporarily to remove herself from the London battleground of litigation and abuse, but the newspapers continued to track her down, and in July reported her at Cowes, "living quite privately with her family." Before leaving London, and from her sequestered refuge on the Isle of Wight, she dashed off letter after letter of colourful comment to Lord Folkestone at his home in Harley Street.

Married at twenty-two, and widowed four years later, Lord Folkestone was a rising radical politician of twenty-nine when introduced to Mrs. Clarke by Colonel Wardle at the beginning of the inquiry, and with her eye firmly fixed on men and the main chance, Mrs. Clarke found him an attractive proposition.

Writing in his diary on December 11th, 1809, Thomas Greevey confided that Lord Folkestone had been induced by Mrs. Clarke to believe that Wardle was an agent of the Duke of Kent, and that in that capacity he had bound himself by promises to be of great service to her, which he afterwards forfeited.

At this point, Sir Herbert Maxwell, the editor of the Creevey manuscripts, interjected a bizarre note of mystery and speculation.

"Creevey goes on to state in terms too little equivocal for modern taste," he wrote with censorious prudery in 1906, "that Lord Folkestone admitted that he had a liaison with Mrs. Clarke while she was under the protection of the Duke of York – a circumstance only worthy of record as throwing light upon the character of the woman who cost His Royal Highness so dearly."

Thanks to the kind co-operation of Major John Blackett Ord, the present owner of the Creevey diaries, it is now possible to elucidate this tantalizing omission, and he confirms that the following are the only words not quoted verbatim by Sir Herbert Maxwell: "In the course of this meeting, Folkestone confides to Western* and myself that he has slept with Mrs. Clarke."

This editorial omission by Sir Herbert Maxwell is an odd example of Edwardian hypocrisy, and Sir Herbert also endeavoured to cast further odium upon Mrs. Clarke by asserting that her intimacy with Lord Folkestone took place whilst she was living with the Duke of York, when, in fact, it could only have occurred either during the inquiry or immediately afterwards.

To be arraigned by Wardle for perjury rankled bitterly with Mrs. Clarke, and in her letters to Lord Folkestone she employed all possible persuasiveness and cunning to sow the seeds of dissension and animosity between the two men.

My Lord,

As you have hitherto held yourself so properly respecting Mr. Wardle and myself by not interfering *keep so still*. As you did not know anything of our concerns at the time you assisted him *you cannot now*. By any interference yourself and friends might create some sort of dislike and odium to which you are not entitled.

I am My Lord with the same sentiments as ever,

Your Most Obedient and Humble Servant,

M. A. Clarke

Still seething with indignation at Wardle's effrontery at charging her with perjury, and perhaps afraid of being convicted, Mrs. Clarke informed Lord Folkestone in unmistakable language what she would like to do with this intolerable Welshman.

---

* Charles Callis, Baron Western – 1767–1844.

Monday.

My Lord,

I have to thank you for not forgetting me. I am glad no one has written you upon the subject, indeed as for Wardle, how can he? Of all things on earth nothing could wound my feelings more than being obliged to go into a Court of Justice. Wardle, who owed me more than any other, was the person, too, that did it . . .

By his own conduct *alone* has he ruined himself as he charges me with perjury. I cannot now think of quitting London till all is finished, and my character cleaned up. I have now a most difficult and dangerous picture of it – it is in the interest of each party to ruin me. I have only to trust to that which bore me through before – TRUTH.

I cannot see that the situation of the Duke of York is at all benefited by what Wardle negotiated with me – for I was not to be paid for *Lies* but *Truth,* and what difference could it make if I was to be made comfortable by giving my evidence against him? Everything I said was corroborated by others – if I had my will of Wardle I would have him dipped in a horse pond for his conduct in subpoenaing me.

I think I must now publish the whole affair and *convince* the world, for I flatter myself they will believe me, that the Duke of Kent is as great a wretch as his brother York; as soon as he has sucked the orange he throws away the rind.

I hope Cobbett will not abuse me; I do not deserve it. I wish it was pointed out to me publicly what course I ought to pursue . . . The only thing to be said for me is that I jumped from the frying pan into the fire. Your seal was not broken. I must now be careful of writing to anyone as a letter might be turned and twisted against me, but to Lord Folkestone I need have no fear.

Yours truly obliged,

M. A. Clarke

Lord Folkestone was a young and highly respected nobleman and it is clear from her letters that Mrs. Clarke was extremely agitated at the thought that he might be induced to support Wardle's charge of perjury. Before leaving London for the Isle of Wight, she again wrote to Lord Folkestone, artfully endeavouring to engender a rift between Wardle and his radical colleagues.

My Lord,

You see what a pretty sort of fool as well as knave Wardle has turned out to be! The more he writes the more he will commit himself. Of course I shall be quiet for the sake of myself and all for the present. I am sure Burdett, your Lordship, and Whitbread will be heartily ashamed of him. He will get himself into such a scrape if he goes on that I should not much wonder but he gets expelled the House. Let me advise one thing to you – *not to write to him,* or to anyone else about him but as little as possible. Of course you can know nothing but from Public Report. The mean little knave has spoiled the whole of the cause and the people had need now to execrate him – all this for the sake of a few hundreds of which he knew he must pay. There are more than five more witnesses to prove his ordering but it was deemed unnecessary to call them – of course the cause is gone as it will be said I was a bribed witness and ought not to be credited. I have not common patience with him.

Adieu! Adieu!

The weather is very bad. I shall leave London in the course of next week.

Wednesday,
Westbourne Place.

As a result of her disclosures, Mrs. Clarke had made many enemies, and at the end of August she wrote to Lord Folkestone asking him to intercede for her with a Colonel Pigot. This is the only occasion on which Colonel Pigot crosses Mrs. Clarke's path, and it has not been possible to discover anything about their quarrel. The National Army Museum records for 1809 contain particulars of Colonel Richard Pigot serving with the 21st Light Dragoons, and Colonel Henry Pigot (also spelt Pigote) of the 82nd Foot Regiment, but which of them Mrs. Clarke wished to placate it is impossible to say.

Cowes, Isle of Wight.
August 26.

My Lord,

Somehow Colonel Pigot has taken it into his head I meant to injure him. (As) I do not wish to lose his friendship the object of my troubling you now is to ask you to write him and say what you please and what you know upon the subject and to tell him I desired it – he will believe what you say and I shall feel happier by his being made acquainted. I mean and always did well toward him. I have come to this place to be quiet till my friend Wardle makes his attack upon my honour.

Your Most Obedient Humble Servant,

M. A. Clarke

Lord Folkestone does not appear to have been prepared to take the full responsibility for patching up Mrs. Clarke's altercation with Colonel Pigot. He seems to have suggested that she should write to the Colonel herself, and send the letter to him to add a few lines of support to her protestations of friendship and goodwill.

Cowes I. of W.
Thurs. evn.

My Lord,

You are very good and very squeamish. Pray write me half dozen lines in Pigot's letter and believe me –

Yours very obediently,
M. A. C.

I hear but do not know nor do I care, that Wardle's indictment will not lay. This is from a counsellor who has ten guineas but he is a friend and thought it would relieve my mind by his making a breach of secrecy but it does not for I had no fears. This is confidential tho' to you my Lord – so adieu.

Mrs. Clarke was not Lord Folkestone's only correspondent, and in September he received from Wardle a querulous letter of recrimination and rebuke.

Dear Lord Folkestone,

I have to acknowledge the receipt of the box of papers and the honour of your Lordship's letter.

Your Lordship is now doubtless aware that I am acquainted with the circumstances of your having been an adviser in the negotiation for the suppression of the Letters Mrs. Clarke was about to publish from the commencement of it to the conclusion, and your Lordship must be equally aware that I had no concern in the promoting or suppressing that publication. It may I think have occurred to your Lordship that in candour I ought to have been informed that such a negotiation was going on, and I certainly did not dream that your Lordship would have sanctioned the concealment of it, especially as there was on my part throughout the Investigation an unreserved communication of every circumstance connected with the transactions of the Duke of York and Mrs. Clarke. I have good reason to know, and at a future day will divulge to your Lordship, how I came to know it, that it has been a leading object with Mrs. Clarke to create a variance between us . . .

Tho' I could not be blind to your Lordship's altered Manners, still I did hope, without my directly seeking it, that an opportunity might present itself for mutual explanation. Whilst waiting in this hope, Sir Richard Phillips, to whom I was only known at the public dinner, was accidentally brought to me by a friend of his, and to my astonishment and regret I learned that, considering your Lordship as my friend, he had entrusted to you, for my information, a circumstance that surely could not fail to be felt by your Lordship as one most important immediately to be known to me, and since that period it has been suggested to me that your Lordship, instead of communicating the fact entrusted to you for me, apprized Mrs. Clarke of the circumstance . . .

It is material to me, as relating to the prosecution I am now instituting, to know minutely the whole of what took place from the commencement of the negotiation for the suppression of Mrs. Clarke's intended publication to its conclusion, and especially what money was paid or agreed to be paid, by whom, for what purpose, and in what manner it was paid and secured, and who were or are intended to be the parties to the Deeds of Security. Your Lordship has it in his power to give me the information and it is with yourself to communicate or withhold it as you see right . . .

Your very obedient and humble servant,

I have the honour to be,

Dear Lord Folkestone,

Gw. Ll. Wardle.

It seems likely that Lord Folkestone had agreed to be either a Trustee or Guarantor in the complex legalities for the suppression of Mrs. Clarke's memoirs, and now alarmed at Wardle's demand to be informed of the full arrangements made, he appears to have written at once to Mrs. Clarke asking to be released from his undertaking. She replied by return confirming that she had asked her lawyer to make the necessary deletion.

Cowes,
My Lord, September 20th.

I have just received your letter and today I write by the same post to Comrie to inform him your Lordship's name must be scratched out if inserted, and that I will defer having the settlement made till I am in London and shall get another.

We are all very well and obliged by your enquiries.

I have the honour to be my Lord,
Your obliged and Obedient,
M. A. Clarke.

The additional lines to Pigot did extremely well. I have not had a single line from anyone about my esteemed friend Wardle and all that I know about him or myself on the score of Law is from the papers – I thought it best to let him proceed quietly.

In the Department of Manuscripts of the British Museum is a copy of an intriguing letter written by Mrs. Clarke from Cowes on July 20th, 1809, and sent to Lord Liverpool "as a characteristic specimen of the writer's style and ingenuity." No information is given about her correspondent, and the name of the man she wished to entice was suppressed "in honour and fairness".

Dear Sir,

I sent the letter you was kind enough to enclose and guess the Baronet would find you one in return which would answer the purpose.

I have hit on a Plan which if you think well of proposing, or being the bearer of a letter to your friend and Patron Mr. A., might put you in a way of exercising your abilities in your profession, and otherwise make you comfortable. If put into practise, or not, you will see the confidence I place in you by penning it, and of course it must ever be a secret to ourselves.

I want to cut out Mrs. Lucy, but privately, and if I were once or twice in your Patron's company, *I am certain of succeeding.* Now, if he as your friend will take you a small house and furnish it, which will not cost him more than five hundred pounds (and what is that trifle to him?) I will be either your *Lodger, Inmate* or *Patient,* and for which I will pay you as much as will enable Mrs. M., with her economy, to keep your house and you shall have the use of my carriage to do as you like with, for a Doctor is nothing without one. All I want, for I am independent, is your friend's

Interest in one affair of mine, and this is not to be gained without, what I said before, *making myself very pleasant* and all that.

All he has to do, *with your permission,* is to call once or twice a week when it is dusk to play a game or two at piquet, or any other game His Worship may be *au fait* at.

His notice of you thus must insure some success, and I have a higher friend than him in a Corner, but he is not a lover, yet the sting of your Patron would, I think, bring him about again.

Think of this well, will you? and fail not writing me tomorrow. And will you take a walk and leave this where directed for

Yours truly,
M. A. Clarke

Your Patron could not meet with such a Disinterested offer every day – he is old now you know – but it is so pleasant to have a great man or two snug.

The reference to her correspondent as a doctor, and to Mrs. M. keeping house, suggest that the letter was probably written to sixty-six year old Dr. Metcalf, who had superseded Dr. Thynne as Mrs. Clarke's medical adviser. Is it possible that His Worship was the Lord Chief Justice, Lord Ellenborough, and that a *tête-à-tête* in the lamplight, as the piquet cards were shuffled and dealt, Mrs. Clarke proposed to enlist his sympathy and support at her approaching trial on Wardle's charge of perjury?

The trial opened on December 10th, and excitement ran high at the prospect of further revelations as Wardle and Mrs. Clarke engaged once more in public combat. By six o'clock people began to gather outside Westminster Hall, and at day-break there was a stampede into the courtroom and every place was immediately occupied.

Lord Ellenborough arrived at ten, and beside him on the bench sat the Dukes of York, Kent and Gloucester, and Lords Moira and Chichester.

In an age when female mendacity and sexual immorality were almost indissolubly linked in the public mind, Wardle's counsel began by reminding the specially empanelled jury of Mrs. Clarke's reckless career of promiscuity. "She has lived under the protection of English, of Irish, and of Scotchmen," he declared, "of navy agents, and of army agents, of persons in and out of Parliament, of Lords and commons. By her art and machinations she wormed herself into the bosom of a royal Duke, where, like the viper in the fable, she had forgotten all his indulgences and all his fostering care, and had treacherously and ungratefully stung her preserver."

In July, on behalf of Francis Wright, the Attorney-General had successfully prosecuted Wardle for debt, and now, in December, Mrs. Clarke had engaged Sir Vicary Gibbs to defend her against Wardle's allegation of perjury. The Attorney-General strenuously cross-examined Wardle about the promises he made to Mrs. Clarke on the excursion to the Martello Towers.

"I wish to know whether in any of your conversations with Mrs. Clarke, the name of the Duke of Kent was mentioned, either by yourself or Major Dodd."

"The name of the Duke of Kent was never mentioned in the presence of Mrs. Clarke, either by Major Dodd or myself, as attached to any promises whatever."

"Did you ever give Mrs. Clarke any money?"

"I did, before she went out of town, to pay the butcher and the baker. I gave her about £100, and after our return about £20 more."

"You have stated that you gave her £100. Did you give her any promises besides?"

"None, but that if she would be a steady friend to the public, I would be a steady friend to her, and there would be no doubt that for any services she might render the public, the public would reward her."

"Can you mean gravely to say that no other promises were held out to her but public acknowledgments as a great and public benefactress?"

"I made her none other whatever."

Wardle had not called Major Dodd in July to corroborate his testimony, probably in the hope of shielding him from public invective and private retribution, but, by December, Dodd was no longer confidential secretary to the Duke of Kent, and Vicary Gibbs harried him relentlessly to explain the incriminating expedition with Mrs. Clarke to inspect the south coast defences.

"I ask you, and do you mean to put your credit upon it, do you mean to say that she did not know that you were private secretary to the Duke of Kent?"

"I do not know whether she did or she did not. She may or she may not."

"So you were several days in her company – you were spending whole days together – and now do you mean to say she did not know it?"

"She knew it in the course of the journey," Dodd conceded.

"Had you any conversation about the intended inquiry?"

"Our conversation chiefly related to the disturbances at Gibraltar."

"I think she borrowed a little of your money, too. Pray how long had you known her before she borrowed money of you?"

"Not long."

"She spared you longer than she did Colonel Wardle. Pray how much did she hit you for?"

"I lent her £5."

"Did you know that £100 was lent her by Colonel Wardle to pay her butcher and baker just before she went on the journey with you?"

"No, I can't say that I did."

"Colonel Wardle, you know, is a family man, you could not think he gave it to her for any improper purposes. What did you understand he gave her the money for?"

"I understood it was to pay her butcher and baker, otherwise she could not accompany us," Dodd admitted.

"Was it a gift or a loan?"

"I should comprehend it was a gift."

"Was it not the impression upon your mind at the time that nothing could be more repugnant to the feelings of the Duke of Kent than that such charges should be made against his royal brother, and do you not know that such have been the uniform sentiments of His Royal Highness?"

"I do."

"Had you at that time constant access to His Royal Highness, and were you not backwards and forwards from Westbourne Place to the presence of His Royal Highness, and from His Royal Highness to Westbourne Place, at that time?"

"Yes, I was frequently at Westbourne Place and with His Royal Highness."

"Did you ever inform His Royal Highness that you were engaged upon this business?"

"No, I did not."

"Did he know that you were daily consulted upon it?"

"No."

"Had his royal mind the least reason to suspect that his private and confidential secretary was engaged in such a business, and did you still continue in his service? Was it consistent with honour and delicacy towards your royal master?"

"I thought it would have been indelicate to have mentioned the subject to His Royal Highness," was all Major Dodd could offer in explanation.

Of the three men who accompanied Mrs. Clarke on her visit to the south coast in November, 1808, the part played by James Glennie is the most ambiguous. He had been dismissed from the Royal Artillery by the Duke of Richmond and, although now employed as a mathematical instructor at the Royal Military Academy, Woolwich, he was undoubtedly an embittered man with a disposition for intrigue and reprisal. He did not agree with his friend Major Dodd that the conversation on the trip to the Martello Towers was confined entirely to the disturbances at Gibraltar nearly six years earlier.

"I tell you in very plain terms," he informed the Attorney-General, "I took down a number of memorandums of what Mrs. Clarke told me of things the Duke of York told her about his own family."

"Then in order that you might not forget them, you wrote them down?"

"I did."

"You did not omit to register or record everything she said?"

"I don't know what you mean by registering or recording. I only took notes, and I thought I had a right to do so. They were very entertaining. Some of them related to making baronets and peers, and carving out districts for generals."

Lord Ellenborough could contain himself no longer. "Common decency and feeling should have induced this man to avoid such enquiries, rather than to seek an exposition so scandalous and defamatory," he interjected, and James Glennie was promptly instructed to leave the witness box before he could comment further on Mrs. Clarke's ribaldry.

Wardle, Dodd and Glennie were an unconvincing trio, but it was the Attorney-General's surprise move in producing Mrs. Clarke's lawyer, Mr. Stokes, that carried the day.

Wardle, Mr. Stokes maintained, had consulted him during the inquiry about calling Francis Wright to the House of Commons to substantiate Mrs. Clarke's evidence, but that he had advised him not to do so in case Wright admitted when cross-examined that

Wardle was to pay for her furniture, when the accusation of bribery from the Government benches would have had disastrous consequences.

Leigh Hunt did not find Mr. Stokes an impressive witness. "Nothing else shall be said but what is known to everybody, viz. that he is a Prostitute's Attorney," he exploded, but in the jury box they entertained no such reservations.

It was late at night before Lord Ellenborough completed his summing-up, and after deliberating for six minutes without retiring the foreman of the jury announced that Mrs. Clarke, they unanimously agreed, was "Not Guilty" of perjury.

For Wardle it was almost the end. He was in serious financial difficulties, and when Parliament was dissolved in 1812 he retired to farm at Southborough, a small Kentish town almost equidistant between Tonbridge and Tunbridge Wells. The Tonbridge parish rate books confirm that he lived in the western part of the town at Culverden House, now known as Great Culverden Farm, and that he remained there for the next eleven years.

Mrs. Clarke wasted no words on Wardle's downfall, and when a friend enquired what had become of him, she dismissed the perfidious Welshman with epigrammatic contempt! "Oh the wretch", she cried, "he has taken to selling milk about Tunbridge*".

* Until around 1900, Tunbridge was invariably spelled with a 'u', but about that time it was generally agreed that Tonbridge should use the 'o', and Tunbridge Wells the 'u'. The old parish of Tunbridge was an exceptionally large one, and included almost all of what is now Tunbridge Wells.

Chapter Eighteen

As reckless with money as any gambler at the faro or baccarat tables at Crockford's, White's or Brooke's, the £10,000 Mrs. Clarke received for the destruction of her reminiscences soon began to ebb away. Rents and taxes were owing, and £1,200 to her lawyer to reclaim her jewels which he had been holding as security; gifts for her family and friends, clothes for herself; the tradesmen to be paid, the balance to Francis Wright, and the exorbitant fee demanded by Sir Vicary Gibbs.

No more was heard of Huxley Sandon's threatened prosecution, and early in 1810, Mrs. Clarke decided to abandon the large, fashionable house in Westbourne Place for an unpretentious cottage in the country at Putney. There was, as always, the need to economise, but of even weightier importance, after a year of turmoil and conflict, was the restless longing to move on in search of new faces and fresh opportunities. Life was a game of chance, and this time, who knew, the ace of trumps and jack of hearts might both be hers.

Her notoriety had also recoiled upon her in a totally unexpected way, leaving her friendless and alone, ostracized by both political parties, the butt of the private joke and the target for the vulgar sallies of the lampoonists, and her isolation at Westbourne Place was an intolerable reminder of the price to be paid for publicising her egocentric life of promiscuity and extortion.

She writhed, too, at the mortification of being forcibly denied the right of regaling the public with her love-letters, and anecdotes of the sexual habits and indiscretions of the royal house of Hanover. Money was a means and not an end, and what remained of the £10,000 was a poor substitute for the splurge she might have made by publishing her memoirs.

If the Government had placed the Duke of York beyond her reach, the Duke of Kent, Wardle, Dodd, Glennie and Croker enjoyed no such immunity, and her exhilaration grew at the prospect of a few more heads rolling in the dust.

Inherently articulate and impelled with animosity, her pen flew over the paper, and in the summer of 1810, under the provocative title of "The Rival Princes", appeared a two-volume narrative "relating to Mrs. M. A. Clarke's Political Acquaintance with Colonel Wardle, Major Dodd, etc. . . . together with a Variety of Authentic and Important Letters, and Curious and Interesting Anecdotes of Several Persons of Political Notoriety."

The Duke of Kent, she claimed, was hand-in-glove with Wardle and Dodd, and Wardle, she said, had informed her that he and Dodd would hold themselves responsible for the Duke of Kent paying her £5,000, an annuity of £400, discharging all her debts, and providing a house furnished in any style and elegance she pleased.

In July, 1809, when Dodd's part in the investigation became public knowledge, the Duke of Kent had put a series of questions to his private secretary. His questions and Dodd's replies were attested by a peer of the realm and privately circulated among the royal family.

Mrs. Clarke's allegations stung the Duke to action, and as a counter-blast the questions and answers were now printed and disseminated for public consumption:

Question: Have I ever expressed to you any sentiment which could induce you to believe that I approved of what was brought forward in Parliament against the Duke of York, or of any proceedings tending to his disgrace?

Dodd to Duke: I have heard your Royal Highness lament the business, and you have made the same communication to me in writing.

Question: Have you ever expressed yourself, in words or writing, either to Colonel Wardle or Mrs. Clarke, or to any other person connected with the Investigation of the Duke of York's conduct, in any way that could give them reason to suppose I either approved the measure or would countenance those concerned in bringing it forward?

Dodd to Duke: Never, but I have on the contrary expressed myself that your Royal Highness would have a very different feeling.

Question: During the ten years you have been my Secretary, when, in the most confidential moments, I have given vent to my wounded feelings on professional subjects, did you hear me express myself inimical to the Duke of York, or that I entertained an expectation of raising myself by his fall?

Dodd to Duke: Never! On the contrary I have heard your Royal Highness frequently express yourself very differently.

In spite of the Duke's protestations, it is stretching credulity too far to believe him guiltless. The feud between the two brothers had been long and bitter, and the Duke of Kent was not the man either to forgive or forget. Mrs. Clarke was well aware that neither Wardle nor Dodd were men of substance or money, and would never have agreed to join them unless convinced that having lost the protection of one Prince she was gaining the financial support of another.

She admitted, too, in a passage of shattering candour, that it was the prospect of financial reward alone that prompted her to support Wardle's charge of corruption.

"I am of opinion that there is not a person in England, at all acquainted with the proceedings of the House of Commons, with respect to the Duke of York and my connection with Wardle and his party, who is so credulous as to believe what Colonel Wardle has lately endeavoured to make the people of England credit as a divine revelation; namely, that I incurred the exposure of myself, children, and family, together with abuse, anxiety of mind, and fatigue of person during my examination in Parliament, from a pure patriotic zeal to serve the public.

"If there should be a person in the country that indulges such an opinion of my patriotism, he must be the most insane, or the most weak man that ever lived . . .

"If I were to tell the same gross falsehood which has issued from the immaculate Colonel Wardle, and compliment myself on having appeared against the Duke of York, without any motives of interest beyond the gratification of serving the public, I am sure the intelligent reader would consider me a most impudent hypocrite, and with great justice, for if I had not been well satisfied of receiving the remuneration agreed upon, not all the Jacobinical parties in Europe should have introduced my letters and person to the notice of Parliament."

No book of denigration makes enjoyable reading and, despite flashes of wit, Mrs. Clarke's subjective style, as she raced along hell-bent on revenege, is an unpalatable obstacle for the reader seeking an authentic account of the origins and background of the inquiry into the conduct of the Duke of York.

Wardle and Lord Folkestone had resolved their differences since the previous summer, and seething with anger at Lord Folkestone's betrayal, Mrs. Clarke attacked him with vindictive bitterness.

"I regret exceedingly that I have mistaken the character of this young nobleman. The reader will see that I have hitherto thought him above the creatures who led me into public notice, but as I find myself deceived, and am now satisfied that he suffers political furor, or the smell of gunpowder, to tarnish the man of honour and the gentleman, I feel justified in shewing the political Lord Folkestone in Colonel Wardle's coat!

"If he be not ashamed to send to me on the event of a challenge, I will readily attend him as a second, and should he at all tremble, I will guide his arm, and pull the trigger, and let it be remembered that if Dodd and Wardle fall in the conflict the world has got rid of two imposters, and the survivor has lost his character for having lent his support to such men.

"As I am not fond of much trouble in these matters, I hope they will choose Wimbledon Common,* as being political ground, which may inspire courage, and not take me far from home."

In 1810 a gossip-conscious public eagerly paid their money for "The Rival Princes" to see what Mrs. Clarke would have to say about it all. For a few weeks it was at the top of everybody's reading list, and there seemed no sphere in which she could not put her talents to work and emerge triumphant. It made no difference that Cobbett rose in furious indignation to declare that "a more flagrant catch-penny never issued from the shop of a low and greedy bookseller."

General Sir David Dundas had superseded the Duke of York as Commander-in-Chief, although Sir Arthur Wellesley believed the appointment to be very much against the wishes of the King's ministers. There was, however, the overriding advantage that at seventy-four he could be quickly and quietly superannuated when it was possible to reinstate the Duke of York. It was also believed that, with the connivance of the King, the army was as much under the command of the Duke after his resignation as it had been before.

On May 25th, 1811, the Duke of York was officially reinstated, and once again the satirists raked out the old scandal and commemorated the occasion in their own derisive style.

---

* No doubt a reference to the duel fought between George Canning and Lord Castlereagh on Putney Heath on September 21st, 1809.

With the berobed figure of the Prince Regent leading the way, George Cruikshank depicted "The Return to Office", with the Duke astride the shoulders of the elderly and decrepit General Dundas, with Perceval running obsequiously ahead clearing the way with a broom. Wardle lies on his back, whilst a perky little dog with Mrs. Clarke's head cleverly superimposed and one leg cocked, stands over him, urinating.

Before the year was out, Mrs. Clarke decided that the time had come for a more permanent and befitting record of her likeness, and in November commissioned the head and shoulders bust in white marble by Lawrence Gahagan.

* * *

Never a woman to tolerate either advice or criticism, she added a prefatory note to the second edition of "The Rival Princes", and dealt with one intemperate reviewer with her habitual threats of blackmail and ruin.

"To the Editors of 'The Press', 'Morning Post', 'The Times', 'Courier', 'The Pilot', and 'Sun', I beg my best thanks for taking up the case of an injured woman without any reference to party politics."

"As M. Bell, the Editor of 'The Weekly Messenger' appears so inspired with the virtues of the honourable Colonel Wardle, that in his estimation my book ought to be consigned to the common hangman, I beg to return him thanks for his recommendation, but will decline to accept the services of that useful Officer of the State, till he has done ample justice to him and every part of his family!"

"Mr. Bell, I suppose, thought his gross and unmanly attack on me (which is not supported by one line of reasoning), was discharging a debt due to the character of the Colonel. If so, I congratulate the Public on the sudden reform in Mr. Bell's principles, who was never known to discharge a debt until he had been arrested, and therefore Colonel Wardle is a lucky man in getting paid so soon!"

"An old Scotch Gentleman whom I have known some years, has furnished me with a great many very curious anecdotes of this Mr. Bell, which as they are authentic and will no doubt amuse the reader, I may be induced to give them publicity if provoked to it!"

It was not, however, Mr. Bell of 'The Weekly Messenger' who at last provoked Mrs. Clarke to the most vicious assault of all, but

William Vesey Fitzgerald, a thirty-year-old Irishman, who, in 1809, had succeeded his father as the Member for Ennis, and who, in 1812, was appointed a Lord of the Treasury in England, and Chancellor of the Irish Exchequer.

A long-standing friendship of nearly fourteen years had existed between Fitzgerald's father and Mrs. Clarke, and, as friend and lawyer, she had entrusted to him for safe-keeping a letter written to her by the Duke of York after their separation promising to educate and provide for her only son.

During the inquiry a large number of letters from the Fitzgeralds were discovered in the collection brought to the House by William Nicholls, and, from an apparent motive of genuine friendship, Mrs. Clarke agreed to their destruction.

The Fitzgeralds were only two of the many aristocratic friends who wished they had never heard of Mrs. Clarke when her life of fraud and promiscuity was the talk of the country, and nothing rankled more than the defection of men who had fawned upon her when she was in a position of grace and favour as mistress of the Duke of York. They abandoned her like rats deserting a sinking ship, and when she wrote to Fitzgerald's father asking for the return of the Duke's letter, she received a curt note informing her that it had been destroyed.

Mrs. Clarke's fury knew no bounds. The letter, she was well aware, had been burnt to protect the Duke of York and curry favour with the Government. Taking up her pen again she struck where it would hurt most, and wrote a sixty-three page letter to the young and ambitious Chancellor of the Irish Exchequer.

Thumbing through her Shakespearian plays she found the quotation that she was looking for, and consumed with hate and anger she began to write:

> Why he can smile, and murder while he smiles,
> And wet his cheeks with artificial tears,
> And frame his face to all occasions.
>
> *Henry VI, Part 3*

"I am anxious in the first place, to caution the Irish nation in particular against the intrigues of one of the most vicious and profligate of men, who at present most mysteriously presides over the finances of that nation, and who is to be its organ in the Imperial Parliament . . .

"The indifference, insolence, and ingratitude with which you have thought fit to treat one whom your duplicity made an unconscious tool to promote your crafty views, may be assigned as a secondary motive, but all your violated protestations of disinterested friendship and service, would not have procured you the honour of this public address from me had you been content to remain in that lowly sphere which is best suited to the mediocrity of your origin, your talents, and qualifications . . .

"On this occasion I am guided by the general principle that has regulated my whole life, never to suffer ingratitude, one of the blackest crimes, to go unpunished, or hypocrisy, sinister artifice, and duplicity, unexposed . . .

"During the memorable investigation before the House of Commons in 1809, Mr. Perceval illegally obtained possession of a considerable number of my papers . . . many of these were addressed to me by your father.

"Aware of the danger to which you were both exposed, after repeated struggles with yourself, you mustered courage sufficient to speak to your friend Colonel Wardle, and to enquire respecting my sentiments and intended conduct towards you. His reply was that he was certain so long as you behaved with propriety, I had no wish to injure or expose either you or your father. Receiving this assurance, overpowered at once with conscious guilt, and joy at the idea that it was likely to escape public detection, you fell swooning into the arms of the immaculate patriot, who having already a sufficient load of his own to bear, could scarcely support the additional weight of you and all your misdeeds . . .

"Thoroughly sensible to your critical situation, and unable to rest from anxiety, irritation of mind, and the dreadful anticipation of impending ruin, you hurried to Westbourne Place at the unseasonable hour of six in the morning, roused my servants, alarmed the whole house, and insisted on seeing me, 'as you had something of the very highest importance to me and my family to communicate.' Then suffusing my drawing-room with those manly tears, the floodgates of which you have so theatrically at your command, with eyes swollen till they could scarcely see, and a voice so stifled with sobs as to be almost inarticulate, you howled forth the guttural complaint of your rending heart, concerning the miserable, deplorable, committed and never to be endured situation of your unhappy father and family, the complete disappointment of all your objects in life . . . and the irretrievable disgrace in which you would all inevitably be involved by the publication of these letters in your father's own handwriting.

"These letters, when committed to your charge by Mr. Perceval, you engaged by a promise the most sacred that can possibly be given, to bring to me to be destroyed, without opening the envelope which contained them, or seeking to learn any part of their contents. This solemn engagement you violated with the most barefaced impudence, first charging me to allow you to read them, and afterwards reconciling the breach of faith to your easy conscience by the pitiful subterfuge of making me read them to you. In consequence of your pertinacious determination to know the contents of everyone of these letters, several hours were occupied in the work of destruction . . .

"It cannot be difficult for anyone to form a just estimate of your pretensions to honourable sentiment and feeling, who is informed of the situation of your aunt, the wife of your father's brother . . . This unfortunate woman is permitted to support her existence by walking the pavé of Dublin, in a state of the lowest and most abandoned prostitution, while you are reaping the golden harvest of moral and political prostitution. This scandal you are not at the pains of removing, because it is a fact of somewhat less notoriety, and less calculated to attract public notice, than the fate of your wretched kinsman, your first cousin, one as nearly allied by blood as it is possible to be, an own brother excepted, who suffered the just sentence of the law for horse stealing.

"Your character, indeed, needs no accessory guilt, no reflected disgrace, it is already so deep a dye as not to require any foreign shadows to heighten its blackness. What must – I will not say every good man – what must the world in general think of him who deliberately seduces the wife of his intimate friend; who, by the exertion of his corrupt influence, causes the husband to be sent to an unhealthy climate, in the flattering hope that disease will speedily sweep him into the grave; who then indulges his licentious passion without restraint; and who, when its facts are likely to become apparent, drugs the unconscious victim of his debauchery, that at the risk of her life he may relieve his apprehensions, by destroying the innocent witness of his guilt, and spare his avarice the sacrifice of a pittance for its support? Gracious God! can such a cold-blooded monster exist . . .

"When the unhappy woman, languishing under the effects of the deleterious drugs administered by your treacherous hand, seemed hastening in the flower of life to a premature grave, fear of the husband's vengeance, and the apprehensions of being called to a public account in the event of her death, impelled you to consult me how you should act, and to intreat me to use my influence to procure a respectable asylum for the unhappy female . . .

"My recommendation would have introduced her into the house of an excellent physician and his amiable and accomplished wife, whose native goodness of heart, exclusive of friendship for me, would have secured her all the attentions that the medical art and humanity can bestow . . .

"It was not long before a still-born infant, a spectacle so frightful that even a medical pen would recoil with horror from the description, attested the virulence of the fatal potion, by which the unhappy mother herself was brought to the brink of the grave . . .

"Though young in years is old in guilt – of the perpetrator of a crime for which our language has no name – of the well convicted, the deliberate destroyer of his own unborn – do you start, Sir, at this picture?

"I would in charity advise you instead of vainly obtruding yourself upon the public notice, instead of proudly aspiring to those distinctions which are the legitimate portion of merit or talents alone, and whose lustre would but render your blackness the more conspicuous, to shrink into the obscurest corner of your native island, and there let your person and your infamy be buried in everlasting oblivion."

The Government was determined that the incorrigible Mrs. Clarke must be brought to book. On February 7th, 1814, she made her final appearance in the Court of King's Bench charged with publishing a libel upon the Right Honourable William Fitzgerald – and this time there was to be no escape.

The "letter" was read to the court by the Deputy Clerk of the Crown Office, "The Times" reported, accusing Fitzgerald of seducing his friend's wife, of procuring the husband to be sent to an unhealthy climate, "and of other matters not fit to be mentioned in a newspaper".

Nothing but the best, and to hell with the cost, had always been Mrs. Clarke's stock response in any situation. Henry Brougham, the man she hoped would extricate her with a cautionary fine, was one of the most redoubtable advocates of the nineteenth century, and six years later he defended Caroline of Brunswick with skilful perspicuity when the Prince Regent wildly attempted to rid himself of an obstructive wife with absurd charges of adultery.

Mrs. Clarke presented Brougham with an impossible brief. On his advice she entered an affidavit admitting her guilt, but the court had little sympathy with either her plea of provocation, or her appeal for leniency.

"Mary Ann Clarke maketh oath that she feels a great concern at having been betrayed into a violation of the law: that she hath been intimately acquainted with the prosecutor and his father for many years: that his father introduced the prosecutor to her previous to his going to College, as from the situation in which this deponent then lived she might do him much service in his progress through life . . .

"That soon after the prosecutor had gained his point, by procuring the destruction of the said letters, he totally withdrew himself from her as a friend and visitor, where he had been previously a constant and almost a daily one, and estranged himself from all friendship towards her, and instead of the reward she had been promised, he, and his father, refused to return her papers which had been deposited in trust . . .

"That this deponent at first pleaded not guilty to the indictment, but being advised she could not defend herself under that plea, withdrew it, and suffered judgment to go by default, and thereby wholly submit herself to the consideration of this honourable Court. That this deponent hath two daughters, one of them approaching the age of womanhood. That she hath hitherto, under many adverse circumstances and misfortunes, given them an education, and brought them up in honour and virtue. And that should this Honourable Court, in its wisdom deprive her said daughters of her protection, they will be left totally destitute, and she humbly hopes, that these circumstances, and the state of her health, and that in the present case she has been actuated by no views of a political nature, but solely by the treatment received from the prosecutor in his private capacity, will be taken into the consideration of the Honourable Court."

Sir Vicary Gibbs had relinquished the office of Attorney-General in 1812, and Sir William Garrow, the new Attorney-General, denounced the libel as a means of extorting money as iniquitous "as if she had commanded a sum to be put under a stone". She had hinted that other volumes dealing with men guilty of ingratitude and broken promises would follow, "so that the whole world is to be at the mercy of Mrs. Clarke's opportunities and circumstances".

He hoped that the sentence of the court would at last teach her to hold her hand.

"Mrs. Clarke conducted herself with her usual flippancy," remarked 'The Times' reporter, and as the Attorney-General sat down she curtseyed to him with ironical insolence.

It is an invidious task for any counsel compelled to appeal for clemency for a client who pleads guilty, and Brougham was ill at ease as he endeavoured to present Mrs. Clarke to the court in a sympathetic light. "This publication arose out of a long connection between the parties," he explained, "commencing with an acquaintance with the prosecutor's father, an intercourse he was not entitled to say, consisting in reciprocal obligations, for the favours seemed all on one side.

"She is a mother, and I entreat your Lordships to reflect on the effects of her punishment on those whom she had, notwithstanding her own errors, brought up in honour and virtue, by giving them that education and those habits of which, if she did not already, she might possibly live to feel the want . . .

"I hope your Lordships will mingle the portion of justice which those considerations might affix with a merciful regard to the interests of the guiltless."

William Mitchell, a man of seventy, was charged with Mrs. Clarke for printing the libel, and "the age and appearance of the companion with whom misery had made her acquainted seemed to entertain her very much," but was probably only a cloak for her embarrassment and fears.

Mr. Justice Le Blanc found Mrs. Clarke's licentious life as appalling as her libellous pen, and had made up his mind that she should have no more opportunities to stir up trouble in the political sphere.

"The Court, in adjusting the punishment which in their duty it will be necessary to inflict upon the prisoners at the Bar, trust . . . that it will be beneficial to the persons who are the objects of punishment", he moralised, "and that during the solitude and restraint to which they must be doomed by the sentence of the Court they will take the opportunity of looking into themselves and looking into their past lives, that they will take the opportunity of those moments that the world has not perhaps hitherto allowed them, to reflect upon what their conduct has been, and what it is that has brought them to the situation in which they now stand . . .

"Taking all the circumstances of the case into consideration the sentence of the Court is, and this Court doth adjudge, that for the several offences of which you have admitted yourself guilty, you, Mary Ann Clarke, be committed to the custody of the Marshal of the Marshalsea of this Court, and be there imprisoned for the space of nine calendar months, and that at the expiration of that time you do give security for your good behaviour for three years by two sureties in the sum of £200 each, and that you, William Mitchell, for this your offence, be committed to the custody of the Marshal of the Marshalsea of this Court and be there imprisoned for the space of four calendar months."

When she realised that she would not be going home but to a prison cell, Mrs. Clarke's composure momentarily deserted her and, lowering her head, she quietly shed a few tears.

The Marshalsea was established originally for the servants of the royal household, but in 1814 was principally a prison for debtors arrested within twelve miles of the Palace of Westminster. It consisted of several old buildings in a poor state of repair, and a committee appointed by the House of Commons the following year reported that "from the confined situation of the prison itself, the scanty yard, the want of a free circulation of air, the quantity of waste water that covers the court, the health of the prisoners may be materially affected . . . It is, however, true that the sewers are generally bad in the Borough." The well water, the committee reported, was strongly impregnated with iron, and that supplied by the London Bridge Company was often so turbid and saline that it was undrinkable.

Mrs. Clarke made her own private protest about conditions in the Marshalsea, and on June 4th wrote to Samuel Whitbread asking him to present a petition to the House of Commons.

It was read on the evening of June 30th, and to those who remembered the vivacity and wit of the woman in the light blue pelisse who had stood so confidently at the bar five years before, it was a sad commentary on human frailty and misfortune.

She had suffered great partiality and oppression from William Jones, the Marshal, Mrs. Clarke protested, to whose ill-treatment she attributed her poor state of health. She was confined in a cell nine feet square, of which her bed occupied a considerable part, and which had only one small window barricaded with iron. The approaches to her room were so obstructed that even her medical attendants found it difficult of access. Below was a place to which the crier, and other subordinate officers of the prison resorted, and from which she was annoyed "with the fumes of tobacco, lamp-oil, and other effluviae equally nauseous and disagreeable". Her illness had brought on a nervous fever, and although so weak that she was hardly able to walk, she was denied fresh air and exercise.

It was agreed that the Petition should lie on the table, and William Fitzgerald rose to explain that he had received a similar application from Mrs. Clarke.

"I feel, as I believe every gentleman even under the circumstances would feel, for a female suffering confinement under the sentence of a court," he commented smugly, "but having taken those proceedings which I adopted from a sense of what was due to my character, as well as to the laws, I felt also that it would ill become me to interfere, even if I were competent to do so."

The following day the Attorney-General informed the House that before Mrs. Clarke had been many days in prison she had complained to the Chief Justice of ill-treatment and discrimination. She had believed herself entitled to certain apartments and had fixed on those she thought most convenient to her, but which had been occupied for a long time by a man imprisoned for debt. She now occupied one of the state apartments, and of the accommodation available she now had the best – "bad enough, certainly, to those who had been accustomed to live in luxury," he remarked wryly.

Mrs. Clarke's major grudge against the Fitzgeralds was the destruction of the Duke of York's letter promising a commission to her son. Whatever his faults, the Duke was good-natured and conciliatory, and was not the man to visit the sins of the mother upon her son. On February 14th, 1814, George Noel Clarke celebrated his sixteenth birthday, and on March 17th, when Mrs. Clarke had been in prison little more than a month, he was appointed, "without purchase", a Coronet (2/Lieutenant) in the 17th Lancers.

When she was discharged from prison in November, 1814, Mrs. Clarke was still only thirty-eight, and almost half her life lay ahead. She knew that in England, at any rate, the party was over and, going once more through the familiar routine of selling her furniture and packing her belongings, she embarked for France.

She had her daughters, her annuity and her memories, but the days of wine and roses belonged to the past, and she was swallowed up once more by the obscurity from which she had so unexpectedly emerged.

The Marquis of Queensberry always called upon her when he was in Paris and held a high opinion of her talents. Her manners, he said, were remarkable, and even in old age she retained pleasing traces of her past beauty. She was lively, sprightly, and full of fun, and regaled him with anecdotes of the royal family "much too scandalous to be repeated."

Mrs. Clarke's main interest was now centred upon her children, and George's military career was steady if scarcely meteoric. On February 2nd, 1815, less than three months after her discharge from prison, he was posted to the East Indies, where he remained for the next five-and-a-half years. On January 1st, 1819, he purchased a lieutenancy in the 17th Lancers,* and on July 7th, 1825, he bought a captaincy in the same regiment, but he resigned his commission in 1832 at the early age of thirty-four.

Like many mothers with an only son, Mrs. Clarke's affections were focused principally upon George, the dashing cavalry captain, but it was, incongruously, the marriage of her highly-strung, cautious daughter, Ellen, to the happy-go-lucky scientist Louis-Mathurin Busson du Maurier, which was to perpetuate her memory.

George du Maurier, Ellen's eldest son, attained a unique position of prestige and affection at the end of the nineteenth century both as an artist and author, and his "Punch" illustrations were as popular as his novels "Trilby" and "Peter Ibbetson."

His son, Sir Gerald, added a new dimension to the du Maurier reputation as one of the most eminent Edwardian actors, and Sir Gerald's daughter, Daphne, enhanced the tradition of authorship begun by her great-great-grandmother, and has been for many years a best-selling novelist of world-wide popularity. The achievements of Mrs. Clarke's descendants must surely owe much to the intel-

---

* George Bingham, the 3rd Earl of Lucan, Cecil Woodham-Smith reveals in "The Reason Why", bought the command of the 17th Lancers in November, 1826, for £25,000, paying £20,000 above the regulation price. Bingham poured money into the regiment, the men had their uniforms specially tailored, and the sartorial spruceness that he achieved resulted in their being nicknamed 'Bingham's Dandies.' He instituted also a repressive regime of drills, parades and inspections, and the regiment groaned under the yoke of his obsessive demand for perfection and his tyrannical discipline.

ligence and vitality inherited from the indomitable girl from Bowl and Pin Alley.

From France, as the years slipped by, with no one to share her memories, and with mixed feelings of nostalgia and regret, Mrs. Clarke watched the passing of her contemporaries.

Of all the prominent men who crossed her path, Spencer Perceval was the first to die. On October 4th, 1809, he had succeeded the Duke of Portland as Prime Minister, an office he held for the next two-and-a-half years in the face of trenchant parliamentary opposition and public disaffection. At a quarter-past-five on Monday, May 11th, 1812, as he entered the lobby of the old House of Commons, a tall man of about forty stepped forward, pressed a pistol against Perceval's chest and fired. Perceval stumbled a few paces forward, gasped "Oh! I'm murdered", and fell face down on the floor.

He was carried immediately into the room occupied by John Rickman, secretary to Charles Abbot, the Speaker of the House, where he was supported partly on a table and partly on chairs. Blood was coming from his mouth, his head fell forward, and, before a surgeon arrived, the Prime Minister was dead, the victim of an assassination unique in British political history.

Mrs. Clarke was too imbued with notions of aristocratic privilege to ally herself with the tap room sentiment that "more of these damned scoundrels must go the same way – and then poor people may live", but she is scarcely likely to have mourned the death of the man who had harried her so relentlessly in the House of Commons.

In August, 1820, came news of the death of the Duchess of York and of her request that she should be buried not in the royal vault at Windsor, but in the parish church of Weybridge beside the wife of Colonel Bunbury, "in testimony of the perfect amity that has cemented our hearts for many years."

The Duchess had always been a much loved figure in the village through her generosity and benevolent interest in the local schools, and as a final tribute the funeral procession was headed by four mutes, followed by twenty-two girls and fourteen boys. Adding a macabre touch to the proceedings, the children "were also permitted to view the awful spectacle of their benefactress lying in state, with which they appeared deeply affected."

In 1826, in the obituary columns of "The Gentleman's Magazine", appeared a bald, two-line announcement of the death of the man who had loved Mrs. Clarke more honestly and faithfully than any other. "William Dowler, Deputy Commissioner of His Majesty's Forces, at Brighton, on September 8th."

The death of Dowler was followed only four months later by that of the man who had loved her, left her, and whose name was forever after to be inescapably linked with her own.

To the end the Duke of York was falling in love, and he gave his heart for the last time to the Duchess of Rutland. Convinced that he would one day succeed his ailing brother as King of England, he ignored, as he always had done, the fact that he was head over heels in debt, and proceeded to build himself a palace in Stable Yard.

The Duchess of Rutland laid the foundation stone, but the Government was soon compelled to bolster the madcap project with financial support, and Thomas Creevey complained bitterly of the Duke's idiotic extravagance.

"To think of these two men – him and his brother, the King," he wrote, "both turned 60, and terribly bad lives, having new palaces building for them! The Duke of York's is 150 feet by 130 feet outside, with 40 compleat sleeping apartments, and all this for a single man . . ."

The Duchess of Rutland died early in 1826, and that summer there were signs that the Duke's heart was slowly deteriorating. As summer gave way to winter, his illness grew progressively more serious, complicated by a dropsical condition and the onset of gangrene in his feet, and he died painfully and bravely in a specially adjustable chair in the home of the Duke of Rutland in Arlington Street on January 5th, 1827, aged sixty-four.

People flocked to pay him homage as he lay in state in St. James's Palace, and he was buried at Windsor on a bitterly cold winter's night. Lord Eldon ruined a new hat by placing it on the ground and putting his feet in it to keep them warm, and George Canning caught a severe chill from which he never fully recovered.

Seven years later, at a cost of £25,000, a statue 137 feet high was erected to the Duke in Waterloo Place, with compulsory contributions, it was said, deducted from the pay of every private soldier.

The statue stands on the site of Carlton House, the scene of so many of his brother's Bacchanalian revelries, the broken dates commemorating his command of the British Army from 1795–1809 and 1811–1827 obliquely reflecting the influence and intrigue of Mary Ann Clarke.

His contemporaries could never forget his reckless improvidence, and at his death his debts were estimated at £300,000, with assets of less than £180,000. "It is a painful part of our duty to refer to the pecuniary embarrassments of the late Duke of York," commented one biographer caustically, "but in reality they form the most prominent feature of his life", and the wits declared that the lightning conductor on the top of the Duke's head, as he gazed from his lofty pedestal in the direction of the Horse Guards, was the file for his unpaid bills.

Wardle was as impecunious as the Duke and, harried by his creditors, he left his Tonbridge farm and fled to Italy. From Florence, in 1827, he issued an appeal for catholic emancipation, which was published in England the following year, and he died in Florence in November, 1833, at the age of seventy-one.

William Fitzgerald was a man of more prudent habits, and when he died at the age of fifty in 1843, after a long illness, he bequeathed his fortune of £150,000 to his two illegitimate children – a speculative sequel to Mrs. Clarke's accusations of seduction and abortion.

Dominigo Corri, "the tormentor of cat gut", lived on until his eighty-eighth year. He sat down one day in the best of health and spirits and ate heartily "till he suddenly fell back in his chair. A rattling was heard in his throat, water was instantly given to him, his neck cloth loosened, etc., but the jaw fell and he was no more. An express was instantly sent off to his son who resides in Hercules Buildings, but ere he arrived he was a corpse."

Mrs. Clarke continued to live in France, but made many visits to England, and on July 9th, 1849, when over seventy, she was writing to John Bidwell of the Foreign Office, from Essex Cottage, Central Hill, Upper Norwood.

Dear Mr. Bidwell,

My lameness and having been visited by my relations from France, whose position has given me great uneasiness, must excuse me from not having seen you since the heavy affliction your dear wife has suffered.

Believe me I feel a great interest in your daughters. I had hoped they would have been settled before her sister left England. As that will not be the case I have enclosed a little letter for Mrs. Marles, which if you think proper I wish you to give her privately.

Not forgetting your former kindness to me.

Believe me always,
Yours very sincerely,
M. A. Clarke

It is a personal letter of little consequence, but there is still the same articulateness, the same touch of confederacy, but there is in addition a mellowness and kindly concern.

Three years later, on June 26th, "The Times" inaccurately reported that Mrs. Clarke had died in Boulogne on the 21st of that month, a date since accepted by authors and the editors of reference books. "The French Times", however, published in Boulogne for the large English-speaking community that had settled there, gave a fuller and more accurate account of her death.

Died, on the 18th instant, Mary Ann Clarke, aged 74 years

"In our obituary of this day will be found chronicled the death of one, who, in her day, played a conspicuous part in public affairs. We allude to the once notorious Mary Ann Clarke, whose knowledge of the War Office enabled Colonel Wardle to bring his charges in 1808–9 against the Duke of York. She died in Boulogne on the 18th instant, and was buried on Thursday last with great privacy before 8 a.m. We hear that she has lived in Boulogne for many years, with the necessaries, but few of the comforts of life."

Her death certificate, attested by a cabinet maker and a publican, and the note of "Indigent" inserted in the column for "Gifts and Legacies" in the register held by the Archivist for the Pas de Calais, reveal that she died alone and in poverty.

"In the year 1852, the 19th June, at 11 a.m., before the Mayor of the City of Boulogne-on-Sea, John Dines, Master Cabinet Maker, 45 years of age, and François Joseph Cordette, publican, 30 years of age, both living in this town, and no relation of the person named above (i.e. the Mayor), made a formal declaration that Mary Ann Mackenzie, of private means, living in this town, born in Oxford, England, 74 years of age, the widow of Mr. Clarke, and the daughter of Robert Farquhar Mackenzie and Ann Elizabeth Vernon (no other information could be given to us with reference to the parents) died yesterday afternoon at three o'clock at her house 9 Rue d'Assas, as we ourselves verified. After their declaration the witnesses signed this document."

Mrs. Clarke was buried in the Cimetière de L'Est, but no trace of her tomb is now to be found. A certificate of indigence was issued by the Mayor of Boulogne on July 7th.

A copy of her memoirs and the Duke's love-letters were entrusted to the Earl of Chichester, who had negotiated their suppression. After his death in 1826 the papers were left in the possession of his son, the 3rd Earl of Chichester, and were burnt by him at 22 Grosvenor Place, London, on May 25th, 1863. The package containing the Duke of York's letters, he deposed, was not opened.

The 3rd Earl also deposed that his father told him that the Duke of Portland considered that Mrs. Clarke's annuity should have been charged to public finances, but that succeeding Governments did not agree, and that it was paid by the Duke of York until his death, and subsequently by Cox and Greenwood, the Army Agents.

As a final ironic touch, it had been suggested also that the annuity should have been paid out of secret service money, but the Duke of Wellington informed the 3rd Earl that this was not possible as the ministers responsible took an oath that such money should only be expended for services performed during the current year!

It has been rumoured that, in defiance of her agreement, Mrs. Clarke published her memoirs in France, but the authorities in Paris disclaim any knowledge of such a publication. It is possible that there has been confusion over the publication in Paris in 1813 of "Les Princes Rivaux, ou Mémoires de Mistress Mary Anne Clarke, favorite du duc d'York", which was simply a translation by J. F. Dauxion-Lavaisse of "The Rival Princes" that Mrs. Clarke had published in England in 1810.

On July 2nd, 1930, an intriguing manuscript was offered for sale by Sotheby & Co., sent to them by an antiquarian bookseller called Michelmore, who has since died.

Lot 600. CLARKE (Mrs. Mary Anne) mistress of Frederick, Duke of York, son of George III. Autographed Manuscript of Recollections, exhibiting the Secret History of the Court of St. James, 204 pp. 4to; with (a) the corrected galley proof of the first few pages of the work, four long slips, (b) a long list of notabilities (autograph) mentioned in the work, six long folio slips; Sheridan the dramatist is mentioned and at the end is Mrs. Clarke's (sic) note: "with a number of other names unnecessary to place here as they will be found in the Recollections", (c) a proof copy, in sheet form, entirely uncut, of Memoirs of Mrs. M. A. Clarke; enclosed in a blue morocco box.

The manuscript was purchased for £15 by a man named Dobson. Despite every effort it has not been possible to trace its present whereabouts, and it remains a tantalizing postscript of mystery and conjecture.

Other and more expensive reminders of this historic scandal echo down the years, and in January, 1968, a commemorative, canary-coloured jug with black transfer prints of Colonel Wardle and Mrs. Clarke was sold at Sotheby's for £85.

But the girl who made a triumphal progression from Bowl and Pin Alley to the royal bed would probably prefer to be remembered in the words of the historian, Sir Charles Oman, who wrote of "the days when the Duke of York, with the occasional assistance of Mary Ann Clarke, managed the British Army."

Appendix

War Office.
30th April, 1804.

Gentlemen,

I have the honour to acquaint you His Majesty has been pleased to approve of your raising Five Thousand Men to be turned over to the Regiments of the line in His Majesty's Service upon the following conditions. The Recruits are to be engaged without limitation as to time and place of service. You will be allowed 13 guineas Levy Money for each recruit finally approved at one of the following Depôts, viz. The Isle of Wight, Dublin, and Edinburgh, out of which Levy Money a sum equal to what may be fixed by the Recruiting Instructions in force at the time, is to be appropriated to furnishing the Recruits with necessaries on their final approval, exclusive of the actual sum which may have been received by the Recruit. The subsistence of the Recruits, the extra allowance to Innkeepers, the Allowance for beer, and any other daily charge will only be allowed to commence from the date of approval of each Recruit, but, with a view to cover any extra expenses that you may incur by the men being enlisted a considerable time before their approval, you will be allowed to enlist ten boys in every 100 Recuits for whom you will receive the same Bounty and Allowances as for Men. The Men and Boys respectively are to be the age and size directed by the General Recruiting Instructions of the Army – no charge for Slop clothing for the Non-Commissioned Officers or Recruits will be admitted, as, on aproval, the latter will be clothed at the Depôts by the Regiments to which they shall be at once attached. No intermediate approval of the recruits is to take place, and, consequently, neither Bounty, Subsistence, nor any other charge will be allowed for such as shall be rejected at the several Depôts. Each Recruit on approval at the Depôt is to sign a certificate that he received the full Bounty promised to him. You will be allowed to appoint 90 Serjeants, 90 Corporals and 60 Drummers, who must be previously approved by an Inspecting Field Officer of a Recruiting District. The Drummers are to be of the age and standard of Boys, as specified in the Recruiting Instructions. The subsistence of the above-mentioned Non-Commissioned Officers and Drummers is to commence from the date of their actual appointment as such. Half of them, if finally approved at the Depôts, are to be reckoned as part of the Complement of the first five hundred recruits for your Levy, and the remainder as part of the first thousand. The Corporals and Drummers are to be given to understand that they are liable to be draughted (sic.) as privates into the Old Regiments.

The whole of the Non-Commissioned Officers and Drummers must, in the first instance, be enlisted and attested as Privates, and their attestation transmitted to this Office immediately on approval. One half of the Serjeants may be enlisted with the conditions of their being discharged at the conclusion of the Levy, which circumstance is to be noticed in their respective attestations. The Bounty of 13 guineas will be allowed for such of the Non-Commissioned Officers and Drummers as shall be finally approved at the Depôts, as part of your Levy. Clothing will be provided under the orders of Government for the Effective Non-Commissioned Officers and Drummers employed as above-mentioned. You will be allowed, during the Levy, the assistance of Ten Officers, whose names are to be stated to His Royal Highness, the Commander-in-Chief for his approbation, and such of these Officers as may be on Half Pay are to receive Full Pay during their service with your Levy, subsequently to such approval as the Men are to be passed at the Depôts, it is not thought necessary to make you an allowance for an Adjutant, Paymaster, Surgeon or Quartermaster, but an Officer above the Ten will be allowed, to be resident at each Depôt during the Levy. In lieu of giving you permission to nominate any Officers for Commissions, an allowance at the rate of Two Guineas per Man over and above the before mentioned Sum of 13 guineas will be made to you whenever 500 Men shall be passed at the Depôts, and, for every 500 Men subsequently passed, the like extra allowance of Two Guineas per Man will be made to you. The stipulated allowance of 13 Guineas each for the approved Recruits will be issued immediately on their approval by the Paymaster resident at the respective Depôts, by Draughts (sic.) upon the Agents of the Corps to which the Men and Boys may be attached, and the Recruits will be afterwards subsisted through the same channel, or by the District Paymaster until they join Regiments. The pay of the Commissioned Officers, Non-Commissioned Officers and Drummers, employed in the Levy is to be received from the Paymasters of the Recruiting Districts in which they shall be respectively stationed, who will draw for the same upon the General Agents for recruiting in London and Dublin respectively, rendering District Pay Lists of their expenditures on this Head to this office. If, however, any of the Commissioned Officers should be on Full Pay in the existing regiments, the District Paymasters will claim for the Pay of such Officers on their respective Regimental Agents in the same manner as for that of other officers employed in the Recruiting Service.

In consequence of this arrangement, it is presumed that your advances on account of the Levy will be so inconsiderable as scarcely to require any imprest of Money into your hands, in the first instance, but if you should find some assistance absolutely necessary, there will be no objection to your receiving a moderate Sum on account, giving security for the immediate repayment thereof when desired. It is to be clearly understood that government reserves to itself the discretion of discontinuing the Levy entirely, in case 4,000 Men are not raised and passed within Nine Months from the date of this Letter, or in case the whole 5,000 Men are not raised and passed within Thirteen Months from the same date. In the execution of this service I am to assure you of every assistance that this office can afford.

I have, etc.,

J. Bragge. (?)

Colonel French, of the late 102nd Foot
and Captain Sandon of the Royal Waggon Train.

Public Record Office reference: WO/4/193

Bibliography

1. *Manuscript Sources*

At the British Museum:

Additional Manuscripts – 38254 Liverpool Papers
40208 Peel Papers
49173–49195 Perceval Papers
37934 Windham Papers
36595
41295U
41315

At the Public Record Office:

Home Office HO/26/18
" " HO/40/1/1
" " HO/42/96

War Office WO/4/193
" " WO/25/784

At the Berkshire Record Office:

Pleydell-Bouverie papers D/EPb 025

2. *Printed Sources*

Newspapers:

"The Boulogne Gazette"
"Corbett's Political Register"
"The Courier"
"The Day"
"The Examiner"
"The French Times"
"The Morning Chronicle"
"The Morning Post"
"The Sun"
"The Times"

Periodicals:

"The Annual Biography and Obituary"
"The Annual Register"
"Cobbett's Parliamentary Debates"
"The Gentleman's Magazine"
'The National Adviser"

Books and Pamphlets:

ASPINALL, A. "The Later Correspondence of George III", Vol. 3, 1798–1801. Cambridge, 1967.

ASPINALL, A. "The Correspondence of George, Prince of Wales", Vol. II, 1789–1794. London, 1964.

AUCKLAND, LORD. "The Journal and Correspondence of William, Lord Auckland". Edited by the Bishop of Bath and Wells. London, 1861.

BASELEY, REV. T. "A Letter to Colonel Wardle in which his Public Conduct is Examined and Illustrated". London, 1809.

BERRY, MARY. "Journals and Correspondence of Miss Berry". Edited by Lady Theresa Lewis. London, 1865.

BIRD, ANTHONY. "The Damnable Duke of Cumberland". London, 1966.

BLAKE, CAPTAIN PATRICK. "A Word to the British Army". Dublin, 1808.

BROUGHAM, LORD. "Historical Sketches of Statesmen who Flourished in the Time of George III". London, 1845.

BROUGHAM, LORD. "Brougham and his early friends – Letters to James Loch, 1798–1809". Collected and arranged by R. H. M. Buddle Atkinson and G. A. Jackson. London, 1908.

BROWN, FORD K. "Fathers of the Victorians". London, 1961.

BURDETT, SIR FRANCIS. "Speech . . . delivered in the House of Commons, March 13th, 1809". London, 1809.

BURNE, LT.-COL. A. H. "The Noble Duke of York". London, 1949.

BURY, LADY CHARLOTTE. "Diary Illustrative of the Times of George IV". Edited by E. Fourmestraux. London, 1838.

CASTLEREAGH, LORD. "The Correspondence and Despatches of Viscount Castlereagh". Edited by the Marquis of Londonderry. London, 1848–53.

CHANCELLOR, E. BERESFORD. "Annals of Fleet Street". London, 1912.

CHANCELLOR, E. BERESFORD. "The Lives of the Rakes", Vol. VI. London, 1925.

CLARKE, MARY ANNE. "The Rival Princes". London, 1810.

CLARKE, MARY ANNE. "A Letter to the Right Honourable William Fitzgerald". London, 1813.

CLARKE, MARY ANNE. "Les Princes Rivaux". Paris, 1813.

CLARKE, W. "The Authentic and Impartial Life of Mrs. Mary Anne Clarke". London, 1809.

COLCHESTER, LORD. "The Diary and Correspondence of Charles Abbot, Lord Colchester". Edited by his son, Charles, Lord Colchester. London, 1861.

COLE, OWEN BLAYNEY. "The Blind Senator – A Biographical Sketch of Francis Burton". Dublin, 1845.

CREEVEY, THOMAS. "A Selection from the Correspondence and Diaries of the late Thomas Creevey, M.P." Edited by Sir Herbert Maxwell. London, 1906.

CRESTON, DORMER. "The Regent and his Daughter". London, 1932.

CROKER, JOHN WILSON. "The Correspondence and Diaries of the late Right Honourable John Wilson Croker, LL.D., F.R.S." Edited by Louis J. Jennings. London, 1884.

CROKER, JOHN WILSON. "The Croker Papers 1808–1857". Edited by Bernard Pool. London, 1967.

CROKER, MISS MARGARET SARAH. "Monody on His Late Royal Highness the Duke of Kent". London, 1820.

DAVIS, J. "Plain Reasons for the re-Appointment of H.R.H. The Duke of York". London, 1811.

DELDERFIELD, ERIC. "The Raleigh Country". Exmouth, 1950.

DRAKARD, J. "The Public and Private Life of Colonel Wardle". Stamford, 1810.

DU MAURIER, DAPHNE. "A Biography of Sir Gerald du Maurier". London, 1934.

DU MAURIER, DAPHNE. "The du Mauriers". London, 1937.

DU MAURIER, GEORGE. "The Young George du Maurier. A Selection of his Letters 1860–67". Edited by Daphne du Maurier. London, 1951.

DYOTT, WILLIAM. "Dyott's Diary 1781–1845". London, 1907.

ELDON, LORD. "The Public and Private Life of Lord Chancellor Eldon". Edited by Horace Twiss. London, 1844.

EVERITT, REV. WILLIAM. "Memorials of Exmouth". Exmouth, 1883.

FORTESCUE, J. W. "The County Lieutenancies and the Army 1803 1814". London, 1909.

FORTECUE, J. W. "A History of the British Army". Vol. II, 1809–1810. London, 1912.

FULFORD, ROGER. "Royal Dukes". London, 1933.

GEORGE, M. D. "Catalogue of Political and Personal Satires". Vols. 8–9. London, 1947–9.

GEORGE, M. D. "London Life in the 18th Century". London, 1925.

GOWER, LORD GRANVILLE LEVESON-. "The Private Correspondence of Lord Granville Leveson-Gower 1781–1821". Edited by Countess Granville. London, 1917.

GRAY, DENIS. "Spencer Perceval—The Evangelical Prime Minister". Manchester, 1963.

GREVILLE, CHARLES C. F. "The Greville Memoirs". Edited by Henry Reeve. London, 1896.

GRONOW, CAPTAIN R. H. "The Reminiscences and Recollections of Captain Gronow". London, 1892.
GRONOW, CAPTAIN R. H. "The Last Recollections of Captain Gronow". London, 1934.
HAGUE, THOMAS. "A Letter to His Royal Highness the Duke of York". London, 1808.
HAGUE, THOMAS. "The Royal Urinead". London, 1808.
HAM, ELIZABETH. "Elizabeth Ham by Herself 1783–1820". Edited by Eric Gillett. London, 1945.
HAMILTON, LADY ANNE. "Secret History of the Court of England". London, 1903.
HERBERT J. and WILSON, W. "Biographical Memoirs and Anecdotes of the celebrated Mary Anne Clarke". London, 1809.
HOGAN, MAJOR DENIS. "An Appeal to the Public and a Farewell Address to the Army". London, 1808.
HOLLAND, LORD. "Memoirs of the Whig Party". London, 1852.
HOLLAND, LORD. "Further Memoirs of the Whig Party, 1807–21" Edited by Lord Stavordale. London, 1905.
HOWARD, JOHN. "The State of the Prisons". Edited by Ernest Rhys. London, 1929.
HUISH, R. "Authentic Memoir of His late Royal Highness Frederick, Duke of York and Albany". London, 1827.
HUISH, R. "Memoirs of George the Fourth". London, 1831.
HUNT, LEIGH, "Autobiography". London, 1850.
HUNT, LEIGH. "Autobiography with Reminiscences of Friends and Contemporaries". Edited by Roger Ingpen. London, 1903.
HUSKISSON, WILLIAM. "The Huskisson Papers". Edited by Lewis Melville. London, 1931.
JAEGER, MURIEL. "Before Victoria". London, 1956.
JERDAN, WILLIAM. "Autobiography". London, 1852–53.
JERDAN, WILLIAM. "National Portrait Gallery of Illustrations and Eminent Personages of the Nineteenth Century". London, 1830.
KING, HORACE MAYBRAY. "Before Hansard". London, 1968.
LAMB, CHARLES. "The Letters of Charles Lamb". Edited by Russell Davis Gillman. London, 1907.
LENNOX, LORD WILLIAM PITT. "My Recollections from 1806 to 1873". London, 1874.
LESLIE, DORIS. "The Great Corinthian". London, 1952.
LEWIS, WILMARTH SHELDON. "Three Tours through London in the years 1748, 1776 & 1797". Oxford, 1941.
M'CALLUM, P. F. "Observations on H.R.H. The Duke of Kent's Shameful Persecution". London, 1808.
M'CALLUM, P. F. 'The Rival Queens, or Which is the Darling?" London, 1810.

MURRAY, AMELIA. "Recollections from 1803–1837". London, 1868.

NEALE, ERSKINE. "Experiences of a Gaol Chaplain". London, 1847.

OMAN, SIR CHARLES. "England in the Nineteenth Century". London, 1920.

OPIE, IONA AND PETER. "The Oxford Dictionary of Nursery Rhymes". Oxford, 1951.

PAPENDIEK, MRS. CHARLOTTE. "Court and Private Life in the Time of Queen Charlotte: Being the Journals of Mrs. Papendiek". Edited by Mrs. Vernon Delves Broughton. London, 1887.

PERCEVAL, SPENCER. "The Substance of a Speech . . . delivered in the House of Commons on the 8th and 9th March, 1809, in the debate on the Inquiry into the Conduct of the Duke of York". London, 1809.

REDDING, CYRUS. "Past Celebrities Whom I Have Known". London, 1866 (1865?).

REID, W. H. "Memoirs of the Life of Colonel Wardle". London, 1809.

ROMILLY, SIR SAMUEL. "Memoirs of the Life of Sir Samuel Romilly". Edited by his sons. London, 1841.

ROMILLY, S. H. "Letters to Ivy from the First Earl of Dudley". London, 1905.

ROSE, GEORGE. "Diaries and Correspondence of the Right Honourable George Rose". Edited by L. V. Harcourt. London, 1860.

SMITH, SIDNEY. "The Letters of Peter Plymley". Edited by G. C. Heseltine. London, 1929.

STACEY, CHARLES BROWNLOW. "The Analysis of Reform: Containing a Review of Mrs. Clarke's Publication". London, 1810.

TAYLOR, ELIZABETH. "Authentic Memoirs of Mrs. Clarke". London, 1809.

VILLIERS, MARJORIE. "The Grand Whiggery". London, 1939.

WALPOLE, SPENCER. "The Life of the Right Honourable Spencer Perceval". London, 1874.

WARDLE, G. W. "Colonel Wardle to his Countrymen – Letter written from Florence, November 3rd, 1827". London, 1828.

WATKINS, JOHN. "A Biographical Memoir of his late Royal Highness Frederick, Duke of York and Albany". London, 1827.

WELLINGTON, DUKE OF. "Civil Correspondence and Memoranda of Field Marshal Arthur, Duke of Wellington, K.G., 1807–1809". Edited by his son. London, 1860.

WILBERFORCE, WILLIAM. "The Correspondence of William Wilberforce". Edited by Robert Isaac Wilberforce and Samuel Wilberforce. London, 1840.

WILBERFORCE, WILLIAM. "The Life of William Wilberforce". Robert Isaac Wilberforce and Samuel Wilberforce. London, 1838.

WINDHAM, WILLIAM. "The Windham Papers". Edited by the Earl of Roseberry. London, 1913.

WOODHAM-SMITH, CECIL. "The Great Hunger". London, 1962.

WOODHAM-SMITH, CECIL. "The Reason Why". London, 1953.

WYNN, (CHARLOTTE WILLIAMS) LADY. "Correspondence of Charlotte Grenville, Lady Williams Wynn, and her three sons, Sir Watkin Williams Wynn, Bart., Rt. Hon. Charles Williams Wynn, and Sir Henry Williams Wynn, G.C.H., K.C.B., 1795–1832". Edited by Rachel Leighton. London, 1920.

YORK, DUKE OF. "The Posthumous Letter of His Royal Highness the Duke of York". Edited by Thomas Clerc Smith. London, 1827.

Anonymous Books and Pamphlets

"A Citizen". "The Claims of Mr. Wardle to the Thanks of the Country". London, 1809.

"An Englishman". "The Duke of York – A Letter to His Royal Highness, or A Delicate Inquiry into the doubt whether he be more favoured by Mars or Venus". London, 1807.

"Anonymous". "The Prince of Wales – A Second Plain Letter to His Royal Highness". London (undated).

"Anonymous". "The Bonne Bouche or Epicurean Rascality". London, 1807.

"Anonymous". "Mentoriana or A Letter of Admonition and Remonstrance to His Royal Highness the Duke of York". London, 1807.

"Anonymous". "The Agent and his Natural Son". London, 1808.

"Anonymous". "The Miss-Led General – A Serio-Comic Satire". London, 1808.

"Anonymous". "A Plain Statement of Facts". London, 1809.

"Anonymous". "A Letter to Mrs. Clarke on her late connection with the Duke of York". London, 1809.

"Anonymous". "A Full Report of the Proceedings at a Meeting of the Citizens of Westminster". London, 1809.

"Anonymous". "Mrs. Clarke's Garland". London, 1809.

"Anonymous". "Trial – The King, on the Prosecution of Gwyllym Lloyd Wardle, Esq., M.P., against Francis Wright, Daniel Wright and Mary Anne Clarke". London, 1809.

"Anonymous". "A Sketch of the Life and Character of His Royal Highness the late Duke of York". Glasgow, 1827.

"Anonymous". "Debts of His Royal Highness the Duke of York – Extracts from the London Daily and Weekly Press". London, 1832.

Index

Burn away! – I would burn half the
You may preserve a copy or two for
private friends –
Burning the Books of curious Arts